William Fortyhands

DISINTEGRATION
AND
REINVENTION
OF THE
SHAKESPEARE CANON

NINE-BANDED
BOOKS

William Fortyhands: Disintegration and Reinvention of the Shakespeare Canon

Copyright ©2016 Samuel Crowell
All rights reserved

Published by

Nine-Banded Books
PO Box 1862
Charleston, WV 25327
www.ninebandedbooks.com

ISBN 10 0-9907335-4-8
ISBN 13 978-0-9907335-4-6

Editorial assistance
Anita Dalton ~ James Nulick ~ Ann Sterzinger

Cover illustration ©2016 by Josh Latta

Cover design by Kevin I. Slaughter

For My Mother
And My Children
And My Teachers, L.B. and A.P.

William Fortyhands

CONTENTS

Preface ~ 13

Chapter 1: The Cloud of Unknowing ~ 15
John Aubrey – Avebury – Problems of Knowing – Discontinuity – Space – Time – Sequence – Revolutionary Potential – Historical Knowledge

Chapter 2: Hidden Persuaders ~ 23
Ben Jonson's Folio – Macaulay's Fable – The First Folio – Later Folios – Later Comments by Jonson

Chapter 3: Elizabeth's Beat Generation ~ 35
The Beat Generation – John Lyly – Thomas Lodge (Gosson) – George Peele – Robert Greene – Thomas Nashe (Harvey) – Thomas Kyd – Christopher Marlowe

Chapter 4: The First Editors ~ 49
Samuel Pepys – Edward Ravenscroft – Nicholas Rowe – John Aubrey – The Shakespeare Mythos – Alexander Pope – Lewis Theobald

Chapter 5: Poets Corner ~ 55
Homer's Iliad – Pope and George Chapman – Michael Drayton – Philip Sidney – Edward Dyer – Mary Sidney – John Davies of Hereford – Samuel Daniel – Poetic Forms – Dactylic Hexameter

Chapter 6: Apotheosis and Evidence ~ 73
David Garrick's Jubilee – Shakespeare's Will – A Groatsworth of Wit Paid with a Million in Repentance – Francis Meres' Palladis Tamia

Chapter 7: Our English Homer ~ 87
The Nature of Attribution Studies – Early Attribution Studies: Homer – Early Attribution Studies: The Bible – Erasmus – Schmucker – Schleiermacher – Hermeneutics – Unitarians versus Analysts – Authorship and Inerrancy

Chapter 8: Toward a Shakespeare Chronology ~ 93
Samuel Johnson – Edward Capell – Edmond Malone – Shakespeare's Chronology – Nashe's Preface to Greene's Menaphon – The Ur-Hamlet – The German Hamlet – Other Ur-plays

Chapter 9: Blood Is a Beggar ~ 99
Sources for the Plays – Philosophical Sources – Montaigne – The Panchatantra – Milkmaid and Bucket – Aesop – Hellenist Philosophy – Epicurus, Zeno, Pyrrho – McCarthy, Sir Thomas North – Marcus Aurelius – Logos – Stoicism – Seneca

Chapter 10: Frauds and Forgeries ~ 107
William Henry Ireland – John Payne Collier – Permanent Damage to Primary Sources – Thomas Carlyle – Of Heroes and Hero Worship – Disraeli's Venetia

Chapter 11: Henslowe and His Crew ~ 113
The Diary of Philip Henslowe – Edward Alleyn – Anthony Munday – Henry Chettle – Thomas Dekker – Thomas Heywood – John Webster – Sir Thomas More Manuscript

Chapter 12: The First Dissidents ~ 121
Joseph C. Hart – Chambers' Edinburgh Review – William Henry Smith – Francis Bacon – Delia Bacon

Chapter 13: Bacon and Ciphers ~ 129
Ignatius Donnelly – Standard Anti-Shakespeare Arguments – Parallelisms – The Cipher – Vedic Expansions

Chapter 14: Turn-of-the-Century Skeptics ~ 139
New Shakespeare Society – Frederick Fleay – J. M. Robertson – George Greenwood – Walt Whitman, Henry James, Mark Twain – Marlowe (Zeigler, Mendenhall) – William Stanley, Earl of Derby – Roger Manners, Earl of Rutland – John Aubrey

Chapter 15: Topical Allusions and Generation J ~ 145
Generation J – Ben Jonson – Beaumont and Fletcher – Philip Massinger – John Ford – John Marston – The "War of the Theaters" – The Parnassus Plays – Satiro-mastix – Political Contexts – Essex Rebellion – Gunpowder Plot – Shakespeare's Absence

Chapter 16: Black Iron Prison ~ 157
Philip K. Dick – "Black Iron Prison" – "Bad Quartos" – Sir Thomas More Attribution – Stipulations About Parallelisms – The "Disintegration" Speech – The Clayton Loan

Chapter 17: Oxford and Marlowe ~ 167
James Looney's Idea – The Life of Edward de Vere, the 17th Earl of Oxford – Prince Tudor Theory – Vedic Expansion – Christopher Marlowe (Hotson)

Chapter 18: Modern Reinventions ~ 175
Context of Discovery, Context of Justification – Kuhn's Paradigm Shift – Gary Taylor – "Shall I die" – Donald Foster – "Funeral Elegy" – Elliott and Valenza – Brian Vickers

Chapter 19: The Oxford Reaction ~ 181
The Growth of Oxfordianism – Accusations of "Hate Virtue" – "Monstrous Adversary" or "Roaring Homo" – Shakespeare "Denialism" – Oxford's Bible (Strittmatter, Anderson) – Sackville, North, and other recent nominations

Chapter 20: The Quarto Plays ~ 189

Chapter 21: The Folio Plays ~ 197

Chapter 22: Apocrypha, Poems, Sonnets ~ 203

CHAPTER 23: SHAKESPEARE BACK TO FRONT ~ 211
Shakespeare's Life – Circumstances and Challenges – Known Activities – Probability of Fitting the Known with the Assumed (Playwriting) – On Poet-Ape

CHAPTER 24: LEGENDS OF THE NOBLE HAND ~ 219
Edward Ravenscroft – The Pinner of Wakefield – Other Oblique References – The Test That All the Candidates Fail – Lack of Direct Evidence – The Likely or Possible Activities of the Earl of Oxford

CHAPTER 25: BEETHOVEN'S STAIRCASE ~ 231
Beethoven's Ninth – The "Death of the Author" – Vickers' Protestations – The Intentional Fallacy – The Genetic Fallacy – Reader Response – Hermeneutics (Dilthey) – Loss of Secure Subject, 20th Century Intellectual Trends – Love's Types of Authorship (Precursory, Executive, Declarative, Revisory)

CHAPTER 26: THE FOLIO UNBOUND ~ 239
Speculations on Henry V – Suggestion of Quartos Being Shakespeare's Revisions – The Case for Hamlet – The Tempest – Individual Play Analysis Advocated for Purposes of Chronology and Context

CHAPTER 27: CONCLUSIONS ~ 253
Traditional Attribution to Shakespeare Is Unassailable – But That Doesn't Make it Unquestionable – Unitarians versus Analysts, Irreconcilable Approaches – Gombrowicz's Ferdydurke – Psychological Reactions to Unknowing: Hate-Virtue, Milkmaid and Bucket or Cascading Assumptions – Chain of Reasoning versus Skein of Reasoning – Forgery and Fraud – Gluttony-Virtue or Vedic Expansions – Black Iron Prison or Epistemic Closure – Accusations of Denial – Traditional Categories: Internal Evidence (Moot) – External Evidence (Title Pages) – Contextual Evidence (Anyone but Shakespeare) – Expand the Pantheon

Acknowledgements ~ 267

Bibliography ~ 269

Index ~ 285

44. Lastly, there are idols which have crept into men's minds from the various dogmas of peculiar systems of philosophy, and also from the perverted rules of demonstration, and these we denominate idols of the theatre. [...]

45. The human understanding, from its peculiar nature, easily supposes a greater degree of order and equality in things than it really finds; and although many things in nature be sui generis, and most irregular, will yet invent parallels and conjugates, and relatives where no such thing is. [...]

46. The human understanding, when any preposition has been once laid down, (either from general admission and belief, or from the pleasure it affords), forces every thing else to add fresh support and confirmation; and although more cogent and abundant instances may exist to the contrary, yet either does not observe or despises them, or gets rid of and rejects them by some distinction, with violent and injurious prejudice, rather than sacrifice the authority of its first conclusions. [...]

>—Sir Francis Bacon,
>   *Aphorisms* from the *Novum Organum* (1620)

PREFACE

This is a book on the Shakespeare authorship controversy, something that I have been reading about since my boyhood in the 1960s. My interest in the subject, as with most of my readings, has been intermittent and desultory. I make no claim, nor do I aspire, to expertise or mastery. However, a couple of years ago I decided to engage the subject a bit more systematically so that I could gain that valuable thing: my own informed opinion. This book is the result.

Simply stated, the Shakespeare authorship controversy (or "problem") is based on the idea that plays and poems normally attributed to William Shakespeare (1564–1616) were not written by him, but by someone else. The controversy has been swirling about since the 1850s and there has been no shortage of possible Shakespeare replacements, although usually the list of candidates is limited to a half dozen or so, the top three being Francis Bacon, Christopher Marlowe, and, nowadays, Edward de Vere, the 17th Earl of Oxford.

Books on the subject have always been enlightening to me but they tend to follow a very predictable curve. First, it is argued that William Shakespeare had many deficiencies and therefore could not have written the plays and poems, and then, after the interval, the new candidate is thrust upon the stage and shown to be a perfect fit. I don't mind this approach but it does get fairly predictable after a while.

Instead, I have chosen to narrate the history of Shakespearean criticism—necessarily, with great brevity—to highlight the ways in which various authors have questioned this or that part of the Shakespearean canon, and to show how their opinions did or did not change as more biographical information about the poet, and more historical information about the Elizabethan theater, emerged in later centuries. I hope to mimic the way one might approach this topic over time in ever widening contexts.

The upshot of this approach is that we should be able to see how the authorship controversy grew out of the history of criticism and document discovery. However one wishes to approach the issue, and no matter how extravagant the claims of various dissident scholars, it is still a part of Shakespearean criticism, and a part, I would argue, that is entitled to respect.

In order to pursue my own theories about historical understanding, and literary criticism, I have allowed myself to introduce a lot of things that normally do not turn up in books of this kind, and I have also allowed myself to introduce a few concepts that I have privately derived in the many decades I have spent musing on this topic.

To do this properly, I have presented a lot of contextual material, including material pertaining to the Elizabethan stage and Shakespeare's contemporaries. This may not seem pertinent at first glance. I can only counsel patience.

The fundamental purpose of this text is to show how the authorship controversy grew out of the history of our knowledge of Shakespeare. It is not meant to refute the candidacy of any one over any other. This does not mean I do not have my own solution to the problem.

In some of our institutions of higher learning there is a pre-graduation custom that consists of strapping forty ounce bottles of malt liquor to the hands of young scholars, with the stipulation that these cannot be removed until all of the liquid is consumed. In order to signify the underlying seriousness of their endeavor, the prospective graduates, in the dead of night, may be obliged to recite Homer's *Iliad* while drinking. Such an aspirant is called Edward Fortyhands.

Of course my title is of a piece with the strangeness of the name of the Poacher of Stratford; thus Shakespeare, Shake-speare, Shake-shaft —all vaguely sexual—perhaps also Shaken-stein (for those who believe he invented the human) or even Loan-Shark (for those who believe he was mostly a money lender). But perhaps it points to my solution, after all.

1 | THE CLOUD OF UNKNOWING

*John Aubrey ~ Avebury ~ Problems
of Knowing ~ Discontinuity ~ Space ~
Time ~ Sequence ~ Revolutionary Potential ~
Historical Knowledge*

On an early January morning in 1649, a young Englishman named John Aubrey went riding with a friend; they were attempting to catch up to a hunting party. Riding across the Salisbury plain, they had to be careful: the chalky soil of the region had allowed large stone blocks to extrude from under the surface, presenting a hazard to both horse and rider. Nearby, there was a hollow containing many such stones (which are called "sarsens" for reasons unknown, though the locals referred to them as "Grey Wethers" because from a distance the stones resembled a flock of sheep[1]).

Riding west they passed through a small village, and then Aubrey came to a stop. He had seen something. He had seen one of these stones standing upright, and then another, and then another. Dismounting, while his friend rode on, Aubrey began to investigate.

What Aubrey was experiencing was a moment of discovery; he was seeing a pattern. We might call this "wonder," as John Donne had described it in his Easter sermon in 1625—a wonder that resolves itself by degrees either into knowledge or belief.[2] It could be compared to the wild surmise that Keats described crossing the face of stout Cortez, in the famous poem he wrote after a friend read to him from George

---

[1] Freely adapted from Aubrey's account in John Britton, *Memoir of John Aubrey*, 30-31.

[2] "If I know a thing, or believe a thing, I do no longer wonder: but when I find that I have reason to stop upon the consideration of a thing, so, as that I see enough to induce admiration, to make me wonder, I come by that step, and God leads me by that hand, to a knowledge, if it be of a natural or civil thing, or to a faith, if it be of a supernatural, and spiritual thing." Sermon XVIII, Easter Sunday, 1625, *Donne Complete Works* (Kindle)

Chapman's translation of Homer's *Iliad*. We might call the phenomenon pattern recognition, fed by such innate human proclivities that have been understood as "patternicity" or "pareidolia," or even "apophenia"—the same sort of thing that causes us to see faces in clouds, as it did also for both Hamlet and Marc Antony.[3]

But Aubrey was not seeing falsely. What he was investigating that January morning was what we now call the stone circle at Avebury, the largest stone circle in Great Britain. And we want to hold onto that image of Aubrey's discovery (just as he, no doubt, held the reins of his horse as he walked around) because it serves to introduce our subject, which is the ongoing argument over the authorship of the plays and poems usually attributed to William Shakespeare.

Casting our eyes over this panorama of ten-foot-tall standing stones, describing a circle some thousand feet in diameter, the first question we ask is: how did this get here? Subsequent analysis strongly suggests that the stones derived from the sarsens, which, by nature, were gradually being exposed to the surface. But who arranged them? And why? No one knows.

So the first thing the Avebury stone circle reminds us is that knowledge is *discontinuous*. This runs counter to what we would normally think. After all, civilization has had an uninterrupted history in Europe going back several millennia. Confronted with something like the stone circle at Avebury, one would expect a narrative of how it got there, if not at least an oral tradition. But there was nothing in Aubrey's time, as he chatted up the local villagers, and nothing since.

This discontinuity touches on a major problem with the life of William Shakespeare (1564–1616), and the story that has him producing 37 plays, 154 sonnets, several other poems, and, according to some, extensive interventions in the plays of others. There is so much we do not know. E.K. Chambers, the most magisterial of Shakespeare authorities, called this lack of knowledge "nescience" and counseled that we must simply accept it.[4] But such uncritical acceptance is anathema to human nature. No one accepts a blind alley, a wall, or a blockage without, somehow, coming up with a way to get around it. And so it

---

3 Michael Shermer coined the term "patternicity" in his book, *The Believing Brain*. It has the advantage over the other terms of being easier to pronounce; "pareidolia" is another term used to describe seeing or hearing things in random stimuli such as clouds or static, while "apophenia" has its roots in the tendency to see patterns, usually of a persecutorial nature, in random data (as such it is a term usually restricted to clinical psychology). (For *Hamlet*, the end of Scene II, Act III, for *Antony and Cleopatra*, the beginning of Scene XIV, Act IV.)

4 Chambers, EK, William *Shakespeare: A Study of Facts and Problems*, I:26

is that a large part of Shakespearean scholarship—and this includes both those who believe he wrote the plays, and those who believe he did not—involves attempts to infer facts where facts do not exist, and to infer causes when causes are not apparent. It is, in a word, human curiosity that propels the authorship controversy.

The second thing that Aubrey's discovery reminds us of is how the progress of knowledge is *sequential*—that it is played out over time and space. Aubrey had to ride through and see the stones in sequence before realizing that he was onto something. He had to inspect the area, to see how they were arranged. He noted the circular pattern, and then he observed the circular ditch that enclosed the stones and indeed a large part of the village itself.

There are two ways the sequential nature of knowledge applies to the authorship controversy. The first concerns the way knowledge is received. Learning is a cumulative activity, but the things we learn at first are also the things that influence our subsequent learning. This is of critical importance both in the way Shakespeare is approached and in the way he is attacked. Conventional "Stratfordians"—as we call those who believe that William Shakespeare wrote the plays and poems (so called because Shakespeare was born and died in the small trading town of Stratford-on-Avon)—always take Shakespeare's authorship for granted, which is only natural, since that is the narrative that is taught to children from their earliest school days as well as in innumerable television shows and films. In the rare instance where Stratfordians choose to address the authorship controversy at all, they rarely endorse the legitimate skepticism of their opponents; instead, they invariably go for the low-hanging fruit of anti-Stratfordian madness or obsessive compulsive cipher seeking.

But anti-Stratfordians (or anti-Strats) are also prone to load their presentation, in part because they are also conditioned by the prevailing belief in sole Shakespearean authorship. Consider the outline of a typical anti-Stratfordian demonstration. First, it will be argued that William Shakespeare could not possibly have written the plays. Thus we encounter a narrative describing Hillbilly Shakespeare growing up in a hovel in Stratford, unschooled, and, based on his six surviving signatures, barely literate. In turn, we are informed that the purported dramatist was also a usurer, who was at the same time dim-witted and easily manipulated by the true creator of the plays. Having thus presented Shakespeare as an object of scorn and ridicule, the second step of course involves introducing the true author. The candidate is almost always a nobleman, because, so the thinking goes, no one but a nobleman would have had the need to use the Stratford man as a front.

There is another way in which knowledge is sequential, not just as we learn things as individuals, but as we learn things collectively in a given culture. In this case, if we use his death as a starting point, there have been intensive efforts to understand Shakespeare and his works for almost 400 years. During that time, much indirect evidence has emerged, yet none of that indirect evidence has widely shaken the orthodox belief that Shakespeare wrote the works that appeared under his name. That is why I want to take a historical approach to this emerging knowledge.

An historical approach to the Authorship Controversy also underlines a third thing about Aubrey's discovery at Avebury: namely, that knowledge, or rather, our more comprehensive grasp of knowledge, what we might call "understanding," is *context-dependent*. Many other names can be used: prepossession, preunderstanding, foreknowledge. Aubrey's recognition of the stone circle at Avebury was certainly influenced by his interest in British antiquities, as well as the imposing presence of the most famous stone circle of them all, Stonehenge, which lies 17 miles to the south on the same plain.

But that is not the only context of knowledge. Let us put the matter another way. If Aubrey had no knowledge of antiquities or Stonehenge, might he have discovered the stone circle at Avebury in any case? Quite possibly, but his prior knowledge could lead him to the discovery in two ways. A passive position would enable him to discern the pattern, but a more active position would have him actually seeking out the pattern. The positions are not the same. We might call the latter a kind of motivated pattern seeking. And such motivated pattern seeking will always lead to more knowledge, and then to a different perception of the object being studied. It seems that Aubrey's discovery was of the passive kind, in that he appears to have merely stumbled upon the stones. But in the authorship controversy it is more typical to have students discover one new thing and then actively seek to make all the other data fit that pattern.

What this means is that the contexts of knowledge change as knowledge is acquired. But that in turn represents another problem, to wit, the way in which the acquisition of knowledge has the potential to change our fundamental beliefs or assumptions about a body of knowledge. While emerging knowledge may challenge the comprehensiveness of a given explanation about a thing, it does not follow that a given explanation will automatically respond to such emerging knowledge. What normally happens is that such emergent knowledge is simply assimilated into whatever explanation already exists, or it is ignored and stepped around—rather like those relentlessly emerging stones on the Salisbury plain, before someone got the bright idea to raise them up and arrange them in a new and more orderly pattern.

With regard to the authorship controversy, the orthodox view of Shakespeare as sole author is only where the story begins. The accumulation of evidence over 400 years created problems for that point of view, and, in my thinking, this was the direct cause of the controversy. It is from this vantage that we begin to see how the authorship controversy actually has an organic relationship with orthodox Shakespearean studies.

In order to make this argument, I will therefore adopt a chronological approach to the subject, focusing above all on questions of authorial attribution.

The first collection of all of Shakespeare's plays was published in 1623, seven years after his death. This edition is universally referred to as the First Folio. In course, we will examine how that body of work underwent metamorphosis during the 17th century, until critical editions of Shakespeare began to appear. Nicholas Rowe attempted the first critical edition of Shakespeare in 1708, being followed by several other editors. The poet Alexander Pope published an edition in 1725, and, after a famous dispute,[5] was followed by William Theobald in the 1730s. Samuel Johnson followed, bringing George Steevens in his train.

All of these editors relied on their predecessors, as well as on the discovery of documents relevant to Shakespeare and his works, the most important discoveries being made in the period 1740–1840. At the close of the 18th century, the synthesis of Edmond Malone appeared. This also featured an attempt at a chronology on how Shakespeare must have written the plays. With minor exceptions, Malone's chronology has continued to inform all subsequent chronologies.

---

5 Theobald found fault with Pope's editing decisions, and Pope retaliated in *The Dunciad*. See Chapter 10.

In the 1840s, following the discovery of the *Sir Thomas More* manuscript[6] as well as the long-delayed publication of Henslowe's Diary,[7] we encounter the first voices of dissent. Joseph C. Hart, in *The Romance of Yachting*, ascribes the plays to any number of other writers, while an anonymous Englishman, in a brief journal article entitled "Who Wrote Shakespeare,"[8] points to the logical implications of Henslowe's Diary. By the 1850s, such skeptical chords are amplified in the works of William Henry Smith and Delia Bacon, whose 1857 book *The Philosophy of the Plays of Shakespeare Unfolded* set the authorship controversy in motion.

In the latter half of the 19th century broad trends emerged. It seemed that Shakespeare critics always questioned the overall integrity of the canon, with virtually everyone flagging this or that play, or group of plays, or lines in plays, that they were confident could not have been by the hand of Shakespeare. Among the orthodox, this tendency reached its apogee in the investigations of Frederick Fleay and J. M. Robertson.[9] Anti-Stratfordians, on the other hand, initially focused on Francis Bacon as the true author. This narrow line of focus held for several decades, until, right at the turn of the 20th century, three new candidates emerged: William Stanley, the Earl of Derby; Roger Manners, the Earl of Rutland; and finally Christopher Marlowe, a contemporary of Shakespeare who was thought to have been killed in 1593. Meanwhile, another group of agnostics emerged, led largely by the writings of George Greenwood[10] (who had no particular favorite alternative). Among the "Greenwoodians" we may note such luminaries as Henry James, Walt Whitman, and Mark Twain.

These trends continued up through the First World War. In the 1920s, new perspectives emerged. This is when we begin to find the notion, exemplified in the writings of James Looney, that the Shakespearean canon was the sole work of Edward de Vere, the Earl of Oxford. This is also when we observe the retrenchment of the orthodox school, an event spearheaded by the writings of E. K. Chambers and his famous speech on "Disintegration" in 1924. Chambers' speech, which signaled

---

6 The MS to *Sir Thomas More* was identified as worthy of attention and published in 1844. See Chapter 11.

7 The "diary" or records of the theatrical impresario and businessman Philip Henslowe was discovered in the archives of Dulwich College in the late 1700s, but was not published until 1846. See Chapter 11.

8 "Who Wrote Shakespeare?" in Chambers' *Edinburgh Journal*, August 1852. See Chapter 12.

9 Fleay and Robertson are discussed in Chapter 14.

10 Greenwood's activities are discussed in Chapter 14.

his emergence as the dean of Shakespeare studies, was also a clear rebuke of the agnostic stance toward the orthodox canon taken by the likes of Fleay and Robertson. In sum, it laid down a position that held sway among orthodox Shakespeareans for the next sixty years, being supported in turn by the sharp skepticism of Samuel Schoenbaum and several others. Another important new perspective tracing to this period, while strictly historical, was the discovery by Leslie Hotson of documents proving beyond most reasonable doubts the circumstances of the death of Christopher Marlowe in May 1593.

In the 1980s, the position of the orthodox school began to change and expand. First, there was the promotion of texts that were attributed to Shakespeare, and which met the usual requirements for attribution, but which were very doubtful in content. Second, there was a reorganization of the canon by the Oxford University Press, which not only created an immense amount of confusion as to what constituted an authentic Shakespearean text but which also added some plays to the canon that had never been included before.

Meanwhile, the anti-Stratfordians, led largely by the labors of Charlton Ogburn, began to succeed in gathering attention to their alternative candidacy of de Vere, the Earl of Oxford. The culmination of this trend is notable not only in many books and articles, but also in television shows and videos, and in widely publicized moot courts.

The new century has led to reaction on both fronts. Some scholars[11] have been fated to play a double role: debunking what they feel are illegitimate additions to Shakespeare on the one hand, while stoutly defending collaborative attributions on the other. Others have made it their calling to refute the anti-Stratfordians, particularly the candidacy of Oxford.[12] Still others have continued to argue in favor either of alternative authorship or the fundamental principle of the validity of the authorship problem.[13] Meanwhile, Gary Taylor, who played a large role in the Oxford University Press reorganization, has championed alternative authorship of several plays, favoring the candidacy of Thomas Middleton, a late contemporary of Shakespeare, at least in a

---

11 Having in mind above all Brian Vickers, whose work in Elizabethan literature extends back to the 1960s, but who in recent decades has also become prominent in authorship debates. See chapters 18 and 25.

12 The most prominent critics of the Oxfordian case are Irvin Matus, Scott McCrae, and James Shapiro in chronological order. Shapiro's *Contested Will* (2011) is the most influential, and, along with John Michell's survey, *Who Wrote Shakespeare?* (1997) is one of the main sources the present text has in view. See also chapter 19.

13 Having in mind William D. Rubenstein and Roger A. Strittmatter; Rubinstein has also co-authored a book arguing an alternative candidacy for Sir Henry Neville, while Strittmatter has emerged as an authoritative Oxfordian. See Chapter 19.

collaborative sense. Anti-Stratfordians have continued with their arguments on Oxford's behalf, but some new and old candidates have also been much discussed, Marlowe chief among them, but also such new candidates as Henry Neville, Thomas Sackville, and Thomas North.

To attempt such a traversal in a brief compass presents a challenge. It is a challenge not only in terms of comprehensiveness but also in terms of simple comprehension. To assist in the latter, it will be necessary to introduce a lot of contextual material. We will also visit many of Shakespeare's contemporaries, and we will engage a number of topical themes that gave rise to much writing in his time. Due attention will thus be devoted to the Marprelate pamphlets, to the "War of the Theaters," and to attribution studies in general (particularly insofar as they touch on Homer and the Bible). It will also be necessary to consider the implicit philosophy of the plays, the deeply entrenched belief in furtive noble contributions to Elizabethan dramaturgy, and, of course, the plays and poems themselves.

The contextual information will be dealt with piecemeal so as not to put undue strain on the reader by introducing all of the characters in the first scene and making it impossible to follow the action. The notes are meant to direct the interested reader to more comprehensive treatments, to expand on a particular point, or simply to comment on the narrative as it unfolds. The evolution of scholarship, tied to the discovery of documents, will set the pace.

At the end of this traversal, a few things should be clear. First, by any normal attribution standard, the plays and poems can only be attributed to William Shakespeare, and no one else. However, this should not be considered a ringing endorsement that Shakespeare actually wrote them, because, by any normal standard of internal or contextual evidence, there is no way William Shakespeare could have written these plays. More: that any single individual could have written them. These conclusions will not settle the matter of authorship; they will, however, emphasize the extent to which the human mind will strain for meaning when confronted with the cloud of unknowing.

2 | Hidden Persuaders

Ben Jonson's Folio ~ The First Folio ~ Later Folios ~ Later Comments by Jonson ~ Origins of Elizabethan Theater ~ Macaulay's Fable

William Shakespeare died on or around April 23, 1616, at his home in Stratford-on-Avon; about 52 years from the day of his birth. There is no record of public reaction to his death.

Yet the most important event of 1616, at least in terms of the history of drama, was the publication by Ben Jonson (1572–1637), of his collected works in folio form. This was the first time that an English dramatist had sought to publish a collection of his works, including plays in a book.[14] The plays were published in the larger and sturdier folio format, and Jonson edited the plays to ensure that only his own writings were included. For example, one of the plays, *Sejanus*, was originally written with a collaborator, but Jonson went back and rewrote the play so that it would reflect only his hand.

Jonson's achievement can be better assessed if we compare it to the development of the theater during the preceding decades, particularly during the reign of Queen Elizabeth I (1533–1603), which began in 1553.

Bands of traveling actors were common in England the 16th century. Numbering perhaps a dozen, but usually fewer, such a troupe would travel from town to town to perform "interludes" or "plays" interspersed with acrobatic or tumbling routines, dances, music, and "jigs" which might feature all of the above as well as a kind of stand-up

---

14 Donaldson, Ian, *Ben Jonson: A Life*, 323–331, describes the preparation of Jonson's folio, and its uniqueness in including plays, as well as some mockery Jonson received as a result. He also duly notes Shakespeare's utter lack of concern for his own plays, while setting out various apologies for his failure to publish them.

comedy. The venues for these early performances would be anywhere a crowd could gather: a town hall or an abandoned monastery (thus, the name of a famous theater, "Blackfriars"), or an outdoor arena that featured blood sports such as bear baiting or cockfighting (thus, the name of another early theater, "The Cockpit"). The first site constructed specifically for theatrical performance came only in 1576, when James Burbage (ca. 1530–1597) built what was naturally enough called "The Theater."[15]

By the time "The Theater" opened, acting troupes were legally required to secure the patronage of a nobleman—who, we might assume, would also help sponsor them financially.[16] As a result, in the 1570s, we find a large number of acting troupes named after nobles: Lord Leicester's Men (a very old group going back to the 1550's), Oxford's Men, Lord Hunsford's Men, Lord Strange's Men, and several others, including an all-star troupe, Queen Elizabeth's Men, known also as just the Queen's Men.[17] By Shakespeare's time—in the early 1590s—many of these groups appear to have disbanded or reorganized themselves for any number of reasons; the death of the noble patron, or the inability to stay afloat during the periodic closing of the theaters due to epidemics, being obvious reasons.[18] While it was typical for theatrical companies to winter in London, all of them traveled. As early as 1585 a small troupe traveled to Elsinore in Denmark; there were travels to Holland and Germany as well, and there were several performances in small towns like Stratford-on-Avon.[19]

By the 1590s, the two main companies in London were the Admiral's Men, who mainly played at a theater called The Rose, and the Lord Chamberlain's Men, who played at The Globe. The latter was the

---

[15] Basic sources include: Chambers, EK, *Elizabethan Stage* (4 vols., ES); Bentley, Gerald Eades, *Jacobean and Caroline Stage* (7 vols., JCS); Fleay, Frederick, *Biographical Chronicle* (2 vols., BC); Fleay, Frederick, *Chronicle of London Stage* (CLS); Pollard, Tanya, ed., *Shakespeare's Theater*. Burbage's theater is usually considered the first such in London, but Pollard, ed., xi, claims 1567, with no reference.

[16] Fleay, CLS, 42-44, Pollard, ed., xv, discuss both the prohibitions and demand for licenses for plays in 1559, as well as the 1572 statute requiring players to have noble (baron or higher) patronage; legislation regulating the use of oaths or irreligious expressions came in 1606 (possibly relevant to our later construal of *Hamlet*.)

[17] Chambers, ES, vol. II provides detailed analyses of individual companies, and see also Andrew Gurr, *Shakespeare's Opposites: The Admiral's Company*, and Scott McMillan and Sally Beth MacLean, *The Queen's Men and their Plays*.

[18] The worst epidemic during the examined period was 1592-1593, just when Shakespeare began to make his appearance. There was another epidemic in 1603, and indeed several others in the first decade of the 1600s.

[19] Fleay, BC and CLS both discuss this; McMillan and MacLean list a visit to Stratford in 1587; trips to the continent are discussed in Chambers, ES, vol. II as well as Simon Williams, *Shakespeare on the German Stage, Volume I* (1990), both indebted to the groundbreaking work of Albert Cohn, *Shakespeare in Germany in the Sixteenth and Seventeenth Centuries* (1865).

company that Shakespeare was affiliated with, although after the death of Elizabeth its name was changed to The King's Men (since at that point they came under the patronage of Elizabeth's successor, King James). There remained several other smaller groups.

The actual plays that were performed are mostly unknown. We have the names of some plays, particularly when a troupe had the good fortune to be called to perform at Court (since Elizabeth was a great lover of the theater), but few texts survive. Matters become a little clearer as we move into the 1580s; we have more titles, and some surviving texts, but even then the names of the authors remain elusive. Even well into the 1590s and beyond we will find the names of plays like *Sir John Mandeville* or *The Black Batman of the North* but no text to match with them.[20]

Part of the problem is that plays were rarely published. This began to change around 1590, but even then published plays were identified primarily by the company that performed them, and rarely by an individual author (when plays were identified by author, such identification was often limited to ambiguous initials). This is not to imply that the theater was in a primitive state. On the contrary, by common acknowledgment two of the most important plays in the evolution of Elizabethan theater were first staged in the mid-1580s: *Tamburlaine* and *The Spanish Tragedy*. Both were published in the early 1590s, but the only reason we know that the first was written by Christopher Marlowe is because of a consensus agreement about the meaning of a few lines of poetry; and the only reason we know Thomas Kyd wrote the latter is because of a stray comment made 20 years later.[21]

All of this suggests that plays were not taken very seriously as a form of literary expression. Poems, sonnet cycles, translations, even polemics might be published under an author's name, but plays rarely were. For example, Robert Greene was a prolific writer, and also a playwright, but while his books were attributed to him, no play was ever published under his name in his lifetime. This began to change during the 1590s, and Shakespeare's plays are a prime indication of that change.

Thus over several decades dramatic works grew in perception from occasional, casual, and ephemeral productions until they at last

---

20 Chambers, ES, volume IV, lists around 80 published anonymous plays, the website lostplays.org lists many more, most known only by name. Brian Vickers, *Shakespeare as Co-Author*, 19, references hundreds.

21 Chambers, ES, volume III, 396 for Kyd, referenced by Heywood, *Apology*, in 1613 (the play is usually dated to 1584–1589). For Marlowe, Chambers, ES, volume III, 421, references Greene's *Perimedes the Blacksmith* of 1588, and Harvey referencing the death of the author in 1593. The Kyd reference in Heywood was not discovered until 1771.

achieved the status of durable works of art. It is fair to say that Jonson's 1616 Folio was a benchmark in establishing plays as works deserving of posterity and also meriting attribution to a specific author. There is more, for Jonson's Folio set the model—as well as the expectation—that would be followed by others. This is important to keep in mind.

We should understand a few things about book sizes. Folio size meant a printing sheet that had been folded in half, producing a page roughly the size of a standard 8.5" x 11" sheet of paper today (or the slightly longer A4 size in Europe). The next step down from folio size is quarto, and in this case the page is folded twice; this was by far the most common size of the texts we will be referring to in this study. Quartos were cheap, and usually issued in soft-cover, yielding something resembling a pamphlet or a slim oversized paperback. Quarto was also the most common size for the printing of plays, as well as novels and romances; lacking boards, they were highly perishable. Folios were more durable, because they were usually in boards, and more statement oriented. Still smaller sizes, e.g., octavo, were also common; octavo involved a three time fold and yielded a text about the size of a smaller 1950s-era paperback.

Jonson's Folio was unique for a dramatist at that time, and contained seven of his dramas (excluding his many collaborations with others), fifteen masques (a kind of dramatic performance meant for courtly or private audiences), half a dozen entertainments for the royal court, and two groups of poems.

At this time, a number of plays with Shakespeare's name printed on the cover were in circulation in London. Evidently, the demand for such plays increased toward the end of the 1610s, so there were a number of plays published with phony dates.[22] This appears to have been the impetus to the publication of the First Folio, preparations for which appear to have begun in 1621.

We do not know many critical facts about the publication of the First Folio. We do not know how its publication was financed or how the various printers involved worked together to produce it. We do not know how the plays were selected, nor what the printed versions were based on (although 20th century scholarship has made large strides in this area). Nor do we know who the driving force behind its publication

---

[22] In 1619, William Jaggard and Thomas Pavier, two printers, issued about ten Shakespeare plays, some with false dates going back to the beginning of the century. These "Pavier Quartos" (sometimes called the "False Folio") appear to have been the stimulus to gather all of the plays (or as many as possible) into a single edition.

was. We know the First Folio was priced at about 1£, which was a considerable amount back then, somewhere around $500–$1,000 today.[23] The print run was somewhere between 500 and 1,000 copies, therefore we can assume some patronage. But the most important thing about the First Folio, aside from its contents, is the front matter, which we will briefly summarize:[24]

1. A dedication to the woodcut of Shakespeare, ten lines in rhyming couplets, signed "B.I." and universally assumed as being by Ben Jonson.

2. The title page, which reads "Mr William Shakespeares Comedies, Histories, & Tragedies: Published according to the True Originall Copies" and "London, Printed by Isaac Jaggard and Ed. Blount, 1623." Between the title and the publication data lies the now famous (or notorious) woodcut of Shakespeare by Martin Droeshout. This is the normal woodcut portrait of Shakespeare that most people are familiar with; it has been harshly criticized for its ungainliness by everyone.

3. After a blank facing page, a two-page dedication to the "most noble" and "incomparable pair of brethren," William Herbert, Earl of Pembroke, and his brother Philip Herbert, the Earl of Montgomery. This is an extremely flowery bit of obsequiousness, but the names of these men are important to the controversy due to the tacit admission that Shakespeare was unable to edit these works himself. It is signed by John Heminge and Henry Condell, who, we know by other sources, were fellow members of Shakespeare's theater company.

4. A single-page appeal "To the great Variety of Readers" that again in flowery language appeals to readers to evaluate the book as they will "but buy it first" (and a bit further on, "what ever you do, Buy"). The appeal also contains the assurance that this version supersedes all previous versions, insofar as "you were abus'd with diverse stolne and surreptitious copies, maimed, and deformed by the frauds and stealthes of

---

23 Approximations for the value of the pound in the examined period range from $1,000 down to about $600, but the purchase power of the pound would have been greater than the nominal value in any case (insofar as quotes for the annual salary of a peasant have been listed as low as one or two £ in some sources).

24 Using Doug Moston, ed. *The First Folio of 1623* (photographic reproduction) as a guide.

injurious impostors." Again, this is signed by Heminge and Condell. Here are some extended excerpts:

> From the most able, to him that can but spell: there you are number'd. We had rather you were weighed; especially, when the fate of all bookes depends upon your capacities and not of your heads alone, but of your purses. Well! It is now publique, & you wil stand for your priviledges wee know: to read, and censure. Do so, but buy it first. That doth best commend a Booke, the Stationer saies. Then, how odde soever your braines be, or your wisedomes, make your licence the same, and spare not. Judge your six-pen'orth, your shillings worth, your five shillings worth at a time, or higher, so you rise to the just rates, and welcome. But, whatever you do, Buy. Censure will not drive a Trade, or make the Jacke go. And though you be a Magistrate of wit, and sit on the Stage at Black-Friers, or the Cock-pit, to arraigne Playes dailie, know, these Playes have had their triall alreadie, and stood out all Appeales ; and do now come forth quitted rather by a Decree of Court, then any purchased letters of commendation.
>
> It had bene a thing, we confesse, worthie to have bene wished, that the author himselfe had lived to have set forth, and overseen his owne writings; but since it hath bin ordain'd otherwise, and he by death departed from that right, we pray you do not envie his Friends, the office of their care, and paine, to have collected & publish'd them; and so to have publish'd them, as where (before) you were abused with diverse stolne, and surreptitious copies, maimed, and deformed by the frauds and stealthes of injurious impostors, that expos'd them: even those, are now offer'd to your view cur'd, and perfect of their limbes; and all the rest, absolute in their numbers as he conceived them.
>
> Who, as he was a happie imitator of Nature, was a most gentle expresser of it. His mind and hand went together: And what he thought, he uttered with that easinesse, that wee have scarse received from him a blot in his papers. But it is not our province, who onely gather his works, and give them you, to praise him. It is yours that reade him. And there we hope, to your divers capacities, you will finde enough, both to draw, and hold you: for his wit can no more lie hid, then it could be lost. Reade him, therefore; and againe, and againe: And if then you doe not like him, surely you are in some manifest

danger, not to understand him. And so we leave you to other of his Friends, whom if you need, can be your guides: if you neede them not, you can lead yourselves, and others, and such readers we wish him.

There are a couple of points to be made about this letter. First, it is commonly argued today that both the Heminge and Condell texts were not written by them, but by Ben Jonson instead.[25] Second, the letter in particular makes a number of statements—stolen and surreptitious copies, scarce found a blot in his papers—which are demonstrably false, depending on other interpretations.[26] Third and finally, the "happy imitator of nature" helps set up a longstanding dichotomy in Shakespeare studies: between the evidently learned author of some of the plays, and the natural untutored poet who, as Milton would later put it, "warbled his wood notes wild."

5. After another blank facing page is the table of contents. It lists 35 plays, but there are actually 36 in the Folio (for reasons that are unclear *Troilus and Cressida* was inserted at the last minute). Fully half the plays were published for the first time in the First Folio, which means that their inclusion is the main evidence, if not the only evidence, for their attribution to William Shakespeare.

6. After another facing page, there is a two-page poem signed by Ben Jonson. Along with the Droeshout engraving, this is probably the most famous element in the First Folio's front matter. Thus a few quotations are necessary:

> [....]
>
> I, therefore will begin. Soule of the Age!
> The applause! delight! the wonder of our Stage!
> My Shakespeare, rise; I will not lodge thee by
> Chaucer, or Spenser, or bid Beaumont lye
> A little further, to make thee a roome:
> Thou art a Moniment, without a tombe,

---

[25] Diana Price, in *Shakespeare's Unorthodox Biography*, quotes several Shakespearean authorities, 170–174. It is also a typical anti-Stratfordian position. The recent biographer of Jonson, Donaldson, also believes Jonson contributed to the open appeal to some degree, 370–376.

[26] The most likely reference to the "stolen and surreptitious copies" is to the Pavier quartos of 1619, but there were many cheap paperback quarto editions of at least half of the plays, and these vary sometimes widely from the Folio versions. Their existence in turn sets up a major tension in Shakespeare criticism, as we shall see.

> [....]
>
> For, if I thought my judgement were of yeeres,
> I should commit thee surely with thy peeres,
> And tell, how farre thou dist our Lily out-shine,
> Or sporting Kid or Marlowes mighty line.
> And though thou hadst small Latine, and lesse Greeke,
> From thence to honour thee, I would not seeke
> For names; but call forth thund'ring schilus,
> Euripides, and Sophocles to vs,
> Paccuvius, Accius, him of Cordova dead,
> To life againe, to heare thy Buskin tread,
> And shake a stage: Or, when thy sockes were on,
> Leave thee alone, for the comparison
> Of all, that insolent Greece, or haughtie Rome
> Sent forth, or since did from their ashes come.
>
> [....]
>
> But stay, I see thee in the Hemisphere
> Advanc'd, and made a Constellation there!
> Shine forth, thou Starre of Poets, and with rage,
> Or influence, chide, or cheere the drooping Stage;
> Which, since thy flight fro' hence, hath mourn'd like night,
> And despaires day, but for thy Volumes light.

The text is very famous in ways that are not always obvious. Anytime anyone refers to Marlowe and his "mighty line" they are quoting this text. "Soul of the Age" and "Monument without a tomb" are also famous catchphrases. The most notorious line refers to Shakespeare's lack of learning—"small Latine, and lesse Greeke"—which lends fuel to the debate about Nature versus Art. One small detail that is frequently cited by anti-Stratfordians is the vocative "Star of Poets"—"Star" in Greek is "aster," which could generate "Poet aster," meaning a poor or incompetent poet.

7. A page containing a sonnet celebrating Shakespeare in general terms, signed Hugh Holland.

8. After another facing page, two more encomiums to Shakespeare, one by "L. Digges" and another by "I.M."

9. Yet another facing page, and then the list of "principall actors" with "William Shakespeare" heading the list.

I am sure that to the casual reader such details about the front matter of the First Folio will seem pedantic, but the fact is that virtually every comma of this text has been worked over by Stratfordians and anti-Stratfordians for hundreds of years in order to yield clues about the nature of the First Folio, Shakespeare, and any alternative candidates for authorship. As a result, it is impossible to not reference it. At the same time, the over-analysis of this front matter does seem excessive, if only because it reads like advertising copy—not much different from the blurbs one could find on any book, not only in Elizabethan and Jacobean times, but down to our own day.[27]

Of course, a number of the statements made in the above quotations about the First Folio have been shown to be inaccurate, but such notes belong to the 20th century. For the moment, the only thing we need to keep in mind is the enormous authority this front matter has invoked, for almost four hundred years.

But that is not the end of the matter. While the first print run of the First Folio was somewhere between 500 and 1,000 copies, a second edition (usually called the Second Folio) was issued in 1632. In 1642 all of the theaters were closed as a result of the Civil War. They remained closed during the Protectorate, not reopening until 1662. Then in 1663 a third edition of the plays (called the Third Folio, naturally) was issued, but this edition included seven new plays: *Pericles, Locrine, The London Prodigal, The Puritan, Sir John Oldcastle, Thomas Lord Cromwell,* and *A Yorkshire Tragedy*. Excepting *Pericles*, none of these are considered authentic Shakespeare plays today. Finally, a Fourth Folio was issued in 1685. This version would be used as the basis for the first 18th century editors of Shakespeare.

Nor is that the end of Ben Jonson, either. In 1618, Jonson went on a walking tour of Scotland (where his father was born), and in early 1619 he visited the Scottish poet William Drummond of Hawthornden (1685-1649). Drummond later published his conversations with Jonson wherein Jonson made two references to Shakespeare. Twice Jonson said that Shakespeare "wanted art," by which he could have meant education, skill, or intelligence. In the second such reference he elaborated by saying that Shakespeare in one of his plays had placed a shipwreck in Bohemia—an obvious mistake, since Bohemia

---

27 That the front matter of the Folio is primarily advertising is not merely an anti-Stratfordian argument. See Kirschbaum, *Shakespeare and the Stationers*, 5 (although Kirschbaum considers it comparatively "honest" for the 17th century).

31

(essentially the modern Czech Republic) is a landlocked country.[28] The usual response to these remarks, by both sides, is to say that at one point Bohemia had a sliver of seacoast on the Adriatic, thus Shakespeare (whoever he was) was right. What is more noteworthy, however, is that the idea of a shipwreck in Bohemia came from a romance by Robert Greene, *Pandosto* (1590, reissued and retitled in 1607),[29] and it is that romance that was adapted into the play *The Winter's Tale* (usually assigned to the early 1600s). So what that quote actually means is that Jonson was not aware that that particular play was borrowed from Greene, and by extension it suggests that Jonson, for all his legendary learning and despite his fulsome praise in the Folio, was largely ignorant not only of Shakespeare's plays but also of the literature of his day.

The next reference Jonson made to Shakespeare comes in a late work, *Timber, or Discoveries*, which is a collection of various observations by Jonson, in many cases based on classical authors. In one, *De nostrati Shakespeare* (About our Shakespeare) Jonson wrote the following:[30]

> I remember, the Players have often mentioned it as an honour to Shakespeare, that in his writing, (whatsoever he penn'd) hee never blotted out a line. My answer hath beene, Would he had blotted a thousand. Which they thought a malevolent speech. I had not told posterity this, but for their ignorance, who choose that circumstance to commend their friend by, wherein he most faulted. And to justifie mine owne candor, (for I lov'd the man, and doe honour his memory (on this side Idolatry) as much as any.) Hee was (indeed) honest, and of an open, and free nature: had an excellent Phantsie; brave notions, and gentle expressions: wherein hee flow'd with that facility, that sometime it was necessary he should be stop'd: *Sufflaminandus erat*; as Augustus said of Haterius. His wit was in his owne power; would the rule of it had beene so too. Many times hee fell into those things, could not escape laughter: As when hee said in the person of Caesar, one speaking to him; Caesar, thou dost me wrong. Hee replyed Caesar did never wrong, but with just cause: and such like; which were ridiculous. But hee redeemed his vices, with his vertues. There was ever more in him to be praysed, then to be pardoned.

---

28 Patterson, R. F., ed., *Ben Jonson's Conversations with William Drummond of Hawthornden*, 5 (wanted Arte), 20 (Shipwrack in Bohemia). Patterson contended that Jonson only complained that Shakespeare wanted art once, and that the contrary perception only arose because other compilers have yoked the two references together, which he felt was inappropriate.

29 *Pandosto, or the Triumph of Time* was originally published in 1588. It was reissued in 1607 as *Dorastus and Fawnia*, and was quite a popular romance. It is usually assumed that the reissue was the source of *The Winter's Tale*.

30 Jonson, "Timber, or Discoveries Made on Men and Matter," *Works of Ben Jonson*, 871.

The above quote is usually taken by orthodox Shakespeareans as proof of Jonson's knowledge of Shakespeare, and his estimation of his plays. Anti-Stratfordians have a bit harder time with the text. Orthodox Stratfordians also usually offer a sententious comment that, whatever the error in *Julius Caesar*, Shakespeare subsequently corrected it in the text. However, a better reading might be that the reference to the garbled speech from *Julius Caesar* means that Jonson actually saw Shakespeare in that role, and saw him forget his lines. This interpretation aligns with later evidence that Shakespeare played kingly roles, but it also suggests that he lacked the sophistication to actually understand his own lines. The other information from the paragraph is that it appears Heminge and Condell thought the "never blotted out a line" phrase was very felicitous, which in turn suggests that Jonson wrote it, before he mocked it.

Before he became a famous historian, Thomas Macaulay wrote articles for the *Edinburgh Review*, which was a popular liberal monthly in 19th-century Britain. In one of these, Macaulay reviewed the work of a minor poet named Robert Montgomery.[31] Macaulay introduced his review by reference to an old Indian story about a Brahmin who went out one day to buy a sheep for sacrifice, but was tricked into buying a dog instead. The story goes that the Brahmin encountered a man who assured him that he had a fine sheep in his sack, but when the Brahmin resisted purchasing what was so clearly a dog, the man suggested that they should accept the judgment of a disinterested third party. Thereupon a confederate of the first man appeared, and assured the Brahmin that the dog was indeed a sheep. Finally a third member of the group appeared, and again confirmed the ovine nature of the dog in question. The Brahmin made the purchase, with predictably unfortunate consequences.

Macaulay used the fable for a lengthy discussion of what he called "puffery," that is, the unscrupulous advertising of second-rate books. But the concept could go in a number of directions. One could talk about majority opinion versus minority opinion, or one could talk about groupthink or cognitive dissonance versus critical voices outside the circle, or one could talk even more generally about public opinion, and how it is shaped, or how general beliefs are shaped, and how they

---

31 Macaulay, Thomas, *Lord Macaulay's Essays*, 131–132. Macaulay's review of Montgomery is notorious for its savagery, but remains an amusing dissection of bad poetry. Montgomery's poetical subjects in *The Omnipresence of the Deity*, and *Satan, or Intellect without God*, tie in well with early 19th century attempts to recapture religious faith, and bear comparison with the discussion of Samuel Schmucker in Chapter 7.

might be shaped on purpose. Usually, as in the case of our unlucky Brahmin, the idea is proposed that there was some kind of conspiracy involved, that those who promote a majority opinion, about anything, much less books, are driven by a conscious desire to deceive. However, one doesn't need recourse to conspiracies to explain human error. Most of the time, when a false belief holds sway, it is more a case of accident than deliberate deception. At any rate, we can be sure of one thing: advertising is not a conspiracy; it is simply an attempt to sell a product.

To sum up, although the front matter in the First Folio is the main proof that Shakespeare wrote the plays (and the only proof that he wrote half of them), its composition was not supervised by him, and we do not know how the texts were assembled, by whom, or from where. The fulsome praise in the dedicatory material appears to have been written mainly by one man, whose private estimation of Shakespeare was equivocal, and whose own Folio volume from seven years earlier clearly provided the model for this one (including the notion that plays deserve preservation in folio format centered on the attribution to a sole author). At the same time, the purpose of the front matter is mainly to guarantee the authenticity of the text, thereby promoting purchase of the book. With this much understood, it is only fair to question the testimonial power of this material.

In 1691, Gerard Langbaine published *An Account of the English Dramatick Poets* which was the first attempt at a history of English drama. The book itself was no great milestone in scholarship, but we will use it to introduce our first group of Shakespeare's contemporaries, all of whom were in London before him. Usually when we speak of groups of writers or artists we designate them in some way; the Lost Generation, the Lake Poets, the Romantics, and so on. The group we want to discuss already has a name, but I prefer to call them the Elizabethan Beats.

3 | ELIZABETH'S BEAT GENERATION

*The Beat Generation ~ John Lyly ~ Thomas Lodge
(Gosson) ~ George Peele ~ Robert Greene ~ Thomas Nashe
(Harvey) ~ Thomas Kyd ~ Christopher Marlowe*

When we read about the postwar Beat Generation in America, we usually have in mind a particular group of individuals and a particular set of literary works, the most iconic being Jack Kerouac's *On the Road*, Allen Ginsburg's *Howl*, and William S. Burroughs' *Naked Lunch*. But when we read further we find that these three writers, along with several others, were centered in New York City, and in particular, at and around Columbia University. We learn that they were addicted to adventure and silly pranks, such as rolling one of their number in a beer barrel down Broadway, or sticking one's head out of a moving subway car (which ended with a tragic decapitation.[32]) We find that they were alienated, disillusioned, and decadent in the style of the poets of *La Belle Epoque* in late 19th century France.[33]

They also had their share of personal problems. Mental illness touched the lives of many Beat writers, and currents of sexual libertinism and ambiguity increased the tension in their milieu and in their relationships. Tragedy and crime also figure in many Beat biographies. A young man named Lucien Carr, a central figure in the Columbia University circle, killed another man over a sexual misunderstanding; Kerouac helped hide the knife. More infamously, before he wrote *Queer* and *Naked Lunch* William Burroughs shot and killed

---

32 Bill Morgan, *The Typewriter Is Holy*; Ann Charters, ed., *The Portable Beat Reader*; David J. Kracijek, "The Last Beat", *Columbia Magazine*, Winter 2012-13.

33 The literary and artistic models of Lucien Carr and his circle seem imitative of the absinthe-laden atmosphere of late 19th century France. Consult in particular the life trajectories of Verlaine and Rimbaud in poetry, van Gogh and Gaugain in painting, and Huysmans and Mirbeau in literature (Mirbeau's *roman à clef* about van Gogh, *In the Sky*, was recently published in Ann Sterzinger's English translation).

his wife in what by most accounts was a "William Tell" stunt gone tragically wrong.

Alcoholism and drug addiction are predominant motifs in the lives of the Beats, leading in many cases to destitution. Indeed, themes of failure and disillusion are resonant in the collective portrait of a generation worn out, discarded, and incapable of fitting into "the Combine," to borrow a concept favored by Ken Kesey (who, while not exactly a beatnik, was an important transitional figure between them and the countercultural efflorescence of the mid to late 1960s). Ground down, beaten, incapable of fitting into a society whose values they no longer believed in: thus, the Beat Generation.

But suppose we didn't call them the "Beat Generation." Suppose we called them instead the "University Wits." Would our image of them change? Probably, because the words we use tend to limit or prejudice our perceptions. Yet the name "University Wits" would certainly be appropriate. After all, the founding members, so to speak, were all centered in Columbia, which is a university, and they were all extremely bright, and therefore, at least in one sense of the word, witty. At the same time "University Wits" just doesn't conjure the same feel for the members of the group. It doesn't leave us with the same impression of alienated men seeking to find a meaningful path through postwar America. Instead, we envision rich kids in monogrammed jackets and immaculately pressed flannel trousers making terrible puns in some dead language before embarking on a predictable life journey, buoyed by sizable trust funds.

As it happens Elizabeth's reign also had a group of young men who emerged from the two English universities at Cambridge and Oxford, and who came to London in the 1570s and 1580s in order to find their place in the world. They were the original "University Wits," though they were far from being cloistered intellectuals with a secure future. On the contrary, most of them came from poor or middling circumstances and sought to make their way in life through writing. One, John Lyly, more or less succeeded. Another, Thomas Lodge, eventually escaped the self-destructive vortex of the group, converted to Catholicism, and became a medical doctor. Four others, George Peele, Robert Greene, Thomas Nashe, and Christopher Marlowe, all died relatively young. Like their 20th century counterparts, they fell victim to their passions, their rashness, and their addictions.

The University Wits are directly relevant to any discussion of Shakespeare because there is no question that their forays into the world of drama created the models that Shakespeare later used. And, depending on who one consults, their writing either lies behind or even within the canon. Thus to these Elizabethan Beats we now turn.[34]

John Lyly (pronounced "Lily") was born in Hampshire in 1554 and was raised in Canterbury. He started at Oxford in 1571, receiving a BA in 1573 and an MA in 1575.[35] He then moved to London and in 1578 published *Euphues: The Anatomy of Wit*, which was something of a literary sensation. He followed it up with a sequel a couple of years later.

At around this time, in the early 1580s, Lyly began working for Edward de Vere, the Earl of Oxford, directing a troupe of boy actors at Blackfriars, a former Dominican monastery that had been converted for various purposes, including the staging of plays. Lyly continued in that capacity for a few years, until there was a falling out (still not understood) between him and Oxford. Lyly was subsequently arrested for debt (which may have been paid off by Oxford[36]). Around the same time, Lyly married an heiress.

We know that Lyly continued to write plays throughout the 1580s (eight comedies in all are known), but he quit the stage writing business in about 1595, retiring to the country. He died in 1606.[37]

Lyly is most famous for inaugurating an ornate and complex writing style called "Euphuism" after the hero of his first books. The following from *Euphues, the Anatomy of Wit* is a fair example:[38]

> As therefore the sweetest rose hath his prickle, the finest velvet his brack, the fairest flower his bran, so the sharpest wit hath his wanton will, and the holiest head his wicked way. And true it is that some men write and most men believe, that in all perfect shapes, a blemish bringeth rather a liking every way to the eyes, than a loathing any way to the mind. Venus had her mole in her cheek which made her more amiable: Helen her scar on her

---

34 For this and all other biographies offered here reliance has been on, first, Chambers, ES, III, and Bentley, JCS, III-IV, as well as *The Dictionary of National Biography* (DNB), first edition, 63 vols. 1885–1900, online at en.wikisource.org

35 According to Jeffrey L. Forgeng, in *Daily Life in Elizabethan England*, 59, the course of study for the Bachelor of Arts degree (BA) normally took four years and involved several terms of Latin, plus rhetoric and disputation (that is, the arts of argument and persuasion, also presumably in Latin), plus terms in music and basic mathematics. The Master of Arts degree (MA) took another three years, and involved Greek and philosophy (including metaphysics), as well as astronomy, geometry, and basic science.

36 Chambers, ES, III: 412.

37 Lyly's works can be accessed in the three-volume edition of R. Warwick Bond, *The Complete Works of John Lyly* (1902). As something of a running thread in this book, these editions of Shakespeare's contemporaries are usually at least a century old.

38 Bond, *Complete Works of John Lyly*, I:184-185 (text has been modernized for spelling and italics).

chin which Paris called cos amoris, the whetstone of love. Aristippus his wart, Lycurgus his wen: So likewise in the disposition of the mind, either virtue is overshadowed with some vice, or vice overcast with some virtue. Alexander valiant in war, yet given to wine. Tully eloquent in his glozes, yet vainglorious: Solomon wise, yet too wanton: David holy but yet an homicide: none more witty than Euphues, yet at the first none more wicked. The freshest colors soonest fade, the keenest razor soonest turneth his edge, the finest cloth is soonest eaten with moths, and the cambric sooner stained than the coarse canvas: which appeared well in this Euphues, whose wit being like wax apt to receive any impression, and having the bridle in his own hands, either to use the rein or the spur, disdaining counsel, leaving his country, loathing his old acquaintance, thought either by wit to obtain some conquest, or by shame to abide some conflict, and leaving the rule of reason, rashly ran unto destruction.

This kind of prolix rhetorical style was not created by Lyly; there had been, and have been, many authors who invoke the style from time to time. However, Lyly was the first to make it a defining characteristic of his own literary output.

Thomas Lodge was the other acknowledged master of the Euphuist manner. He was born in about 1558. His father was a grocer who had once been Lord Mayor of London, as had ancestors on his mother's side. Lodge was thus a self-styled "gentleman," not noble, but not a commoner either. He also attended Oxford, where he earned his BA in 1577. In 1578 he began his studies at Lincoln's Inn, which was one of the four "Inns of Court" where one trained for a law career. However, his law career was interrupted by a quarrel in print with Stephen Gosson (1554–1624).

Gosson had been a playwright in the 1570s but had a change of heart, embracing the moral austerities of the Puritans. He then turned on his former literary productions and wrote *School of Abuse* (1579), a scathing attack on the theaters and the dramatic arts generally. Lodge fired back with *Defence of Playes* (1580), a rather poorly arranged pamphlet that was euphuistic in style and heavily encrusted with classical references. Gosson then countered with *Plays Confuted in Five Actions* (1582), a polemic laced with personal abuse and accusations against Lodge.[39]

---

[39] Gosson's *School of Abuse* is available in a modernized "Renascence Edition" at the website luminarium.org; *Plays Confuted in Five Actions* is very rare, thus Tanya Pollard, *Shakespeare's Theater*, provides almost the entire text. Pollard is careful to note that while Gosson embraced Puritan values he was not a Puritan: later in life he became a minister in the Church of England.

Despite the largely groundless basis for Gosson's attacks on Lodge, we do know that Lodge got into some kind of trouble since he was called before the Privy Council in 1581. Other sources indicate that he was disinherited for failing to practice law. We do know that he began writing—including playwriting—in the mid 1580s, while he maintained his address at the Inns of Court until at least 1585.

We can also be fairly certain that Lodge had troubles with debts. The primary source for this is his *Alarum against Usurers* (1585), a tract in which relevant autobiographical detail may be discerned. Between the late 1580s and early 1590s he went on two voyages, one to the Canaries in 1589 (during which he is supposed to have whiled away the time by writing *Rosalynde: Euphues Golden Legacy*), and again from late 1591 to mid-1593 (which yielded *A Margarite for America*). Several other books followed, and by 1595, when he published *Wit's Miserie*, he had quit London, and the stage. It was around this point that Lodge also converted to Catholicism, spending several years outside of England, mostly in France. In 1600 he became a physician, assuming his MD at Oxford.[40]

Although Lodge was active in defending the stage, we know very little about his own dramatic output. Only two plays under his name survive. One is *The Wounds of Civil War*, a Roman play that was published in 1594 (but probably written years earlier). The other, listed as having been co-written with Robert Greene, is *A Looking Glass for London and England*, which was also published in 1594 (but usually backdated to 1590). There has been some speculation about his involvement as an actor, since the name "Lodge" appears in a later theatrical document, but the case remains unproved. He is frequently mentioned as a possible author of many anonymous plays as well as some Shakespeare plays.

Lodge's greatest fame however lies with *Rosalynde*, since the play *As You Like It* is heavily based on it. The book is a curious Euphuistic mixture of poetry and prose. A sample:[41]

> Aim your deeds by my honorable endeavors, and show yourselves scions worthy of so flourishing a tree, lest, as the bird Halcyones, which exceed in whiteness, I hatch ones that surpass in blackness. Climb not, my sons: aspiring pride is the vapor that ascendeth high,

---

40 Lodge's collected works can be found in the four-volume edition of Edmund W Gosse, *The Complete Works of Thomas Lodge* (1883).

41 Lodge, Thomas, *Rosalynde, or, Euphues' Golden Legacy*, 3–4.

but soon turneth to a smoke; they which stare at the stars stumble on stones, and such as gaze at the sun (unless they be eagle-eyed) fall blind. [....] Take heed, my sons, the mean is sweetest melody; where strings high stretched, either soon crack, or quickly grow out of tune.

Note the metaphor featuring the exotic bird. This is what "euphuistic" mainly means, that is, the appropriation of obscure, or even false, natural history in the service of larger generalizations. However, in later times the word has been invoked to encompass all species of excessively ornate prose.

Shortly after the above excerpt, Lodge shifts into verse:[42]

> In choice of wife, prefer the modest-chaste,
> Lilies are fair in show, but foul in smell:
> The sweetest looks by age are soon defaced;
> Then choose thy wife by wit and living well.
> Who brings thee wealth and many faults withal,
> Presents thee honey mixed with gall.

We now turn to Robert Greene, the player who most fully embraced the bohemian lifestyle of the Wits. Born in 1558, Greene went to Cambridge, earning his BA in 1578 and his MA in 1583. There is some evidence that he may have been a vicar in Essex for a time[43] (Greene himself claimed that he traveled all over Europe[44]). What we do know is that Greene ended up in London, where, based on book dedications and other evidence, he was probably in the employ of the Earl of Oxford for some time. Though he wrote plays, Greene was probably most notorious for various books or pamphlets focusing on the underside of London life—the world of petty thieves and prostitutes, which he immortalized in such titles as *A Defence of Cony Catching*.[45]

---

42 Lodge, Rosalynde, 6.

43 Chambers, ES, III: 323 cites evidence that a Robert Greene was a vicar in Essex, 1584–85; part of the force of that evidence is that it ties into the identification of the author of the *Pinner of Wakefield*, which is discussed below.

44 In *A Notable Discovery of Cozenage* (1591), Greene claims to have been to France, Germany, Poland, and Denmark, and to have had contact with Spaniards and Italians. The references to Germany, Poland, and Denmark suggest that he followed a known route for players along the Baltic. See also Williams, *German Stage* and Cohn, *Shakespeare in Germany*.

45 Editions of Greene's writings, mainly his dramatic and poetical works, may be found in Alexander Dyce's edition, *The Dramatic and Poetical Works of Robert Greene & George Peele* (1883), Dyce's edition of *The Dramatic Works of Robert Greene* (2 vols., 1831), J. Churton Carlton's *The Plays & Poems of Robert Greene* (1905), and finally the much rarer *Life and Complete Works in Prose and Poetry of Robert Greene* (15 vols, 1881–86) edited by Alexander Grosart. About 40 of Greene's numerous prose works have been painstakingly converted to modern type and spelling by Nina Green, at oxford-shakespeare.com, and have been frequently consulted if not necessarily quoted.

According to the usual story, Greene deserted his wife and children, married the prostitute daughter of a petty thief named Cutting Ball, had a son, who he named Fortunatus, and then, after writing his last pamphlet, *Groatsworth of Wit*, died in the fall of 1592.

Greene's dramatic work is again hard to measure. A handful of plays, all published posthumously in the 1590s, named him as author.

For reasons that will become apparent, Robert Greene provides a useful transition to the next member of the group, Thomas Nashe. But Nashe is best introduced through the person of Gabriel Harvey (1550–1631), a Cambridge scholar and a rough contemporary of the poet Edmund Spenser. Harvey comes into our story for several reasons. He had a brother who wrote on astrology; he himself wrote several verses and was attempting to invent a hexameter style for English (hexameter being the poetical style of Homer and copied by Vergil and others subsequently); and, the relevant point for now, because of his running feud with Thomas Nashe.

The bad blood appears to have started around 1580 when Edmund Spenser published some of Harvey's attempts at hexameter verse. One of these, the "Mirror of Tuscanismo" contained a parodic description of someone who slavishly followed Italian fashions. John Lyly considered it a description of the Earl of Oxford, even though Harvey strenuously denied this. Meanwhile, Gabriel Harvey's brother Richard (the one with an interest in astrology) was making disparaging comments about Robert Greene (who was also on the Earl of Oxford's payroll) and finally Greene retaliated against the Harvey brothers with the pamphlet, *Quip for an Upstart Courtier* (1592), in which Greene revealed the mortifying information that Harvey's father was a rope maker from the village of Saffron Walden. It was one of Greene's last publications, and he died by the end of the year.

Enter Thomas Nashe. Nashe was born in 1567, and was therefore the youngest of the Elizabethan Beats. He came from a minister's family. He matriculated at Cambridge in 1582, got his BA in 1585, staying on for some time. His writings imply that he took a tour of France and Italy at some point, but by 1588 he was living in London, following the path of a writer. His first published writing under his own name was a preface to a book by Greene, *Menaphon* (1589), which we will reference later because of its significance in dating *Hamlet*. Several other items followed.

Nashe appears to have won his spurs in the London intellectual world through his contributions to the "Martin Marprelate Controversy," which involved a series of some seven pamphlets written by Puritans under the name "Martin Marprelate" attacking the hierarchy of the Church of England. The pamphlets were published covertly on a roving printing press over a six month period from late 1588 to the summer of 1589. Along with several other writers, Nashe was engaged in rebutting these pamphlets and his efforts soon earned him a reputation as a raucous and sarcastic debater with a distinctive prose style. As the Marprelate controversy was dying down, Robert Harvey (the astrologer brother) stepped in with some critical remarks directed at Lyly, Greene, and Nashe over their conduct in the pamphlet war. This led to Nashe's pamphlet, *Pierce Penniless, his Supplication to the Devil* (1592) which would later be revised.[46]

This brings us back to Gabriel Harvey's quarrel with Greene. After Greene's death, Harvey published *Four Letters and Certain Sonnets* (1592)[47] which contained an explicit attack on Greene along with some sorry details about his last days. Nashe followed in 1593 with his sardonically titled *Strange News of the Intercepting of certaine Letters and a Convoy of Verses as they were going privily to victual the Low Countries* (implying that Harvey's pamphlet had been intercepted on the way to the outhouse). Gabriel Harvey soon responded in kind with *Pierce's Supererogation*, which included several attacks on Nashe. This back and forth went on until Nashe backed down, offering a kind of apology in his *Christ's Tears in Jerusalem* (1594). While Harvey tried to fuel the public quarrel with his *New Letter of Notable Contents* in 1595, Nashe moved onto other projects for a time. But in 1596 Nashe would return to the ring with *Have with you to Saffron Walden*, which essentially meant "Gabriel Harvey, go home." Nashe's ostensible final volley came laced with another series of scurrilous broadsides.[48]

---

46 There are two standard editions of Nashe's works, one in six volumes by Grosart (1883–84), *The Complete Works of Thomas Nashe*, and the edition by Ronald B. McKerrow (1904–05), *The Works of Thomas Nashe* in three to four volumes (the fourth volume was announced but apparently only three were printed). As with Greene, over 20 of Nashe's works have been modernized and uploaded by Nina Green, at oxford-shakespeare.com, due to her belief that both Greene and Nashe were fronts for the Earl of Oxford.

47 Harvey, *Four Letters and Certain Sonnets, Especially Touching Robert Greene and Other Parties by Him Abused* (1592, 19th century reprint, nd, "Yellow Series"); also see Grosart's *Works of Gabriel Harvey* (3 vols, 1883).

48 Which included a woodcut of an Elizabethan gentleman in contorted posture, with the caption, "The picture of Gabriell Harvey as he is readie to let fly upon Ajax" ("Ajax" being slang for toilet). The explanation in the body of the text reads, "let them behold his lively counterfeit and portraiture, not in the pantofles of his prosperity, as he was when he libelled against my Lord of Oxford, but in the single-soled pumps of his adversity, with his gown cast off, untrussing, and ready to bewray himself upon the news of the going in hand of my book."

In late 1597, while Nashe was in prison, Harvey attempted to get the last word in with *The Trimming of Thomas Nashe*. The row might have gone on, but in 1599 the Archbishop of Canterbury stepped in, ordering that all of the pamphlets involved in the quarrel be destroyed and never printed again. Of course, copies of the pamphlets survived, and the prevailing sense among scholars since is that Nashe won the argument, at least in terms of style.

Here is a sample of Nashe's prose, written shortly before his quarrel with Harvey to introduce a book of poetry by the deceased Philip Sidney (here, *Astrophel*):[49]

> The sun for a time may mask his golden head in a cloud, yet in the end the thick veil doth vanish, and his embellished blandishment appears. Long hath Astrophel (England's sun) withheld the beams of his spirit from the common view of our dark sense, and night hath hovered over the gardens of the nine sisters, while ignis fatuus and gross fatty flames (such as commonly arise out of dunghills) have took occasion, in the middest eclipse of his shining perfections, to wander abroad with a wisp of paper at their tails like hobgoblins, and lead men up and down in a circle of absurdity a whole week, and never know where they are. But now that cloud of sorrow is dissolved which fiery love exhaled from his dewy hair, and affection hath unburdened the labouring streams of her womb in the low cistern of his grave; the night hath resigned her jetty throne unto Lucifer, and clear daylight possesseth the sky that was dimmed; wherefore break off your dance, you fairies and elves, and from the fields with the torn carcasses of your timbrels, for your kingdom is expired. Put out your rush candles, you poets and rimers, and bequeath your crazed quartorzains to the chandlers, for lo, here he cometh that hath broken your legs.

Nashe was involved in several other literary projects. He wrote *The Terrors of the Night* (a study of dreams and oneiromancy), and *The Unfortunate Traveler* (a picaresque novel). He was also involved in playwriting, though—as with most of the Elizabethan Beats—it is hard to tell how much. Only one play survives under his own name, *Summer's last Will and Testament*. It was published in 1600, but its dialog shows a creditable linkage to the verbal jousting and wordplay that

---

[49] Nashe, Preface to Sidney's *Astrophel and Stella* ("Somewhat to Read for them that List"), using Nina Green's transcription.

we find in the comedies of Lyly and Shakespeare.[50] It should be noted that Nashe also completed and had published one of Marlowe's plays, *The Tragedy of Dido, the Queen of Carthage*. Nashe also introduced the dildo into English literature with his poem, *The Choice of Valentines*. The action of that poem concerns a young man who, wishing to see his Valentine, goes to the whorehouse where she works. When the hero is unable to perform, despite the best efforts of his beloved, he is resigned to the role of voyeur as she produces the engine of self-pleasuring and takes matters into her own hands. The description is remarkable for its length and detail.[51]

In the summer of 1597, Nashe helped write a play called *The Isle of Dogs*. The play was almost immediately suppressed for being seditious, and both Nashe and Ben Jonson were imprisoned briefly. Immediately upon release, Nashe left London and moved to the eastern coast where he wrote *Nashe's Lenten Stuffe*. He was dead by 1601.

The next member of the group is George Peele (1558–1597). His father was a clerk in London who also wrote a book about book-keeping. Peele went to Oxford and received his BA in 1577 and his MA in 1579. Returning to London, he followed the general trajectory of London writers: widely varied productivity and extreme poverty. His first play, *The Arraignment of Paris*, was apparently written in 1580, but although he was active in the London theater for almost two decades, very few plays survive under his name. In addition to *The Arraignment*, Peele is credited with *The Famous Chronicle of Edward I*, a typical Elizabethan history play heavily indebted to Holinshed's *Chronicles*; *The Battle of Alcazar*, written in a style meant to capitalize on the popularity of Marlowe's *Tamburlaine*; *The Old Wives' Tale*; and *The Love of King David and Fair Bathsheba*.

Peele also wrote poetry in a variety of styles. His name is attached to *The Merry Conceited Jests of George Peele*, which was not published until 1605, eight years after his death. The *Jests* and associated texts describe Peele as a redhead with a high voice and fun loving disposition: sort of an Elizabethan Carrot Top. One such jest involved the occasion in which Peele sought to fool a hog drover into thinking his

---

50 *Summer's Last Will and Testament* is supposed to have been written in the early 1590s. Its publication in 1600 suggests Nashe's recent death as well as the presence of literary remains in the wake of the decease of other impecunious writers.

51 The dildo is unnamed, compare "Steely Dan" in Burroughs' *Naked Lunch*, although *The Choice of Valentines* is not referenced in Ingleby's *Shakespeare Allusion Book*. The McKerrow edition of Nashe (vol. 3) contains a description of the text along with a discussion of the simple substitution code for some passages; however, Nina Green's website has the complete text with modernized spelling.

pigs were sheep; the drover demurred, and Peele suggested that they ask a third party, who was Peele's friend and in on the joke. As with the MacCaulay story of the Brahmin mentioned earlier, we already know how the story will turn out.[52]

By 1596, Peele appears to have been seriously ill. On one occasion, he had his ten-year-old daughter carry a copy of an old manuscript of verses to a patron, no doubt in the hopes of some reward. He was dead by the end of the year.

The last two members of the group under discussion are Thomas Kyd (1557–1595) and Christopher Marlowe (1564–1593), who will be discussed in tandem because they shared apartments at around the time of Marlowe's death.

Thomas Kyd was the son of a scrivener, that is, a copyist and stenographer. He received a good grammar school education at Merchant Taylors' School in London. Kyd was well educated and knew Latin, French, Italian, and some Spanish. His main claim to fame is *The Spanish Tragedy*, a revenge tragedy, complete with a ghost, in the style of Seneca's tragedies. It was apparently written sometime in the 1580s, and it was enormously popular, even being exported to the Continent, which is why in the 19th century there was a great deal of attention paid to Kyd by Dutch and German scholars. Only one play was published under Kyd's name, *Cornelia*, in late 1593. Beyond that his output is measured by occasional writings with the telltale initials "T. K." and by various attributions.[53]

Christopher Marlowe was from Canterbury, the son of a shoemaker.[54] He received financial assistance for his education from childhood onward. Attending Cambridge from 1580, he received his BA in 1583 and his MA in 1587. The award of his MA was held up because at some point Marlowe had been sent to the Continent, specifically to Rheims, where he was employed as a spy on English Catholics. There is no question that he was in London by 1587, because that is where *Tamburlaine* was put on the stage.

---

52 The biographical details and reference to the Merry Conceited Jests both from the memorial essay in Dyce's *Complete Works of Robert Greene and George Peele*.

53 Boas, ed., *The Works of Thomas Kyd*, xiii-cvii.

54 Marlowe is the one member of the group to receive fairly constant attention; compare Frederick Boas, *Marlowe and his Circle*(1929) with modern treatments such as David Riggs, *The World of Christopher Marlowe* (standard contextual academic biography), Charles Nicholl, *The Reckoning: The Murder of Christopher Marlowe* (highly detailed and focusing on Marlowe's connection with the Elizabethan secret service and spy network), Park Honan, *Christopher Marlowe, Poet & Spy* (self-explanatory academic biography), and Daryl Pinksen, *Marlowe's Ghost*, which argues that Marlowe wrote the plays.

Tamburlaine tells the story of the shepherd Tamerlane, a historical figure,[55] who later becomes the emperor of Asia Minor. As such it introduces a typical Marlovian theme of a single individual who overcomes obstacles to attain absolute power. Such plots were enormously popular, but what really carried the play was Marlowe's stunning command of blank verse and his extraordinary verbal sequences; thus, in the second part of the play, Tamburlaine enters the stage leading a group of Asian monarchs in chains, with his chariot pulled by two kings with bits in their mouths, while Tamburlaine delivers this speech:[56]

> Holla, ye pamper'd jades of Asia!
> What, can ye draw but twenty miles a-day,
> And have so proud a chariot at your heels,
> And such a coachman as great Tamburlaine,
> But from Asphaltis, where I conquer'd you,
> To Byron here, where thus I honour you?
> The horse that guide the golden eye of heaven,
> And blow the morning from their nostrils,
> Making their fiery gait above the clouds,
> Are not so honour'd in their governor
> As you, ye slaves, in mighty Tamburlaine.
> The headstrong jades of Thrace Alcides tam'd,
> That King Aegeus fed with human flesh,
> And made so wanton that they knew their strengths,
> Were not subdu'd with valour more divine
> Than you by this unconquer'd arm of mine.
> To make you fierce, and fit my appetite,
> You shall be fed with flesh as raw as blood,
> And drink in pails the strongest muscadel:
> If you can live with it, then live, and draw
> My chariot swifter than the racking clouds;
> If not, then die like beasts, and fit for naught
> But perches for the black and fatal ravens.
> Thus am I right the scourge of highest Jove;
> And see the figure of my dignity,
> By which I hold my name and majesty!

---

55 Tamerlane (ca. 1330–1405), also known as Timur and similar variants, ruled the Timurid empire from 1370 until his death.

56 *Tamburlaine the Great—The Second Part*, Act IV, Scene III, in M. G. Scarsbrook, ed. *The Life & Complete Works of Christopher Marlowe* (Kindle).

Such an over-the-top style is one of the reasons why Marlowe is sometimes faulted for bombast.[57]

Marlowe immediately became the most popular playwright of his time, and five other plays of his have come down to us: *Edward II*, *The Jew of Malta*, *The Massacre in Paris*, *The Tragedy of Dido*, and perhaps the greatest of all Elizabethan dramas, *Doctor Faustus*. Most of these were published posthumously: in the case of the *The Jew of Malta*, not until 1633.

In addition to being a great playwright, Marlowe was also a poet of some distinction, and a translator of Latin poets. He also had a knack for getting into difficulties. He was in a knife and sword fight, which got him into trouble with the authorities. He was involved in an attempt to counterfeit coins.

He was also suspected of defacing a Dutch church and other locations in London with threatening verses—an event which created the circumstances of his death. Marlowe was arrested in May 1593. He was then released with instructions to be available for further questioning. Two weeks later, in Deptford, he was killed in a knife fight, the exact circumstances of which would not be understood for over three hundred years.[58]

There is a sequel. Because he had lived with Marlowe for a time, Kyd was arrested after Marlowe's death and was tortured. A document was found in Kyd's possession that was anti-Christian in nature; this was attributed to Marlowe. Kyd eventually wrote a letter accusing Marlowe of atheism. Meanwhile, a Richard Baines produced a document itemizing Marlowe's various blasphemies, such as:

- That Moses was but a juggler, and that one Heriots, being W. Raleigh's man, can do more than he.
- That Christ was a bastard and his mother dishonest.
- That all that love not tobacco and boys are fools.[59]

Of course, these are cartoon blasphemies, or the kind of things someone would come up with if they wanted to accuse someone of

---

57 The quote was also much parodied, thus, Pistol in *Henry IV, Part 1*: "These be good humours, indeed! Shall packhorses, And hollow pamper'd jades of Asia, Which cannot go but thirty mile a day" and even as late as *Eastward Ho!* in 1605: "Quick. Eastward Ho! "Holla, ye pampered jades of Asia!" Touch. [aside] Drunk now downright, a' my fidelity!"

58 Riggs, *World of Christopher Marlowe*, 306, notes that there were several literary remains.

59 Pinksen, *Marlowe's Ghost*, 24–26 seems to provide the complete list of charges; the document is dated three days before Marlowe's supposed death.

blasphemy.[60] That is why the circumstances of Marlowe's death remain suspicious; to this day there are those who believe he was murdered, or even that his death was staged. The scandals surrounding Marlowe's death would leave him branded as an atheist and a homosexual thereafter. The stigma was an issue in Marlovian criticism until such characterizations became matters of no consequence in the 20th century.

Kyd, who had always lived in poverty, died a broken man from his torture in 1595.

Lyly, Lodge, Greene, Nashe, Peele, Marlowe, and Kyd were among the intellectual elite in London in the 1580s, at least among non-nobles. All of them were well educated (only Kyd failed to attend university), and all were highly intelligent and extremely talented writers. All were involved in the London stage. Yet the dramatic output for all seven only amounts to about two dozen plays over a period of roughly two decades. Partly for this reason, and partly for stylistic reasons, all of them have had parts of the Shakespearean canon attributed to them over the years.

There are some other characteristics that seem to unite the group. They wrote extensively, and often, in all available genres (Greene and Nashe in particular were known to write very spontaneously). Many of their writings were originally published anonymously. Lyly, Greene, Peele, and Nashe were all probably at one time or another patronized by the Earl of Oxford. All of them were poor, all of them had problems with debts (failure to pay debts was a criminal offense that could lead to imprisonment in this era), and several had problems with a dissolute and promiscuous lifestyle. Only Lyly and Lodge managed to escape, but all of them, except Lodge, would be dead by 1606. Each of these men would have been available for impromptu writing assignments throughout the 1580s and 90s. And they would have left behind literary remains that would later be passed on to others.

We can now turn to the first editors of their greatest contemporary, William Shakespeare.

---

60 Michell, *Who Wrote Shakespeare?*, 234.

4 | THE FIRST EDITORS

Samuel Pepys ~ Edward Ravenscroft ~ Nicholas Rowe ~ John Aubrey ~ The Shakespeare Mythos ~ Alexander Pope ~ Lewis Theobald

The theaters were closed from 1642 to 1662 as a result of the conflict that led to the English Civil War, the execution of Charles I, and the Protectorate of Oliver Cromwell. We can assume the twenty-year hiatus had a detrimental effect on the continuity of historical memory. When the theaters reopened in the 1660s, in any case, the evidence suggests that a rather casual attitude prevailed regarding the past. Reading *The Diary of Samuel Pepys*, for example, shows an amusing disregard for Shakespeare's plays: *Romeo and Juliet* is "the worst I ever heard in my life," *Midsummer Night's Dream* is "the most insipid ridiculous play that I ever saw in my life," *Twelfth Night* is a "silly play," and so on. On the other hand, Pepys saw *Macbeth* no less than four times, because it was one of the "best plays...for variety of music and dancing," and while he also disparaged *The Tempest*, he liked the tune of the seaman's dance, which he eventually was able to commit to memory. Beyond amusement, however, such comments should remind us of one thing: that a Shakespeare play is much more than the words of which it is composed.[61]

John Dryden, the leading poet of the Restoration, also wrote in reference to Shakespeare, and he appears to have been the first to call Shakespeare Homer, as the "father of our dramatic poets." Dryden also appears to have furthered the Nature vs. Nurture debate by opining

---

61 Basic source for Shakespearean criticism in the 18th century is Vickers, *Critical Heritage* (6 vols.). For Pepys, Vickers, *Critical*, 1: 30-32

that Shakespeare "needed not the spectacles of Books to read Nature."[62]

John Milton seemed to precede Dryden, for in his *L'Allegro* he referenced "sweetest Shakespear, fancies childe" among the good things in life, to be left to "warble his native Wood-notes wilde."[63] But already in this period we begin to see a glimmering of the future controversy. In 1678, Edward Ravenscroft published a revised version of *Titus Andronicus* with the following note:[64]

> I think it is a greater theft to Rob the dead of their Praise than the Living of their Money: That I might not appear Guilty of such a Crime, 'tis necessary I should acquaint you, that there is a play in Mr. Shakespeare's volume under the name of Titus Andronicus, from whence I drew part of this. I have been told by some anciently conversant with the Stage, that it was not Originally his, but brought by a private Author to be Acted, and he only gave some Master-touches to one or two of the Principal Parts or Characters; this I am apt to believe, because 'tis the most incorrect and indigested of his Works; it seems rather a heap of Rubbish than a Structure.

It took almost a century after Shakespeare's death before an attempt was made to codify his works. The first attempt was made by Nicholas Rowe, who was himself a playwright, best known for *The Fair Penitent* (1703) which introduced the character of Lothario into the popular lexicon as a byword for a philanderer.

Rowe's edition used the Fourth Folio, which, as we have noted, contained 43 plays. Another fault to Rowe's edition is that he only consulted a couple of the sizable number of quarto editions of the plays (to repeat, about half of the plays in the First Folio had quarto editions, some several, and there were differences among these). On the other hand, Rowe was the first to attempt a biographical essay about William Shakespeare. Among the sources he may have used were notes that had been gathered by John Aubrey (1626–1697), the same John Aubrey we encountered at Avebury.[65] In addition to his archaeological interests, Aubrey was a great gossip who enjoyed having his house-guests regale him with tales about contemporary celebrities. These notes would not

---

62 Vickers, *Critical*, 1:139.

63 Milton, *L'Allegro*, lines 133–134, *The Poetical Works of John Milton* (Kindle).

64 Vickers, *Critical*, 1:238–239.

65 It is also possible that Rowe and Aubrey both consulted the same source: Thomas Betterton, (ca. 1635–1710), a prominent actor; another actor, William Beeston, was a known source for Aubrey but died in 1682.

be published in full until 1898. The entry for Shakespeare is brief, and reads as follows:[66]

> Mr William Shakespeare was borne at Stratford upon Avon in the County of Warwick. His father was a Butcher, and I have been told heretofore by some of the neighbours, that when he was a boy he exercised his father's Trade, but when he kill'd a Calfe he would doe it in a high style, and make a Speech. There was at this time another Butcher's son in this Towne that was held not at all inferior to him for a naturall witt, his acquaintance and coetanean, but dyed young.
>
> This William, being inclined naturally to Poetry and acting, came to London, I guesse about 18: and was an Actor at one of the Playhouses, and did acte exceedingly well: now B. Johnson was never a good Actor, but an excellent Instructor.
>
> He began early to make essayes at Dramatique Poetry, which at that time was very lowe; and his Playes tooke well. He was a handsome, well-shap't man: very good company, and of a very readie and pleasant smoothe Witt. The Humour of the Constable in Midsomernight's Dreame, he happened to take at Grendon, in Bucks (I thinke it was Midsomer night that he happened to lye there) which is the roade from London to Stratford; and there was living that Constable about 1642, when I first came to Oxon. Ben Johnson and he did gather Humours of men dayly where ever they came.
>
> One time as he was at the Tavern at Stratford super Avon, one Combes, an old rich Usurer, was to be buryed. He makes there this extempory Epitaph:
>
> > *Ten in the Hundred the Devill allowes,*
> > *But Combes will have twelve he sweares and vowes:*
> > *If anyone askes who lies in this Tombe,*
> > *Hoh! quoth the Devill, 'Tis my John o' Combe.*
>
> He was wont to goe to his native Countrey once a yeare. I thinke I have been told that he left 2 or 300 pounds per annum there and thereabout to a sister.
>
> I have heard Sir William Davenant and Mr Thomas Shadwell (who is counted the best Comoedian we have now) say that he had a most prodigious Witt, and did admire his naturall parts beyond all other Dramaticall writers.
>
> His Comoedies will remaine witt as long as the English tongue is understood, for that he handles mores hominum. Now our present

---

[66] Basic guide for Shakespeare remains Chambers, *William Shakespeare: A Study of Facts and Problems* (2 vols, *WS*) which contains all relevant material for either biography or the plays and poems.

writers reflect so much on particular persons and coxcombeities that twenty yeares hence they will not be understood. Though, as Ben Johnson sayes of him, that he had little Latine and lesse Greek, he understood Latine pretty well: for he had been in his younger yeares a schoolmaster in the countrey.

He was wont to say that he never blotted out a line in his life. Sayd Ben Johnson, I wish he had blotted-out a thousand.

The biographical details that Rowe and others provided are part of what is known as the "Shakespeare Mythos" and are usually accepted with a critical spirit by historians, because most of these details have no substantiation. Even so, much subsequent scholarship has been devoted either to proving or disproving these details.

Among other details of the Mythos that Rowe did not include: that Shakespeare attended grammar school in Stratford but was forced to quit when his father's fortunes declined, that he worked for his father from the age of 14, that he was the eldest of ten children, that he was forced to flee Stratford following an episode of deer poaching, that he started out in London holding the horses for noblemen who were attending the theater.[67]

Other stories claim that Shakespeare retired to Stratford and received a thousand pounds a year, and that he sent two plays to London annually. It is also claimed that he took part in drinking contests, and that he was engaged in such a bout in Stratford (with Michael Drayton and Ben Jonson) when he contracted his fatal illness. The fact that many of the stories do not put Shakespeare in a particularly good light, at least by the standards of prior biographers, reinforces the tendency towards skepticism.

Rowe's edition was printed by the Tonson family, who owned the copyright to the plays. Their control of the plays determined the later editors. Rowe was selected because of his eminence as a playwright. Fifteen years later, owing to his fame as a poet, Alexander Pope would be selected to edit a new edition.[68]

A more learned editor than Rowe, Pope went to the trouble of obtaining copies of almost all the plays that were published in quarto. This allowed Pope to refute the claim that Shakespeare "never blotted out a line," since the quartos differed from the Folio versions of several plays

---

67 Chambers, *WS*, II:238–302, itemizes 58 sources for the Mythos.

68 Taylor, Gary, *Reinventing Shakespeare*, 52–53, 68–75, 87–88.

(usually being significantly shorter). Pope also showed a preference in many cases for the quarto versions, claiming they contained beautiful passages omitted from the Folio, which he felt contained "whole heaps of trash." He also questioned the authorship of some of the plays. For example, he rejected all of the seven plays added in the later Folios, as well as *Titus Andronicus*, *Love's Labour's Lost*, and *Winter's Tale*. He was also convinced that *Richard II* had been tampered with, because he felt a large number of couplets in that play simply did not fit.[69]

Pope had a twofold theory for the mixed nature of the plays. On the one hand, he felt that non-Shakespeare plays had been added because "pieces produced by unknown authors or fitted up for the Theater while it was under his administration; and no owner claiming them, were adjudged to him, as they give strays to the Lord of the Manor."[70] In addition, Pope was convinced that the players themselves had mutilated the plays by adding extraneous text; in part, this was to explain the brevity of the quarto versions relative to the usually more expansive versions found in the First Folio. The most memorable feature of Pope's edition is that he dropped about 1,500 lines into footnotes, indicating his belief that they had been added by other hands.

Negative reactions to Pope's edition were not slow in coming. He was criticized anonymously for portraying the players as ignorant buffoons who had ruined the plays with their additions. More substantive criticism came from Lewis Theobald (1688–1744), who published *Shakespeare Restored* in 1726. Theobald found fault with many of Pope's edits and restored the text of the plays with minute care. That in turn led Theobald to publish his own edition of Shakespeare in 1733. Pope's reaction was to incorporate many of Theobald's corrections, and also to mock Theobald, who became "Tibbald, the King of the Dunces" in his famous satire *Dunciad*.[71] Theobald was a good scholar who promoted fidelity to the text, but there was perhaps an inborn contrast between his disinterested point of view as a scholar and Pope's aesthetic point of view as a poet.

In the early views of Shakespeare we have unanimity that they were the works of one man, the "poacher from Stratford." At the same time, however, virtually all agreed that some of the attributions were

---

69 Vickers, *Critical*, 2: 403.

70 Vickers, *Critical*, 2: 413.

71 Pope's *Dunciad* was first published anonymously in two versions (1728–29) and then in two expanded editions in 1742–43; Theobald was a main target in the earlier editions but was later superseded.

inauthentic, and that in some cases the text had been corrupted. These would become constant themes in subsequent criticism. Another common divide concerned the learning which the plays did or did not exhibit. This was often expressed as a problem of Nature opposed to Art, though we would now frame the issue more in terms of Nature and Nurture, or better, spontaneity and education. However it is characterized, the problem has been a constant in Shakespearean criticism ever since.

5 | Poets' Corner

Homer's Iliad ~ Pope and George Chapman ~ Michael Drayton ~ Philip Sidney ~ Edward Dyer ~ Mary Sidney ~ John Davies of Hereford ~ Samuel Daniel ~ Poetic Forms ~ Dactylic Hexameter

Alexander Pope made his reputation as a poet, specifically for his translation of Homer, which was done by subscription.[72] Pope's Homer, presented in a form called "heroic couplets," was meant to supersede the translation done a century earlier by George Chapman. Before we move on to a more thoroughgoing discussion of Chapman and some of the other poets active in Shakespeare's time (all of whom are relevant to the authorship question), we should pause to consider the differing approaches taken by Pope and Chapman in their translations of Homer.

Homer's *Iliad* is about the Trojan War, and specifically about a series of events that follow an incident involving Achilles. Here is how Pope renders the opening:[73]

> Achilles' wrath, to Greece the direful spring
> Of woes unnumber'd, heavenly goddess, sing!
> That wrath which hurl'd to Pluto's gloomy reign
> The souls of mighty chiefs untimely slain;
> Whose limbs unburied on the naked shore,
> Devouring dogs and hungry vultures tore.
> Since great Achilles and Atrides strove,
> Such was the sovereign doom, and such the will of Jove!

---

[72] In other words, the works were translated and published in a manner analogous to modern day crowd-sourcing, e.g., Kickstarter.

[73] Pope's beginning to the *Iliad*, at gutenberg.org.

We can compare this to the opening of George Chapman's version, published in 1611. This is the version that caused John Keats to write his famous sonnet, "On First Looking into Chapman's Homer" in 1816.[74]

> Achilles' banefull wrath resound, O Goddesse, that imposed
> Infinite sorrowes on the Greekes, and many brave soules losd
> From breasts Heroique–sent them farre, to that invisible cave
> That no light comforts; and their lims to dogs and vultures gave.
> To all which Jove's will gave effect; from whom first strife begunne
> Betwixt Atrides, king of men, and Thetis' godlike Sonne.

There is no question that Chapman's translations of Homer were the main achievement of his career. Born in 1559, he appears to have spent some time at Oxford, leaving without a degree. By the 1580s he was in London, working on his translations and seeking noble patronage: in this last he was never successful, as Chapman lived in debt and poverty his entire life. He was well known to other London authors of the period, being praised for his intelligence and moral bearing. Two portraits of Chapman survive, showing a sharp nose and penetrating eyes under a massive domed forehead.

Chapman first made a name for himself as a poet, writing *The Shadow of Night* in 1594; he is also credited with finishing *Hero and Leander*, a poem which Marlowe left unfinished at his death; Chapman's continuation is so well done that it provides a rationale for some to claim that Marlowe was not in fact killed in 1593.[75]

Chapman was also involved in writing for the theater. He was well known for his plotting, and he has at least a dozen plays to his credit. These are about equally split between comedies and tragedies. His successful stage works began with *The Blind Beggar of Alexandria*, a comedy, and continued with such tragedies as *Bussy D'Ambois*. Chapman's style is comparable to other Elizabethan dramatists of the time, except that his erudition and moral and philosophical speculations tend to obtrude. He has occasionally been put forth as a co-author of some Shakespearean plays, notably *Macbeth*. Chapman did collaborate with Ben Jonson on a play, *Eastward Ho!* (1605), that made fun of the Scots; as a result both he and Jonson were briefly imprisoned. George Chapman died in London in 1634.

---

74 Chapman's beginning to the *Iliad*, in Shepherd, Richard Herne, ed., *The Works of George Chapman*. Here as elsewhere the main sources for biographical information will be Chambers, ES, Bentley, JCS, and *DNB*.

75 As with Nashe's *Summer's Last Will and Testament*, the existence of *Hero and Leander* points to literary remains that ended up in other hands.

Michael Drayton (1563–1631) was a close contemporary of Chapman, but rather more successful in receiving patronage for his poetical efforts. Drayton published poems throughout the 1590s, and in the 1600s published the *Poly-Olbion*, a massive travelogue describing every county in England and Wales with digressions, all of it in Alexandrine couplets.

Drayton is perhaps best remembered for being from Shakespeare's home county of Warwickshire. It is Drayton who is supposed to have accompanied Shakespeare on his last drinking binge, and even if we dismiss that story as apocryphal, it is true that Shakespeare's son-in-law, Dr. John Hall, treated Drayton in the 1620s. Drayton also provided a memoir of Shakespeare in one of his poems, written in 1627. I am going to provide a longer excerpt than usual to put the comments about Shakespeare in proper context:[76]

> Neat *Marlow* bathed in the *Thespian* springs
> Had in him those brave translunary things,
> That the first Poets had, his raptures were,
> All ayre, and fire, which made his verses cleere,
> For that fine madnes still he did retaine,
> Which rightly should possesse a Poets braine.
>
> And surely *Nashe*, though he a Proser were
> A branch of Lawrell yet deserves to beare,
> Sharply Satirick was he, and that way
> He went, since that his being, to this day
> Few have attempted, and I surely thinke
> Those words shall hardly be set downe with inke;
> Shall scorch and blast, so as his could, where he,
> Would inflict vengeance, and be it said of thee,
> *Shakespeare* thou hadst as smooth a Comicke vaine,
> Fitting the socke, and in thy naturall braine,
> As strong conception, and as Cleere a rage,
> As any one that trafiqu'd with the stage.
>
> Amongst these *Samuel Daniel*, whom if I
> May spake of, but to sensure doe denie,
> Onely have heard some wisemen him rehearse,
> To be too much *Historian* in verse;
> His rimes were smooth, his meeters well did close,

---

[76] From "Of Poets and Poesie" from the "Elegies on Sundry Occasions" (1627) in *Minor Poems of Michael Drayton*, Cyril Brett, ed. (Oxford, Oxford:1907), 110–111.

> But yet his maner better fitted prose:
> Next these, learn'd *Johnson*, in this List I bring,
> Who had drunke deepe of the *Pierian* spring,
> Whose knowledge did him worthily prefer,
> And long was Lord here of the Theater,
> Who in opinion made our learn'st to sticke,
> Whether in Poems rightly dramatique,
> Strong Seneca or Plautus, he or they,
> Should beare the Buskin, or the Socke away.
> Others againe here lived in my dayes,
> That have of us deserved no lesse praise
> For their translations, then the daintiest wit
> That on Parnassus thinks, he highst doth sit,
> And for a chaire may mongst the Muses call,
> As the most curious maker of them all;
> As reverent *Chapman*, who hath brought to us,
> *Musaeus, Homer*, and *Hesiodus*
> Out of the Greeke; and by his skill hath reard
> Them to that height, and to our tongue endear'd,
> That were those Poets at this day alive,
> To see their bookes thus with us to survive,
> They would think, having neglected them so long,
> They had bin written in the English tongue.

Drayton was also involved in the stage for several years in the late 1590s and early 1600s. We know from various sources that he was involved in about two dozen plays but only one of these, *Sir John Oldcastle*, has survived, and that was a collaboration with three other writers.

Among poets surveyed so far, Chapman, Drayton, and William Shakespeare were all about the same age; born around 1560. But there was another generation of poets born a decade earlier. We have already encountered two of these: Gabriel Harvey and Edward de Vere, the Earl of Oxford. Edmund Spenser (1552–1599), author of the famous epic *The Faerie Queen*, was probably the most celebrated poet of the age, but he has no direct relevance to Shakespeare or the stage. More direct is the career of Sir Philip Sidney (1554–1586), whose reputation in poetry, romance, and literary criticism was enormous.

Born in 1554, Sir Philip Sidney received all of the benefits of the high nobility, including a university education (although he left Oxford before taking a degree). His youthful acquaintances included Fulke

Greville (1554–1628), who went on to have a long career in the government under both Elizabeth I and James I, and Sir Edward Dyer (1543–1607), a minor poet who was advanced as a candidate for the Shakespearean canon in 1943.[77] Dyer only left behind about a dozen poems, perhaps the most famous being, "My Mind to me a Kingdom Is" which runs as follows:

> My mind to me a kingdom is;
> Such perfect joy therein I find
> That it excels all other bliss
> Which God or nature hath assign'd.
> Though much I want that most would have,
> Yet still my mind forbids to crave.
>
> No princely port, nor wealthy store,
> No force to win a victory,
> No wily wit to salve a sore,
> No shape to win a loving eye;
> To none of these I yield as thrall,—
> For why? my mind despise them all.
>
> I see that plenty surfeit oft,
> And hasty climbers soonest fall;
> I see that such as are aloft
> Mishap doth threaten most of all.
> These get with toil and keep with fear;
> Such cares my mind can never bear.
>
> I press to bear no haughty sway,
> I wish no more than may suffice,
> I do no more than well I may,
> Look, what I want my mind supplies.
> Lo! thus I triumph like a king,
> My mind content with anything.
>
> I laugh not at another's loss,
> Nor grudge not at another's gain;
> No worldly waves my mind can toss;
> I brook that is another's bane.
> I fear no foe, nor fawn on friend,
> I loathe not life, nor dread mine end.

---

[77] Alden Brooks wrote two books on the subject, *Will Shakspere, Factotum and Agent* (1938) and *Will Shakspere and the Dyer's Hand* (1943) promoting Dyer's candidacy. The latter is essentially a much expanded version of the former, which makes me think that the latter was written first, and then cut down to size, and then reissued in original form.

> My wealth is health and perfect ease,
> And conscience clear my chief defence;
> I never seek by bribes to please,
> Nor by desert to give offence.
> Thus do I live, thus will I die,—
> Would all did so as well as I!

The poem is an excellent example of the introspective nature of the Elizabethan Renaissance, and indeed of the Renaissance as such. Another reason the poem is worth quoting is Dyer's authorship has been contested; since 1975, it has been argued that the verse was actually written by Edward de Vere, the Earl of Oxford.[78]

Sir Philip Sidney was also a friend and patron of Gabriel Harvey and Edmund Spenser. As a popular courtier, he also traveled widely in Europe: in fact, Sidney, a devout Protestant, had the misfortune to be in Paris during the St Bartholomew's Day Massacre, beginning August 23, 1572, when thousands (or tens of thousands) of protestant Huguenots were killed by Catholic mobs. He also traveled extensively in Italy and even Eastern Europe. In the 1580s, reckless for military service, he went to the Netherlands to take part in the decades-long rising of the Dutch against the Spanish, was wounded by a bullet in the leg during the battle of Zutphen in 1586, and died after three weeks. At the time of his death, Sidney was only 31 years old.

Sidney is remembered for four literary works, none of which were published during his lifetime. The first of these was the *Defense of Poesy* (1579 to 1581), which was written as a direct response to Stephen Gosson's *School of Abuse*—this was the same pamphlet against which Lodge wrote his maiden tirade. *The Defense of Poesy* was not published until 1595, but it was widely circulated in manuscript form before then. Sidney's main argument is that literature, as a form of imitation, can inspire virtuous and moral conduct. He describes the London stage in the following section, quoted with some interpolations:[79]

> Our tragedies and comedies not without cause cried out against, observing rules neither of honest civility nor of skilful poetry, excepting Gorboduc,—again I say of those that I have seen. Which

---

[78] Steven W. May argued for de Vere's (possible) authorship in "The Authorship of 'My Mind to Me a Kingdom Is'" in *The Review of English Studies*, v. 26, n. 104 (Nov, 1975). The claim has been a staple of Oxfordian arguments ever since, although May is not an Oxfordian. May later elaborated on his attribution in a longer study of the poetry of Oxford and Essex in "The Poems of Edward de Vere, Seventeenth Earl of Oxford and Robert Devereaux, Second Earl of Essex" in *Studies in Philology*, v. 77, n. 5, 1980.

[79] All of the extracts from the "Defense of Poesy" from the text in Smith, *Critical Essays*, v. 1, 148–207.

> notwithstanding as it is full of stately speeches and well-sounding phrases, climbing to the height of Seneca's style, and as full of notable morality, which it doth most delightfully teach, and so obtain the very end of poesy; yet in truth it is very defectious in the circumstances, which grieveth me, because it might not remain as an exact model of all tragedies. For it is faulty both in place and time, the two necessary companions of all corporal actions. For where the stage should always represent but one place, and the uttermost time presupposed in it should be, both by Aristotle's precept and common reason, but one day; there is both many days and many places inartificially imagined.

Histories of Elizabethan drama usually cite *Gorboduc* (1561) as the first of the modern Elizabethan dramas, and it was the first to have been written entirely in blank verse. Co-authored by Thomas Norton (1532–1584) and Thomas Sackville, the Earl of Dorset (1536–1608),[80] *Gorboduc* is a tragedy drawing on the same sources in Celtic history as *King Lear*.

> But if it be so in Gorboduc, how much more in all the rest? where you shall have Asia of the one side, and Afric of the other, and so many other under-kingdoms, that the player, when he cometh in, must ever begin with telling where he is, or else the tale will not be conceived. Now ye shall have three ladies walk to gather flowers, and then we must believe the stage to be a garden. By and by we hear news of shipwreck in the same place, and then we are to blame if we accept it not for a rock. Upon the back of that comes out a hideous monster with fire and smoke, and then the miserable beholders are bound to take it for a cave. While in the mean time two armies fly in, represented with four swords and bucklers, and then what hard heart will not receive it for a pitched field?

Notwithstanding the good humor of his phrasing, Sidney's complaint about time and place was common enough. It was felt that Elizabethan drama failed to respect the "classical unities" of time, place, and action. Seneca's tragedies, referenced in the first paragraph, were held to be the superior model. The final sentence of this paragraph is a direct anticipation of the opening chorus of *Henry V*, and just for that reason tends to suggest that that play, or some version of it, was prepared in the 1580s (rather than being delayed until 1599 as traditional dating has it). More:

---

80 Sackville would be suggested as an author of the Shakespeare canon in 2011 by Sabrina Feldman in *The Apocryphal William Shakespeare* (discussed in Chapter 24).

Now of time they are much more liberal. For ordinary it is that two young princes fall in love; after many traverses she is got with child, delivered of a fair boy, he is lost, groweth a man, falleth in love, and is ready to get another child,—and all this in two hours' space; which how absurd it is in sense even sense may imagine, and art hath taught, and all ancient examples justified, and at this day the ordinary players in Italy will not err in. Yet will some bring in an example of Eunuchus in Terence, that containeth matter of two days, yet far short of twenty years. True it is, and so was it to be played in two days, and so fitted to the time it set forth. And though Plautus have in one place done amiss, let us hit with him, and not miss with him. But they will say, How then shall we set forth a story which containeth both many places and many times? And do they not know that a tragedy is tied to the laws of poesy, and not of history; not bound to follow the story, but having liberty either to feign a quite new matter, or to frame the history to the most tragical conveniency? Again, many things may be told which cannot be showed,—if they know the difference betwixt reporting and representing. As for example I may speak, though I am here, of Peru, and in speech digress from that to the description of Calicut; but in action I cannot represent it without Pacolet's horse. And so was the manner the ancients took, by some Nuntius to recount things done in former time or other place.

[....]

But, besides these gross absurdities, how all their plays be neither right tragedies nor right comedies, mingling kings and clowns, not because the matter so carrieth it, but thrust in the clown by head and shoulders to play a part in majestical matters, with neither decency nor discretion; so as neither the admiration and commiseration, nor the right sportfulness, is by their mongrel tragi-comedy obtained. I know Apuleius did somewhat so, but that is a thing recounted with space of time, not represented in one moment; and I know the ancients have one or two examples of tragi-comedies, as Plautus hath Amphytrio. But, if we mark them well, we shall find that they never, or very daintily, match hornpipes and funerals. So falleth it out that, having indeed no right comedy in that comical part of our tragedy, we have nothing but scurrility, unworthy of any chaste ears, or some extreme show of doltishness, indeed fit to lift up a loud laughter, and nothing else; where the whole tract of a comedy should be full of delight, as the tragedy should be still maintained in a well-raised admiration.

The reference to mingling kings and clowns sounds like *King Lear*, which according to the standard chronology was not written until 1606, but which was preceded by another play, *King Leir* [sic!], which was published in 1605, having been entered in the record of potential publications (in effect, registered for printer's copyright) in 1594. The problem then is that there is no fool in *Leir*.

Sidney's next contribution was a sonnet cycle, *Astrophel and Stella*, comprising over 108 sonnets written when he was in his twenties about a young woman he was in love with at the time. It was initially published in 1591 with a preface by Thomas Nashe (the selection of Nashe's prose offered earlier is from this text) with some additional poems, including some verse by the Earl of Oxford. Sidney used the Petrarchian model for sonnets, with an octet of alternate rhymes followed by a sestet of alternate rhymes ending in a couplet. The Petrarchian model, adapted by Sidney, was also used for many other sonnet cycles in the Elizabethan era, including Lodge's *Phillis*, Daniel's *Delia*, the anonymous cycle, *Emaricdulfe* (sometimes attributed to the Earl of Oxford), and of course Shakespeare's sonnets.

Sidney's third major contribution, unfinished at his death, was *Arcadia*, which was revised and published by his sister, Mary Sidney (1561–1621), and hence is generally known in her version, published in 1593 as *The Countess of Pembroke's Arcadia*. It was an enormously popular romance.

Sidney's remaining contribution was an attempt to translate the Psalms. This was another project that would be taken up by his sister after his death, so we should pause to consider her role in greater detail.

Mary Sidney received an extensive education and attended Queen Elizabeth at court. In 1577, at the age of sixteen, she married Henry Herbert (who was in his forties). She had two surviving sons: William, who went on to become the 3rd Earl of Pembroke, and Philip, who became the Earl of Montgomery, and the 4th Earl of Pembroke after his brother's death. These two brothers were the "incomparable pair" to whom the First Folio was dedicated.[81]

Mary's interests were wide and varied. She studied chemistry, medicine, languages, literature, and she apparently took an active interest in esoteric arts, since her name is typically linked to John Dee (1532–1609), an astrologer and alchemist who is sometimes held to be a model

---

81 For Mary Sidney Herbert there is a recent biography by Robin P. Williams, *Sweet Swan of Avon: Did a Woman Write Shakespeare?* (2011). The theory is discussed in Chapter 24.

for Prospero in *The Tempest*. She also hosted a circle of artists and writers at her country estate at Wilton, the so-called "Wilton Circle," which, interestingly, lies just five miles south of the most imposing stone circle of all, Stonehenge (and thus, 20 miles south of Avebury). She wrote in all forms, including drama. Her play, *The Tragedie of Antonie*, may have had some influence on Shakespeare's *Anthony and Cleopatra*, but hers was a book-play (or closet play, meant to be read rather than performed). In addition to her own literary work and as executor to her brother's work, she also completed his translations of the Psalms, presenting a copy to Queen Elizabeth in 1599.

The copyist of the presentation copy of the Psalms was John Davies of Hereford (1565–1618). Davies was from the Welsh borderlands, and Hereford was Welsh-speaking at that time. Davies was a famous copyist and writing-instructor; in other words, he was usually hired by well-to-do or noble families to teach people how to write. According to contemporary accounts, he had enormous skill with quill—not just in terms of the rapidity with which he could write but also his ability to master several different styles or hands. He was also a poet of some ability. Here is an example of a sonnet he wrote:[82]

> The Frosty Beard, inclining al to white,
> The Snowy Head: or Head more white than Snow,
> The Crow-foot neere the Eyes, Browes, Furrow'd quite,
> With Trenches in the Cheeks, Experience show.
> These are the emblems of Authority;
> Which joyned to those do much augment her might:
> These are the signes of Reasons Soveraignty,
> And Hyerogliphicks, spelling judgment right.
> These are the trophies rear'd by Times left hand
> Upon the spoils of Passion, and her Powres:
> We, by these Symbols, Wisedome understand,
> That us directeth, and protecteth ours:
> All these in me begin to come in sight,
> Yet can I hardly rule my selfe aright.

Davies is largely forgotten today, but while his extensive poetry may lack that final spark of brilliance his focus on moral and theological concerns remains interesting. The reference to "hieroglyphics" in the above poem, for example, suggests that the Wilton Circle

---

[82] *The Complete Works of John Davies of Hereford*, ed. Grosart, 1:xviii. The edition, privately published in 1878, comprised two volumes.

was engaged in esoteric and "Hermetic" studies. Like Lodge, Davies frequently wrote (usually in rhyme) about what he considered to be the excesses of his age, notably in such works as *The Scourge of Folly* (1611) and *Wit's Bedlam* (1617). The latter contained several observations about his poetical and dramatic peers, including the following epigram about Shakespeare, entitled "To our English Terence, Mr. Will Shakespeare":[83]

> Some say good *Will* (which I, in sport, do sing)
> Had'st thou not plaid some Kingly parts in sport,
> Thou had'st been a companion for a *King*;
> And, been a King among the meaner sort.
> Some other raile; but raile as they think fit,
> Thou hast no rayling, but, a raigning Wit:
> *And* honesty *thou sow'st, which they do reape:*
> *So, to increase their* Stocke *which they do keepe.*

The "Terence" in the title of the epigram refers to a Roman comic playwright who had a reputation for being a beard for other authors (this will have relevance later). The body of the epigram is inevitably cited as proof of Shakespeare's dramatic activity, although the last four lines are very hard to interpret. One point that deserves notice is that Shakespeare is being characterized as a "King." This fits in nicely with Jonson's memoir of Shakespeare as "Caesar," as well as the apocryphal story that Shakespeare played the ghost of the king in *Hamlet*.

As for the last four lines, we may note the apparent pun on *raile/rayling* where "raile" is first meant to imply the sounding of complaint, and then as having "no railing" ("no rayling") in terms of having no limits (suggesting an ambitious individual). The part about sowing honesty remains incomprehensible: the only context in which honesty would seem to have a role is in fair dealing, but what kind of dealing would Shakespeare have been engaged in? I do not think it means that Shakespeare picked up the bar tab when he was pumping Davies for information about the colloquial Welsh that he would later use in *Henry IV*.

Another member of Mary Sidney's Wilton Circle was Samuel Daniel (1564–1619). Daniel was the son of a music master, and he had a brother named John who was also a professional musician. Daniel attended Oxford as a commoner and studied there for three years,

---

83 Davies, *Complete Works*, Grosart ed., 1: lv.

leaving without a degree in 1582. For many years he was a tutor to Mary Sidney's sons (Daniel would later claim that Mary Sidney taught him how to write poetry). He was a friend of Thomas Nashe. He wrote a book on crests in 1585 and traveled to Europe, including Italy, at some point in the 1580s.

Daniel first gained fame with his popular sonnet cycle, *Delia*. For many years he labored over a verse history of the War of the Roses, which was published in 1595 as the *First Four Books of the Civil Wars*. There is no question that Daniel was dealing with the same subject matter as Shakespeare in his history plays; to read Daniel is to be immediately plunged into the world of *Henry VI* and *Richard II*. Here are a couple of excerpts:[84]

> Sing the Civil Wars, tumultuous Broils,
> And bloody factions of a mighty Land,
> Whose people haughty, proud with foreign Spoils,
> Upon themselves turn back their conqu'ring Hand.
> Whilst Kin their Kin, Brother the Brother foils,
> Like Ensigns all, against like Ensigns band,
> Bows against Bows, the Crown against the Crown;
> While all pretending Right, all Right's thrown down.
>
> [....]
>
> Like when some Mastiff-Whelp, dispos'd to play,
> A while confused Herd of Beasts doth chase,
> Which with one vile Consent run all away;
> If any hardier than the rest, in place
> But offer Head that idle Fear to stay,
> Back straight the daunted Chaser turns his Face,
> And all the rest (with bold Example led),
> As fast run on him, as before they fled:
>
> So, with this bold Opposer rushes on
> This many-headed Monster, Multitude:
> And He, who late was fear'd, is set upon,
> And by his own (Actaeon-like) pursu'd;
> How own, that had all Love and Awe forgone;
> Whom Breath and Shadows only did delude,
> And newer Hopes, which Promises persuade,
> Tho' rarely Men keep promises so made.

---

84 *The Poetical Works of Mr. Samuel Daniel*, vol. II, 5, 47 (London: 1718). Alexander Grosart also edited a four-volume edition published in 1885, *The Complete Works in Verse and Prose of Samuel Daniel*.

The linkage with Shakespeare on *Richard II* is sufficiently close that a friendship between Daniel and Shakespeare is sometimes suggested, although there is no actual evidence. Even so, discussions of *Richard II* invariably address Daniel's parallel treatment.

Daniel also had an interest in the stage. In 1593 he published a book play called *Cleopatra* as a companion to Mary Sidney's *Tragedie of Antonie*, and he got into trouble with Court for his 1599 tragedy *Philotas*, which was believed to be seditious. Around 1603, he was involved in court masques. Ben Jonson said that Daniel was married, but apparently had no children; in a letter he referred to John Florio as his "brother" but whether this means he was married to Florio's sister, or if Florio was married to his sister, or something else entirely, is unclear. His collected works were published in 1618, along with a portrait featuring Daniel with arms akimbo and an amused expression on his face. He died on his country farm in 1619.

Daniel also took part in the ongoing debates about the value of poetry, including dramatic poetry. In his *Defense of Rhyme* (which he dedicated to his former student William Herbert, the Earl of Pembroke), Daniel concluded:[85]

> Next to this deformitie stands our affectation, wherein we always bewray our selues to be both vnkinde, and vnnaturall to our owne natiue language, in disguising or forging strange or uvnvsuall wordes, as if it were to make our verse seeme an other kind of speach out of the course of our vsuall practise, displacing our wordes, or inuesting new, onely vpon a singularitie: when our owne accustomed phrase, set in the due place, would expresse vs more familiarly and to better delight, than all this idle affectation of antiquitie, or noueltie can euer doe. And I can not but wonder at the strange presumption of some men that dare so audaciously aduenture to introduce any whatsoeuer forraine wordes, be they neuer so strange; and of themselues as it were, without a Parliament, without any consent, or allowance, establish them as Free-denizens in our language. But this is but a Character of that perpetuall reuolution which wee see to be in all things that neuer remaine the same, and we must heerein be content to submit our selues to the law of time, which in few yeeres wil make al that, for which we now contend, *Nothing*.

Daniel, Davies, and Mary Sidney were all poets who would repair

---

85 Smith, *Critical Essays*, 2:384.

to Salisbury to comprise the Wilton Circle. Drayton and Chapman were poets who were frequently on hire for dramas in London. Philip Sidney, Spenser, Greville, and Dyer have little further relevance to our story; the others will be revisited.[86]

Before we leave the Elizabethan poets we should say something about the verse forms of the Elizabethan era, since they will be used by later commentators to identify the chronology of the Shakespeare plays. The basic form was blank verse, that is, non-rhyming verse, in iambic pentameter, which comprises five feet of two syllable iambs, or a stressed and unstressed syllable. For example:

> Now is the winter of our discontent,
> Made glorious summer by this son of York

is typical iambic pentameter, as is:

> The evil that men do lives after them,
> The good is oft interred with their bones

when we give three syllables to "interred." Both of these examples are called "masculine" rhymes because they are exactly ten syllables. This kind of line is also called "end stopped." Another form of iambs would be:

> To be, or not to be: that is the question:
> Whether 'tis nobler in the mind to suffer
> The slings and arrows of outrageous fortune,
> Or to take arms against a sea of troubles,
> And by opposing end them? To die: to sleep;

This is actually a sequence of eleven syllable lines, the extra syllable making them "feminine" lines, with the nature of such lines tending to be run on (the technical term for this is "enjambment").

Here's an example from *The Winter's Tale*, which is usually dated late in Shakespeare's career:

> I know't too well.
> Give me the boy: I am glad you did not nurse him:
> Though he does bear some signs of me, yet you
> Have too much blood in him.

---

86 Spenser has some indirect relevance to the authorship question. Essentially, Spenser has named characters in his poems and these characters can be variously identified as Shakespeare himself, or Oxford, or Stanley, or someone else. But all such readings are speculative; they do not advance the authorship problem, nor support any particular unitarian thesis. Michell, *Who Wrote Shakespeare?*, 192–195, explores the Spenser connection in detail, especially as it refers to Stanley.

The syllabification of the above is 4, 12, 10, and 6. Furthermore, while iambic pentameter allows for some inversion of stress, the above examples have several inversions.

Finally, here's a passage from *Henry VIII*, generally considered one of Shakespeare's last plays:

> As I belong to worship and affect
> In honour honesty, the tract of every thing
> Would by a good discourser lose some life,
> Which action's self was tongue to. All was royal;
> To the disposing of it nought rebell'd.
> Order gave each thing view; the office did
> Distinctly his full function.

This is a good example of hypermetric lines (that is, lines that are only loosely pentameter), feminine lines, enjambment, and sheer incomprehensibility.[87]

These examples serve a broader point. Since Edmond Malone advanced the argument at end of the 18th century, it has been held that the chronological order of the plays can be established by observing the general change from strict end-stopped, masculine ending, iambic pentameters to a less controlled and more free verse. There is some sense to this since Marlowe kept generally to the masculine, end-stopped, pentameter form. On the other hand, while we can concede a greater freedom of verse as the 1590s went on, it is hard to see how such freedom of verse would lead to such humdrum and incoherent verses as we find in the excerpts from *Winter's Tale* and *Henry VIII*. The other point to make here is that the more the verse breaks the form, the more the verse becomes indistinguishable from prose. To put it another way: prose authors are not deaf, and would also keep an ear on meter as they wrote. This was especially true in the Elizabethan era.

There are a few other poetic forms worth mentioning. The excerpt from Chapman quoted at the beginning of this chapter was in iambic heptameter, which comes out to fourteen syllables (hence verse in this form is sometimes called "Fourteener") and is considered an earlier

---

[87] Quoted in Shapiro, *Contested Will*, 252.

form of iambic rhyme.[88] Another form is "Alexandrines" or iambic hexameter: 12 syllables per line. A form that alternates heptameter and hexameter is called "poulter's measure" in reference to the varying number of eggs one might receive at the farmer's market. Returning to Homer, his epics were composed in dactylic hexameter, that is, six feet of three dactylic syllables, most typically referenced in English by Longfellow's *Hiawatha* ("This is the forest primeval, the murmuring hemlocks and pines"). But the versification in Homer was based on vowel quantity, not stress. A fair example of an attempt in English to approximate vowel quantity based on dactylic hexameter would go something like this:[89]

> Since *Galateo* came in, and *Tuscanisme* gan vsurpe,
> Vanitie aboue all: Villanie next her, Statelynes Empresse.
> No man, but Minion, Stowte, Lowte, Plaine, swayne quoth a Lording:
> No wordes but valorous, no workes but womanish onely.
> For life Magnificoes, not a beck but glorious in shew,
> In deede most friuolous, not a looke but Tuscanish alwayes.
> His *cringing side necke, Eyes glauncing, Fisnamie smirking,*
> With *forefinger kisse,* and braue *embrace to the footewarde.*
> Largebelled Kodpeasd Dublet, vnkodpeased halfe hose,
> Straite to the dock, like a shirte, and close to the britch, like a diueling.
> A little Apish Hatte, cowched fast to the pate, like an Oyster,
> French Camarick Ruffes, deepe with a w[h]it[e]nesse, starched to the purpose.
> Euery one A per se A, his termes, and braueries in Print,
> Delicate in speach, queynte in araye: conceited in all poyntes:
> In Courtly guyles, a passing singular odde man,
> For Gallantes a braue Myrrour, a Primerose of Honour,
> A Diamond for nonce, a fellowe perelesse in England.
> Not the like *Discourser* for Tongue, and head to be found out:
> Not the like *resolute Man*, for great and serious affayres,
> Not the like *Lynx*, to spie out secretes, and priuities of States.
> *Eyed*, like to *Argus, Earde,* like to *Midas, Nosd,* like to *Naso,*
> Wingd, like to *Mercury,* fittst of a Thousand for to be employde,
> This, nay more than this doth practise of *Italy* in one yeare.

---

[88] Because the 14 syllables of iambic heptameter are identical to the 14 lines in a sonnet, it is difficult to tell whether the terms "fourteener" or "quatorzain" are meant to refer to this meter or to sonnets, as in the Nashe excerpt quoted earlier. A characteristic of iambic heptameter is that there is a natural break in the middle, thus the part of Chapman's Homer in this meter, as with most of the poetry of Emily Dickinson, can be sung to the tune of "The Yellow Rose of Texas."

[89] Nelson, *Monstrous Adversary*, 225–228; the scan and italics from Haslewood, ed., *Ancient Critical Essays*, II: 269–270.

> None doe I name, but some doe I know, that a peece of a tweluemonth:
> Hath so perfited outly, and inly, both body, both soule,
> That none for sense, and senses, halfe matchable with them.
> *A Vulturs smelling, Apes tasting, sight of an Eagle,*
> *A spiders touching, Hartes hearing, might of a Lyon.*
> *Compoundes* of wisedome, witte, prowes[s], bountie, behauiour,
> All gallant Vertues, all qualities of body and soule:
> O thrice tenne hundreth thousand times blessed and happy,
> Blessed and happy *Trauaile, Trauailer* most blessed and happy.

The text is hard to understand because of the attempt to stay with the quantity; the text is also intrinsically difficult, partly because of words that are difficult to translate into modern English. But it is possible to get the sense of the passage, a detailed description of a slightly effeminate fop with Italian affectations. This text is in fact by Gabriel Harvey. It is entitled *Speculum Tuscanismi* (The Mirror of Tuscanism) and it was just this text that earned the enmity of the Earl of Oxford, leading to the long-running quarrel discussed earlier.

6 | Apotheosis and Evidence

David Garrick's Jubilee ~ Shakespeare's Will ~ A Groatsworth of Wit Paid with a Million in Repentance ~ Francis Meres' Palladis Tamia

Shakespeare's popularity increased throughout the 18th century for a variety of reasons: the growth of Shakespearean criticism, the issuance of new editions of his works, perhaps even due to nationalist considerations. However, another factor must have been the growing popularity of the plays as performance pieces, and the most important person in this development was the actor David Garrick (1717–1779). Garrick introduced a style of acting that was more character-centered than previous styles, and he was sensational in a number of Shakespearean roles. In 1769 Garrick arranged a Jubilee for Shakespeare at Stratford. The festival was attended by thousands. There were numerous events, including the performance of a chorus honoring Shakespeare, and a masked ball. When heavy rains and flooding from the Avon cut the festival short, the spectacle was moved to London and put on stage, with 90 performances following. Garrick's Jubilee was one of the key events signaling Shakespeare's installation into the British pantheon as the Great National Poet, or simply The Bard.

But even as public celebrations of Shakespeare's works were taking place, evidence was being sought—and discovered—about Shakespeare the man. In this chapter we will discuss three particularly important discoveries: Shakespeare's Will, Greene's *Groatsworth of Wit*, and Francis Meres' *Palladis Tamia*.

Shakespeare's Will

The Last Will and Testament of William Shakespeare was discovered somewhere in Stratford in 1747 by Joseph Greene. It was first published in 1767. For the Stratfordian school it is an awful document, providing no support for Shakespeare's status as poet and playwright. This was recognized by Joseph Greene himself, who wrote at the time:

> The Legacies and Bequests therein, are undoubtedly as he intended; but the manner of introducing them, appears to me so dull and irregular, so absolutely void of the least particle of that Spirit which Animated Our great Poet, that it must lessen his Character as a Writer, to imagine the least Sentence of it his production.
>
> The only Satisfaction I receive in reading it, is to know who were his relations, and what he left them, which perhaps may just make you also amends for the trouble of perusing it.[90]

The Will begins thus:[91]

> In the name of god Amen I William Shackspeare, of Stratford upon Avon in the countrie of Warr., gent., in perfect health and memorie, God be praysed, doe make and ordayne this my last will and testament in manner and forme followeing, that ys to saye, ffirst, I comend my soule into the hands of God my Creator, hoping and assuredlie beleeving, through thonelie merites, of Jesus Christe my Saviour, to be made partaker of lyfe everlastinge, and my bodye to the earth whereof yt ys made.

After this the three-page will is chiefly concerned with various bequests; the fourth to the last being:

> Item, I gyve & bequeath to [Mr Richard Tyler thelder] **Hamlett Sadler** xxvj^s viij^d to buy him A Ringe, **to William Raynoldes gent xxvj^s viij^d to buy him A Ringe**, to my godson William Walker xxs in gold, to Anthonye Nashe gent xxvj^s viij^d, & to Mr John Nashe xxvj^s viij^d [in gold], **& to my ffellowes John Hemynge Richard Burbage & Henry Cundell xxvj^s viij^d A peece to buy them Ringes**.

The brackets indicate crossouts and the boldface indicates an interlinear addition: of course, Heminge, Burbage, and Condell were fellow actors in the King's Men theater company (previously the Lord

---

90 Schoenbaum, Samuel, *Shakespeare's Lives*, new edition (1993), 92–93.

91 All quotations from the Will in Chambers, *WS*, II: 169–180.

Chamberlain's Men). The third to last bequest I will quote in full, primarily because it is absolutely stupefying:

> Item, I gyve, will, bequeath, and devise, unto my daughter Susanna Hall, for better enabling of her to performe this my will, and towards the performans thereof, all that capitall messuage or tenemente with thappurtenaunces, in Stratford aforesaid, called the New Place, wherein I nowe dwell, and two messuages or tenementes with thappurtenaunces, scituat, lyeing, and being in Henley streete, within the borough of Stratford aforesaied; and all my barnes, stables, orchardes, gardens, landes, tenementes, and hereditamentes, whatsoever, scituat, lyeing, and being, or to be had, receyved, perceyved, or taken, within the townes, hamletes, villages, fieldes, and groundes, of Stratford upon Avon, Oldstratford, Bushopton, and Welcombe, or in anie of them in the saied countie of Warr. And alsoe all that messuage or tenemente with thappurtenaunces, wherein one John Robinson dwelleth, scituat, lyeing and being, in the Balckfriers in London, nere the Wardrobe; and all my other landes, tenementes, and hereditamentes whatsoever, To have and to hold all and singuler the saied premisses, with theire appurtenaunces, unto the saied Susanna Hall, for and during the terme of her naturall lief, and after her deceas, to the first sonne of her bodie lawfullie yssueing, and to the heires males of the bodie of the saied first sonne lawfullie yssueinge; and for defalt of such issue, to the second sonne of her bodie, lawfullie issueing, and to the heires males of the bodie of the saied second sonne lawfullie yssueinge; and for defalt of such heires, to the third sonne of the bodie of the saied Susanna lawfullie yssueing, and of the heires males of the bodie of the saied third sonne lawfullie yssueing; and for defalt of such issue, the same soe to be and remaine to the ffourth [sonne], ffyfth, sixte, and seaventh sonnes of her bodie lawfullie issueing, one after another, and to the heires males of the bodies of the bodies of the saied fourth, fifth, sixte, and seaventh sonnes lawfullie yssueing, in such manner as yt ys before lymitted to be and remaine to the first, second, and third sonns of her bodie, and to theire heires males; and for defalt of such issue, the said premisses to be and remaine to my sayed neece Hall, and the heires males of her bodie lawfullie yssueinge; and for defalt of such issue, to my daughter Judith, and the heires males of her bodie lawfullie issueinge; and for defalt of such issue, to the right heires of me the saied William Shackspeare for ever.

This was a man who was obsessed with having sons: it is also the testament of a man who is very concerned with the disposition of property over time, and nothing besides.

Immediately after this we have the next-to-last item, an interlineation that has been the source of mockery for over 200 years.

> Item, I gyve unto my wief my second best bed with the furniture,

We can assume that Shakespeare was at the time dying in the best bed. Incidentally, this is the only reference to Shakespeare's wife in the entire document.

The Will might be compared to the Will of John Davies of Hereford; here is a brief excerpt:[92]

> Item, I give and bequeathe unto my sonne Silvanus Davies all my books. Item, I give and bequeathe unto my wel-beloved wife Margaret the lease of the house and the garden wherein I nowe dwell in St. Martin's Lane, together with all such brasse, pewter, and ymplements of household stuffe whatsoever as my saied wife at the tyme of her marriage brought unto me, and also such plate and jewells as were hers before marriage, and to the sole use and behoofe of the saied Margaret my saied wife. Likewise I give unto her my picture.

Davies' will goes on for another page, with his son and wife frequently mentioned. Incidentally, Davies' portrait survives; he resembled the Welsh actor Hugh Griffith, who won an Oscar in 1959 for his portrayal of a sheik in *Ben-Hur*.

It is worth mentioning that Shakespeare's Will contains no reference to books among the bequests, but then again, it appears that his descendants were all illiterate so there would have been no need to mention them, if he had had any.[93]

GROATSWORTH OF WIT

The next two documents were both discovered by Thomas Tyrwhitt, a leading scholar of the day. The first of these was the discovery of a passage in an obscure pamphlet published under the name of Robert Greene; the second comprised the references in Frances Meres' *Palladis Tamia*.

---

92 Davies, *Complete Works*, Grosart ed., xvii.

93 Sometimes it is claimed that Shakespeare's daughter Susanna was literate, because a labored signature survives, while her sister Judith still signed with a mark. On the other hand, their husbands, Dr. John Hall, and Thomas Nash (a lawyer) were clearly literate, and Dr. Hall at least was known to have books and a two-volume case book of his practice (in Latin; one volume has since been lost) but no remains have ever been traced to the Bard, which further compounds the mystery of the bookless Shakespeare.

When we last discussed Robert Greene he was making his living writing plays (none of which were published in his own lifetime) as well as numerous pamphlets portraying the life of the criminal underworld in Elizabethan England.[94] We now find him in the summer of 1592 having a luncheon of pickled herring and Rhine wine with Thomas Nashe and a mysterious figure named Will Monox. As recorded by Nashe, it was on this occasion that Greene fell ill. He died on September 2, 1592.[95] *Greene's Groatsworth of Wit Bought With a Million of Repentance* was entered in the Stationers Register less than three weeks later.

The pamphlet is a framed, or stacked, narrative in which one story leads into another. This is a fairly common narrative technique used to tie diverse narratives together; Far Eastern folk tales or animal fables are similarly constructed.[96] Greene's outer story tells of two sons—one of whom is left the family fortune, while the other receives only a groat (that is, a few pence) and is instructed to find wisdom. There are various adventures and then the story shifts to Roberto, who tells of how he wandered to London, recounting his own misadventures and misdeeds. The story culminates in a call for repentance. After delivering a number of maxims on how to conduct oneself in a proper godly manner, Greene provides this long passage:[97]

> To those Gentlemen his Quondam acquaintance,
> that spend their wits in making Plaies, R. G.
> wisheth a better exercise, and wisedome
> to prevent his extremities.
>
>   IF woeful experience may move you (Gentlemen) to beware, or unheard of wretchedness entreat you to take heed; I doubt not but you will look back with sorrow on your time past, and endeavor with repentance to spend that which is to come. Wonder not (for

---

94 Gamini Salgado's *The Elizabethan Underworld* is a lively review of this aspect of Shakespeare's time, and is unsurprisingly based on writings by Robert Greene and Thomas Dekker, among others.

95 By inference, the luncheon probably took place at the Steelyard, which was a German enclave of the Hanseatic League in London; Nashe's description comes from *Strange News*. Many Oxfordians claim that Will Monox was actually the Earl of Oxford but there is no evidence for this. Nina Green believes that Green and Nashe were both fronts for Oxford, which suggests that the Earl of Oxford, Nashe, and Greene all went to the Steelyard and the host asked, "Table for one, Milord?" although actually the claim is that Greene was a front for Oxford's writings, and the occasion of this luncheon was to announce that henceforth Nashe would have that job. This conjures the image of the restaurant assassination in *The Godfather*, except that here, the Earl of Oxford leaves Greene and Nashe at table and goes to the washroom, returning with a pickled herring.

96 One could also argue for a similar structure in Homer: compare the narrative of Odysseus' scar in the *Odyssey*. The notion of the importance of framed narratives is a core insight by McCarthy, *North of Shakespeare*, so I am introducing it up front.

97 All quotes from a version of Greene's *Groats-worth of Wit* in a transcribed "Renascence Edition" at the website luminarium.org. The transcription is keyed to the original 1592 publication.

with thee will I first begin), thou famous gracer of Tragedians, that Greene, who hath said with thee (like the fool in his heart) There is no God, should now give glory unto his greatness: for penetrating is his power, his hand lies heavy upon me, he hath spoken unto me with a voice of thunder, and I have felt he is a God that can punish enemies. Why should thy excellent wit, his gift, be so blinded, that thou shouldst give no glory to the giver? Is it pestilent Machiavellian policy that thou hast studied? O peevish folly! What are his rules but meer confused mockeries, able to extirpate in small time the generation of mankind. For if Sic volo, sic iubeo, hold in those that are able to command: and if it be lawful Fas & nefas to do anything that is beneficial, only Tyrants should possess the earth, and they striving to exceed in tyranny, should each to other be a slaughter man; till the mightiest outliving all, one stroke were left for Death, that in one age man's life should end. The brother of this Diabolical Atheism is dead, and in his life had never the felicity he aimed at: but as he began in craft, lived in fear, and ended in despair. Quàm inscrutabilia sunt Dei iudicia? This murderer of many brethren, had his conscience seared like Caine: this betrayer of him that gave his life for him, inherited the portion of Judas: this Apostate perished as ill as Julian: and wilt thou my friend be his Disciple? Look unto me, by him persuaded to that liberty, and thou shalt find it an infernal bondage. I know the least of my demerits merit this miserable death, but willful striving against known truth, exceedeth all the terrors of my soul. Defer not (with me) till this last point of extremity; for little knowst thou how in the end thou shalt be visited.

With thee I join young Juvenal, that biting Satirist, that lastly with me together wrote a Comedy. Sweet boy, might I advise thee, be advised, and get not many enemies by bitter words: inveigh against vain men, for thou canst do it, no man better, no man so well: thou hast a liberty to reprove all, and none more; for one being spoken to, all are offended, none being blamed no man is injured. Stop shallow water still running, it will rage, or tread on a worm and it will turn: then blame not Scholars vexed with sharp lines, if they reprove thy too much liberty of reproof.

And thou no less deserving than the other two, in some things rarer, in nothing inferior; driven (as myself) to extreme shifts, a little have I to say to thee: and were it not an idolatrous oath, I would swear by sweet S. George, thou art unworthy better hap, sith thou dependest on so mean a stay. Base minded men all three of you, if by my misery ye be not warned: for unto none of you (like me) sought those burrs to cleave: those Puppets (I mean) that speake from our mouths, those Anticks garnisht in our colours. Is it not strange that I, to whom they all have been beholding: is it not like that you, to whom they all have beene beholding, shall (were ye in that case that I am now) be both at once of them forsaken? Yes, trust them not: for there is an upstart Crow, beautified with our feathers, that with his Tygers hart wrapt in a Players hyde, supposes he is as well able to bombast out a blanke verse as the best of you: and being an absolute Iohannes fac totum, is in his owne conceit the onely Shake-scene in a countrey. O that I might intreate your rare wits to be imploied in more profitable courses: & let those Apes imitate your past excellence, and never more acquaint them with your admired inventions. I know the best husband of you all will never prove an Usurer, and the kindest of them all will never seeke you a kind nurse: yet whilest you may, seeke you better Maisters; for it is pittie men of such rare wits, should be subiect to the pleasure of such rude groomes.

In this I might insert two more, that both have writ against these buckram Gentlemen: but let their owne works serve to witnesse against their owne wickednesse, if they persevere to mainteine any more such peasants. For other new-commers, I leave them to the mercie of these painted monsters, who (I doubt not) will drive the best minded to despise them: for the rest, it skils not though they make a ieast at them.

But now returne I againe to you three, knowing my miserie is to you no news: and let me hartily intreate you to bee warned by my harms. Delight not (as I have done) in irreligious oathes; for from the blasphermers house, a curse shall not depart. Despise drunkennes, which wasteth the wit, and maketh men all equall unto beasts. Flie lust, as the deathsman of the soule, and defile not the Temple of the holy Ghost. Abhorre those Epicures, whose loose life hath made religion lothsome to your eares: and when they sooth you wit htearmes of Mastership, remember Robert Greene, whome they have often so flattered, perishes now for want of comfort. Remember Gentlemen, your lives are like so many lighted Tapers, that are with care delivered to all of you to maintaine: these with wind-puft wrath may be extinguisht, which drunkennes put out, which negligence let fall: for mans time is not of it selfe to short, but it is more shortned by sinne. The fire of my light is now at the last snuffe, and the want of wherwith to sustaine it, there is no substance left for life to feede on. Trust not then (I beseech yee) to such weake staies: for they are as changeable in minde, as in many attyres. Well, my hand is tired, and

> I am forst to leave where I would begin; for a whole booke cannot contain their wrongs, which I am forst to knit vp in some few lines of words.
>
> Desirous that you should live,
> though himselfe be dying,
> Robert Greene.

I have given a fuller excerpt than one normally finds since most authors who refer to the text tend to focus solely on the "Shake-scene" paragraph, which will be discussed in due course.

A few less controversial comments first. The playwrights whom Greene addresses in the first three paragraphs are usually assumed to be, in sequence, Christopher Marlowe, Thomas Nashe, and George Peele. The inferences are not hard to establish. Marlowe had a reputation for atheism and was known to reference Machiavelli in his plays. Nashe was already well-known as a young satirist. And that leaves George Peele, in a paragraph that references "St. George" (Lodge was at sea and Lyly was a more successful member of the establishment).[98] The "two more" that Greene could have inserted appears be a reference to authors who had written against the theater, or usury, or both: which brings to mind Gosson, Anthony Munday, and Thomas Lodge.

The overwhelming focus of the text however has always fallen on the "upstart Crow" who "beautified with our feathers" and "supposes he is as well able to bombast out a bank verse as the best of you." Because of the reference to "tiger's heart wrapped in a player's hide," which alludes to a well-known line in *Henry the Sixth, Part 3* ("tiger's heart wrapped in a woman's hide"), and the reference to "Shake-scene," the passage is usually taken to be about Shakespeare. This reading is not, however, universally accepted, and the interpretation does not always break down along party lines; there are Stratfordians who believe the passage is a reference to Shakespeare as a plagiarist, and there are anti-Stratfordians who insist that this is a reference to Edward Alleyn, a prominent actor of the day.[99]

The passage itself has also been the subject of extensive scrutiny, including minute lexical and semantic analysis. For example, "beautified

---

[98] There was once a common view that Lodge was the "young Juvenal," probably on the strength of the one known play collaboration between Lodge and Greene (*A Looking Glass for London*, published in 1594). If Nashe was the "young Juvenal," however, that raises the question of a supposed Greene-Nashe collaboration, which suggests, for example, *Henry VI, Part 1*, parts of which are occasionally assigned to Nashe.

[99] A typical exposition of this idea can be found in Chiljan, Katherine, *Shakespeare Suppressed: The Uncensored Truth About Shakespeare and his Works*, 107–129.

with our feathers" certainly sounds like a reference to plagiarism, and furthermore ties into the characterization of Shakespeare as "Terence" in Davies' epigram twenty years later. On the other hand, "bombast out a blanke verse as the best of you" sounds like a reference to an original, albeit imitative, writer. Perhaps the simplest reading of the paragraph is that it refers to an actor who uses other people's texts as a basis for his own. Yet this interpretation raises the ire of both sides since most approaches in the controversy imply sole authorship, with advocates either arguing that "beautified with our feathers" merely means that Shakespeare borrowed their "forms" of writing (a particularly tepid exegesis followed by Jonathan Bate and James Shapiro[100]) or else they argue that the paragraph does not refer to Shakespeare at all. That's part of the reason for providing longer extracts, so the reader can make up his or her own mind. To further complicate matters, there is also a school of analysis that argues that the offending passage wasn't even written by Greene, but rather by the publisher of *Groatsworth*, Henry Chettle. Concerning the point at issue this is completely irrelevant.

What is relevant is the wider context of *Groatsworth*. The narrative concerns an educated young man who is hired by a well-dressed actor to write plays for him. He falls into debt, gets sick, and dies. So the initial premise of Roberto's story is that the young playwright, because of his poverty, has become indentured to his employer, who is the actor. It is at this point in the narrative that Greene steps in and starts giving explicit advice to his peers, to avoid writing for the players, to "seek better masters," to avoid their usury (i.e., bondage through indebtedness), and, by the way, Greene could mention two others who had written against them (the "buckram gentlemen"). So the overall context is that Greene is exhorting his fellow playwrights to stop writing for players to whom they become indebted and who end up changing their scripts anyway.

There is another text that is relevant. After *Groatsworth* was printed there was some controversy, insofar as some of the three playwrights took offense (remember, these are usually identified as Marlowe, Nashe, and Peele). In December of 1592, Chettle published another little book, *Kind-Hearts Dreame*, to which he prefaced an epistle describing the controversy:[101]

---

100 Bate, *Soul of the Age*, 34–36; Shapiro, *Contested*, 234–235.

101 Chettle, Henry, *Kind-Hearts Dreame*, 1592 (originally published as by "H.C."), using the transcription of Nina Greene, 2001. Italics added.

> About three months since died Master Robert Greene, leaving many papers in sundry booksellers' hands, among other his *Groatsworth of Wit*, in which a letter written to divers play-makers is offensively by one or two of them taken, and because on the dead they cannot be avenged, they wilfully forge in their conceits a living author, and after tossing it to and fro, no remedy but it must light on me. How I have, all the time of my conversing in printing, hindered the bitter inveighing against scholars, it hath been very well known, and how in that I dealt I can sufficiently prove. With neither of them that take offence was I acquainted, and with one of them I care not if I never be. The other, whom at that time I did not so much spare as since I wish I had, for that as I have moderated the heat of living writers, and might have used my own discretion (especially in such a case), the author being dead, that I did not, I am as sorry as if the original fault had been my fault, because myself have seen his demeanour no less civil than he excellent in the quality he professes. Besides, divers of worship have reported his uprightness of dealing, which argues his honesty, and his facetious grace in writing, that approves his art.

Thus Chettle wrote that two of the three playwrights had taken offense at Greene's exhortation. He characterized one of them as someone he did not know and did not care to know (presumably, Marlowe), while the other has been variously identified as Shakespeare or even the Earl of Oxford. However, neither of these identifications makes much sense because Chettle describes how he "hindered the inveighing against scholars," which is not Oxford's most notable characteristic and applies not at all to Shakespeare. That means it is more likely that the second offended party was either Nashe (who we know was sharply critical of the pamphlet) or George Peele.

Meres' *Palladis Tamia*

Francis Meres (1565–1647) was a protestant divine who wrote the *Palladis Tamia* (also known as "Wit's Treasury") in 1598. It is essentially an almanac or digest about English and classical literature, the most famous part of which is a section of extremely vacuous comparisons. We will list half a dozen excerpts to set forth the pattern of Meres' formulaic prose, the data relevant to this study, as well as some comments about characters already introduced:[102]

> As the Greeke tongue is made famous and eloquent by Homer,

---

[102] The quotes from Meres in Smith, *Critical Essays*, Volume 2, 308–324.

> Hesiod, Euripedes, Æschylus, Sophocles, Pindarus, Phocylides, and Aristophanes; and the Latine tongue by Virgill, Ouid, Horace, Silius Italicus, Lucanus, Lucretius, Ausonius, and Claudianus: so the English tongue is mightily enriched and gorgeously inuested in rare ornaments and resplendent abiliments by Sir Philip Sydney, Spencer, Daniel, Drayton, Warner, Shakespeare, Marlow, and Chapman.

This is simply a list of contemporary British poets; Shakespeare's name is just one of many.

> [...]

> As the soule of Euphorbus was thought to liue in Pythagoras: so the sweete wittie soule of Ouid liues in mellifluous and hony-tongued Shakespeare, witnes his Venus and Adonis, his Lucrece, his sugred Sonnets among his priuate friends, &c.

Venus and Adonis and *Lucrece* are two narrative poems that were published in 1593 and 1594 respectively. Both were popular and both were published with dedications by William Shakespeare. The bit about "sugared sonnets among his private friends" is usually taken as reference to Shakespeare's sonnets, which were published under rather odd circumstances in 1609 (we will discuss this in due course). This particular reference is taken by some to indicate that Meres must have known Shakespeare personally, but I think it is more likely a reference to *The Passionate Pilgrim*, a collection of twenty poems for which we have a title page dated 1599 "by W. Shakespeare" (but which may have been published earlier; Meres' book was entered for publication in early September, 1598). Of the twenty poems in *The Passionate Pilgrim*, modern scholarship has determined that only five were by Shakespeare (including two of the canonical sonnets); the others are variously assigned or unknown.[103]

> [...]

> As Plautus and Seneca are accounted the best for Comedy and Tragedy among the Latines: so Shakespeare among the English is the most excellent in both kinds for the stage. For Comedy, witnes his Gentlemen of Verona, his Errors, his Loue Labors Lost, his Loue Labours Wonne, his Midsummers Night Dreame, and his Merchant

---

103 Mark Anderson, in his *'Shakespeare' By Another Name* (232–233) describes the provenance of one of the poems in *The Passionate Pilgrim*, suggesting it originated in the time when de Vere, the Earl of Oxford, was maintaining his circle at his residence in Fisher's Folly. Like most Oxfordian arguments, however, this takes a legitimate attribution and overextends it.

of Venice; For Tragedy, his Richard the 2, Richard the 3, Henry the 4, King Iohn, Titus Andronicus, and his Romeo and Iuliet.

This is the critical paragraph: a list of six comedies and six tragedies, all ascribed to Shakespeare. This means that, absent other information, plays not listed here must have been written in 1599 or later; at least, that is the traditional view. But note that the *Henry VI* plays are not listed; that inclines one to think that they were collaborations.

[...]

As Decius Ausonius Gallus, in libris Fastorum, penned the occurrences of the world from the first creation of it to his time, that is, to the raigne of the Emperor Gratian: so Warner, in his absolute Albion's Englande, hath most admirably penned the historie of his own country from Noah to his time, that is to the raigne of Queen Elizabeth. I haue heard him termd of the best wits of both our Vniversities our English Homer.

This is perhaps the Ur-reference to someone as the English Homer, to be followed by Dryden, Pope, and many others (although the meaning of the attribution would change).

The best Poets for Comedy among the Greeks are these, Menander, Aristophanes, Eupolis Atheniensis, Alexis Terius, Nicostratus, Amipsias Atheniensis, Anaxandrides Rhodius, Aristonymus, Archippus Atheniensis, and Callias Atheniensis; and among the Latines, Plautus, Terence, Næuius, Sextus Turpilius, Licinius Imbrex, and Virgilius Romanus: so the best for Comedy amongst vs bee Edward, Earle of Oxforde, Doctor Gager of Oxforde, Master Rowley, once a rare scholler of learned Pembrooke Hall in Cambridge, Maister Edwardes, one of Her Maiesties Chappell, eloquent and wittie Iohn Lilly, Lodge, Gascoyne, Greene, Shakespeare, Thomas Nash, Thomas Heywood, Anthony Mundye, our best plotter, Chapman, Porter, Wilson, Hathway, and Henry Chettle.

This is an important paragraph because it is frequently cited in the form of "Meres said that the Earl of Oxford was 'the best for comedy'" which is supposed to prove that Oxford wrote plays, and that he was renowned for his comedic writing. However, arguments based on this inference take the matter largely out of context, since any author cited must be compared with over a dozen other names.

> [...]
>
> As Achilles tortured the deade bodie of Hector, and as Antonius and his wife Fuluia tormented the liuelesse corps of Cicero: so Gabriell Haruey hath shewed the same inhumanitie to Greene, that lies full low in his graue.

This paragraph is listed only because it is a direct reference to Gabriel Harvey's tasteless attacks on the dead Greene in *Four Letters and Certain Sonnets*, as discussed earlier.

> [...]
>
> As Iodelle, a French tragical poet, beeing an epicure and an atheist, made a pitifull end: so our tragicall poet Marlow for his Epicurisme and Atheisme had a tragical death. You may read of this Marlow more at large in the Theatre of God's judgments, in the 25th chapter entreating of Epicures and Atheists. As the poet Lycophron was shot to death by a certain riual of his: so Christopher Marlow was stabd to death by a bawdy Servingman, a riual of his in his lewde loue.

This is a reference to the death of Marlowe in 1593. It's pretty much the model of his death that later authors referenced until the 20th century.

Overall, it is a little surprising that Shakespeare scholarship has come to depend on such a superficial and vacuous work, which reads like a cramming guide for an Elizabethan version of Trivial Pursuit or *Jeopardy!* ("I'll take 'Best for Comedy' for two hundred, Alex"). But the reliance on this book simply underscores how little we know about the English theater in the reign of Queen Elizabeth.

To sum up, as the popularity of Shakespeare increased in the 18th century, so did curiosity about his career, and this led to the unearthing of historical documents. The three documents we have reviewed here—Shakespeare's Will, *Groatsworth*, and Francis Meres' *Palladis Tamia*—are, if not the three most important documents, certainly the three most widely referenced documents about Shakespeare.

And yet, the documents are ambiguous in their support for Shakespeare's career and accomplishments. If we accept the identification, *Groatsworth* proves that Shakespeare was active in London by 1592; the Will, if we accept the interlineation to the three actors, proves that Shakespeare was involved with the stage; and the testimony of

Meres attributes twelve plays to him. On the other hand, Meres' attributions leave out some plays that we know came before this date, and mention Shakespeare as merely one of many poets and dramatists; the Will mentions no books nor literary remains and carries no hint of the putative poet and philosopher of the plays; and *Groatsworth* suggests that Shakespeare was a plagiarist.

7 | OUR ENGLISH HOMER

The Nature of Attribution Studies ~ Early Attribution Studies: Homer ~ Early Attribution Studies: The Bible ~ Erasmus ~ Sch mucker ~ Schleiermacher ~ Hermeneutics ~ Unitarians versus Analysts ~ Authorship and Inerrancy

Setting aside the emerging evidence for a moment, the Shakespeare authorship controversy is simply a variation of ordinary attribution studies. To be sure, in attribution studies we usually are simply attempting to figure out the provenance of a single text, not the provenance of an entire body of work. But before we continue we should pause to consider this field of study since it is directly relevant to our subject. This is especially so since attribution studies began over two thousand years ago and concerned the authorship of the Homeric poems. The suggested solutions to that problem had a direct bearing on how people conceptualized the Shakespeare authorship controversy in later times.

Attribution studies require a body of literature that can be consulted; therefore, in Harold Love's survey of the subject, the key was the development of the library in Alexandria, which enabled the comparison and analysis of literature. But as Love also noted, as far back as Aristotle there were disputes as to which ancient texts could be ascribed to Homer.[104]

It doesn't require a lot of imagination to understand how misattributions could have taken place: attribution confers authority and status on a text, and as a result attribution will also confer market value. The landmark in Homeric studies was the publication in 1795 of the

---

[104] Love, Harold, *Attributing Authorship: An Introduction*, 25–26. Shapiro, *Contested*, 69–73, also discusses the topic of Homeric authorship, with much contextual detail but somewhat out of chronological sequence.

Prolegomena ad Homerum by the German philologist Heinrich Wolf, which argued that Homer was a composite. Wolf's core argument was that the texts could not have been written down at the time of any reputed composition, since reliable Greek texts come from about the 6th century BCE, far too late for the subject of the *Iliad* and *Odyssey*, which describe, however inaccurately, events that took place five hundred years earlier. Therefore they must have been compiled at a later date from a collection of songs, sagas, and lays.

Wolf's argument went hand in hand with Enlightenment tendencies to review all old texts critically and skeptically. However, perhaps an even more relevant contributor was David Hume, whose *Enquiry Concerning Human Nature* (1741) set the model for modern empiricism, particularly in the English-speaking world. These two tendencies, toward skepticism on the one hand and analysis on the other, had far-reaching effects that would inevitably carry over into the discussion of Shakespeare.

Homeric studies after Wolff broke down into two camps: "unitarians" and "analysts." Unitarians believe that the Homeric poems (principally the *Iliad* and *Odyssey*, but also including some smaller works) were more or less written by one person. Analysts believe that the Homeric works were compiled, or stitched together, by an editor in about the 6th century BCE. The argument has been going on ever since.

In my opinion, the analysts have the stronger case, not only because of the demonstrable absence of a writing tradition in Greece before the 7th century BCE, but also because of 20th century arguments that the Homeric poems follow a pattern discerned in the transmission of oral poetry elsewhere. But even today one can find experts who will insist that "Homer" (whoever he or she was) was largely the sole author of the poems.

Besides Homer, the Bible was also a candidate for skepticism and analysis. Of course, skepticism expressed as mockery of the Bible had been common (as we know from the attributed remarks of Christopher Marlowe), but outspoken Biblical skeptics often died violent deaths for heresy so it is a little harder to trace the tradition. We know that Voltaire made several mocking comments about the Bible in his *Philosophical Dictionary* and that Hume wrote with insufficient piety in *The Natural History of Religion*, but looking back from a 21st century perspective the grounds for skepticism seem obvious. For example, there are numerous miracles and events that even then appeared unlikely: Moses and the parting of the Red Sea, the plagues of Egypt, Jonah and the whale, and the many miracles attributed to Jesus Christ in the New Testament. In addition, there are numerous structural problems; for example, there are two tales of creation in the book of Genesis, two versions of the Sermon on the Mount (Sermon on the Mount, Sermon on the Plain), and there are numerous apparent contradictions between moral teachings in the Old Testament and the New. Most believers are aware of such inconsistencies.

Above and beyond the issue of inconsistencies in the Bible there are issues of attribution, something which has become much more of an issue in the postwar 20th century after the discovery of the Dead Sea Scrolls and the Nag Hammadi manuscripts, two large caches of documents which describe the literary prehistory of the Bible. Naturally, the question arises: Shouldn't these books be included in the Biblical canon? The short answer is no, because those debates about inclusion were settled long ago.

In brief, the attribution of the books of the Bible was a centuries-long process of assessment, consensus, and authority, completed by about the end of the 4th century. Even today there is a large group of books, the Apocrypha, which are accepted as canonical biblical texts by some Christian denominations but not by others. The main point is that the acceptance of the attribution of a specific text, even when the stakes are as high as they would be in the establishment of a religious tradition, is very vague: it is not, or rarely has been, based on empirical proof as we would normally use that term, but rather on a process of initial attribution, discussion, and eventual consensus. Initial attributions, on the other hand, can frequently be spurious, as Erasmus recognized in 1516:[105]

> The man who is satisfied with the name of the author on the title page regardless of how it got there will read fourteen Gospels, I think, instead of four. Nothing is easier than to place any name you want on the front of a book.

The status of the Bible raises another point. Regardless of the diversity of the sources involved, it is, by fiat, a unified text. Therefore the burden is upon the reader to reconcile the texts. Put another way, when dealing with diverse texts the reader can make independent decisions about which works to include or exclude from a group. But with a

---
105 Quoted in Love, *Attributing*, 20.

canonical arrangement, as with the Bible, or the First Folio, it is up to the reader to reconcile the assembled texts. This calls for a much more active textual engagement where reconstruction and imagination are in play. The science, or method, of this project is called hermeneutics, from the Greek word for "interpretation."

The figure who is usually brought up at this point is Friedrich Schleiermacher (1768–1834), a German protestant theologian who popularized the idea that a proper interpretation of the Bible involved a constant back and forth between the parts of the text under discussion (grammar, syntax, the meaning of words) and then the larger text, in terms of verse, chapter, book, and so forth. Such back and forth has two aims: one is to understand the text, the other is to try to understand what the author of the text was attempting to do with the text. The latter inevitably involves a psychological conceit, in terms of attempting to decipher the author's intentions.

To take a typical example, Proverbs 22:28 enjoins, "Do not move an ancient boundary stone set up by your forefathers." In the first order, we could say that this means what it plainly says—that literal stones set by our literal ancestors should not be displaced. But we could also say that it means one should never alter the environment, or that we should always honor our ancestors, or always maintain tradition. Yet all of these interpretations are removed from context. The meaning of the text is actually "Do not steal," but to arrive at this understanding we must know that boundary stones determine the size of one's holdings.[106] In other words, hermeneutics is the science of interpretation, but it is also the science of putting things into progressively wider contexts in order to achieve the proper interpretation. This constant back and forth from text to surrounding context has come down to us as the "hermeneutic circle."[107]

With reference to our subject, there are two things to add about hermeneutics. The first is that, when we have discussed Shakespearean commentators who promote fidelity to the text, we are discussing something akin to the approach of Biblical hermeneutics. No Biblical scholar, for example, would propose arbitrarily dropping 1,500 lines of text into footnotes: the text is assumed inerrant, and if there is a problem with understanding it, the problem lies with the reader, not with

---

106 Virkler; Ayayo, *Hermeneutics: Principles and Processes of Biblical Interpretation*, 81–82.

107 Roy J. Howard's *Three Faces of Hermeneutics* is a very accessible guide and describes the "hermeneutic circle" in various contexts, 10, 20, 107, 149, 165.

the text. The second point is that, precisely because the hermeneutic circle moves from part to whole and back again, it is no longer a simple process of understanding. On the contrary, we are now discussing an intellectual process that is dynamic, sequential, and played out across time: in a word, phenomenological. Thus the hermeneutic circle becomes a spiral. This will become a larger issue in the 20th century.

In addition to hermeneutics, another result of 18th century Biblical skepticism was the continued questioning of the historical reality of much of the content of the Bible. This pertains particularly to the biography, and even the existence, of the historical Jesus. In reaction to this brand of skepticism, a number of books were written that questioned the historical reality of other historical figures. Among these we may count a book that questioned whether Napoleon ever existed, and, more directly relevant to our subject, a book by S.M. Schmucker, an American protestant theologian, that questioned the historical reality of Shakespeare.[108]

These books by Christians in opposition to Humean skepticism do not have much relevance to our subject, but Schmucker's book is frequently brought up by Stratfordians in order to upset their opponents. James Shapiro, for example, made Schmucker's ostensible thesis a centerpiece in his recent book defending Shakespeare as author, calling Schmucker's text a veritable "playbook" for the anti-Stratfordians. Needless to say, Schmucker's *Historic Doubts* was tongue-in-cheek: his main point was that anyone who would accept the absurdity of skepticism with regard to Jesus Christ and his miracles would also have to question the existence of Shakespeare.

It could be said that the glee of Stratfordians in raising S.M. Schmucker is misplaced. Bible narratives are accepted as a matter of faith, not rational analysis. On the other hand, to propose faith as a necessary precondition to accepting William Shakespeare as the author of the First Folio is to concede the main point of Shakespeare skeptics. Shapiro makes a good observation concerning the fact that the influence of the Bible, and therefore assumed Biblical inerrancy, has only recently begun to be considered with respect to the Shakespeare canon. We can expect that further analysis in this direction will also lead to a questioning of the fundamental Shakespearean tenet of title page attribution.

---

108 Schmucker, Samuel Mosheim, *Historic Doubts Respecting Shakspere; Illustrating Infidel Objections Against the Bible* (1853) and *Historic Doubts Relative to Napoleon Buonaparte*, 3rd edition (1827, no author). The Napoleon book is a response to Hume's *On Miracles* and Whig reform.

This brief review of attribution studies has focused primarily on the Bible and Homer, and we draw different conclusions from them. On the one hand, Biblical analysis and criticism yield the science of interpretation, or hermeneutics, while Homeric criticism yields the binary split between "unitarians" on the one hand and "analysts" on the other. I would like to borrow and modify the terms of Homeric criticism and apply them to Shakespeare. We will thus consider those who believe that Shakespeare wrote all of the works attributed to him as "unitarians." Those who believe that all of the works were written by some other one person, but not Shakespeare, we may consider "unitarian revisionists." Those who believe that the works were assembled from many different sources we may term "analysts." In terms of nomenclature, this book is written from an extreme "analyst" point of view.

Aside from introducing the term hermeneutics, Biblical analysis has little direct connection with Shakespeare (except insofar as it has allowed us to raise, and dispense with, Schmucker's book). Yet there are two ways in which Shakespeare scholarship does mimic Biblical study. The first pertains to the issue of inerrancy: to the extent, for example, that Theobald insisted on the accuracy of Shakespeare's received word, he was not merely defending the pristine nature of the text, and the canonicity of the First Folio; he was also obtruding an almost superstitious approach to the accuracy and authority of his source.

8 | Toward a Shakespeare Chronology

*Samuel Johnson ~ Edward Capell ~ Edmond
Malone ~ Shakespeare's Chronology ~ Nashe's Preface
to Greene's Menaphon ~ The Ur-Hamlet ~ The German
Hamlet ~ Other Ur-plays*

After the editions of Rowe, Pope, and Theobald, there were no less than six further editions of Shakespeare published in the 18th century, most of them under the control of the Tonson family.[109] Meanwhile the fame and celebration of Shakespeare intensified. During this period there were continued debates concerning authorship of parts of the canon, continued revelations about sources, and continued revelations about *Hamlet*. In the next two chapters, we will consider these points and also consider the sources of the philosophical attitudes supposedly unique to the plays. In turn, we will introduce a conceptual shortcoming in the field of authorship studies.

The Shakespeare editions of Thomas Hanmer (1744) and William Warburton (1747) had little impact, but the edition of Samuel Johnson (1765), who was chosen on the strength of his *Dictionary of the English Language*, deserves greater notice. Johnson was the greatest literary mind of the day, and his editorial investment in the Shakespeare corpus was impressive, providing not only detailed—and still interesting—commentary on the plays,[110] but also a healthy dose of incisive criticism; he was no hagiographer. While Hanmer questioned the authorship of *Two Gentlemen of Verona*, Johnson accepted it, but still found it uneven. Johnson traced *Measure for Measure* back to the

---

109 Taylor, Gary, *Reinventing Shakespeare* (1989), 52–53, 68–75, 87–88, 128–129, for references to the Tonson family.

110 *Samuel Johnson on Shakespeare*, see Kindle edition.

Italian novelist Cinthio (the same source as *Othello*), believing some other text must have come between the source and the final play. He felt that *Love's Labour's Lost* contained much that was "mean, childish, and vulgar" but was convinced that Shakespeare wrote it. He regarded *Titus Andronicus* as a "spurious" attribution. He felt that the choruses to *Henry V* didn't fit the play, and that the last act was problematic (presumably because of the long seduction scene conducted partly in French). Johnson also commented that *Richard II* had been "apparently revised" from a prior text, suggesting plagiarism from Rafael Holinshed's *Chronicle*, a large folio of English history that was published in two editions in 1580 and 1587.

Johnson's main contribution to future scholarship comes with respect to the *Henry VI* plays. Both Theobald and Warburton questioned the attribution (Warburton decisively). While Johnson demurred, he did agree that the versions of *Henry VI*, Parts 2 and 3, which were published under other titles in the early 1590s, were inferior to the versions in the First Folio, believing them to be copies taken down by some auditors who then filled in the gaps as best they could. In this way, Johnson created the conceptual framework for the idea of "bad quartos" which would fully emerge 150 years later.

Edward Capell's (1768) version of Shakespeare came next. Capell has a justified reputation for scholarship and a clear and penetrating style, but like Theobald he is something of a Shakespeare apologist (or an unapologetic unitarian). In terms of our overall theme, he defended the attribution of all of the plays to Shakespeare.

Capell was followed by George Steevens in 1773, who was then followed by Edmond Malone (1741–1820), whose various editions culminated after his death in the twenty-volume "Third Variorum Edition." Malone's contribution was twofold. First, he synthesized the textual analysis, source criticism, and document discovery of his predecessors. Second, he sought to provide a chronology for the plays.

From this point forward, with a few exceptions, authoritative editions of Shakespeare became the province of academic consensus.

Recall that 18 of the 36 plays were published before the First Folio. The dates of publication for the quartos could, in several cases, explain when the plays were written, on the assumption that they would have been written a year or two prior to publication. The plays that were published only in the Folio—fully half—had to be interpolated by other means: printed references (such as Meres' list of plays), or mentions in the Stationers Register (the record of texts certified for publication, usually in the printer's name as a form of copyright). To these could be added Malone's theory of developing style, moving more and more toward irregular meter or free verse as time went on. Finally, all of the plays had to be fit into a time bracket from about 1590 to 1613, when the Globe burned down during a performance of *Henry VIII*, three years before Shakespeare's death. Malone's chronology was followed by Chambers in 1930, as well as by Taylor and Wells in 1986; it is essentially unchanged.

In the first phase of this imagined chronology the *Henry VI* plays come largely on the basis of Greene's remark in *Groatsworth*. None of the *Henry VI* plays were referenced by Meres, so Malone considered collaboration or at least later revision. Then we get *Richard III*, followed by miscellaneous plays (*Titus, Shrew, Two Gentlemen*), followed by a hypothetical period during which Shakespeare wrote largely in verse (*Romeo and Juliet, Richard II, Midsummer Night's Dream,* and *King John*).

The Merchant of Venice followed, presumably because it was a more mature work, then *Henry IV*. Meres' list terminates here, so now Malone had to depend on the Stationers Register and quarto publications. *Much Ado, Henry V,* and *Julius Caesar* were supposed to have all been written in 1599, although only *Henry V* was actually published in 1600. The remaining plays were assigned to later dates.

The chronology is not without problems. As noted, the quartos are frequently shorter than the Folio versions, which raises the question as to who revised and expanded these plays, and why. A second problem involves contemporary analogues. *Taming of the Shrew*, if dated to 1595, is preceded by another play, *Taming of a Shrew*, which was published in 1594. As a result there has been a modern tendency to date this play as far back as 1590.

But the largest problem concerns *Hamlet*. The story goes that Malone was set to assign *Hamlet* to about 1595 on the basis of some other references, but then he came across the preface to Greene's *Menaphon*, written by Thomas Nashe in 1589:[111]

> It is a common practice now-a-days amongst a sort of shifting companions, that run through every art and thrive by none, to leave the trade of *noverint* whereto they were born and busy themselves with

---
111 Smith, *Critical*, Vol. 1, 311–312; compare Nina Green's transcription.

the endeavours of art, that could scarcely Latinize their neck-verse if they should have need; yet English Seneca read by candlelight yields many good sentences, as Blood is a beggar, and so forth, and if you entreat him fair in a frosty morning, he will afford you whole *Hamlets*, I should say handfuls, of tragical speeches. But O grief! Tempus edax rerum, what's that will last always? The sea exhaled by drops will in continuance be dry, and Seneca, let blood line by line and page by page, at length must needs die to our stage, which makes his famished followers to imitate the kid in Aesop, who, enamoured with the fox's newfangles, forsook all hopes of life to leap into a new occupation, and these men, renouncing all possibilities of credit or estimation, to intermeddle with Italian translations, wherein how poorly they have plodded (as those that are neither Provencal men, nor are able to distinguish of articles), let all indifferent gentlemen that have travailed in that tongue discern by their twopenny pamphlets.

Thereupon Malone decided that *Hamlet* could not be back-dated to 1589, and thus the *Ur-Hamlet* was born—that is, a hypothetical version of *Hamlet*, but not by Shakespeare, whose quarto version was first published in 1604 (the Folio version is a bit shorter). However, in 1828, several years after Malone's death, a 1603 quarto of *Hamlet* was discovered. This version, also published under Shakespeare's name, was half the length of the 1604 version and had radically shortened versions of the many tragical speeches; thus, "To be or not to be, I there's the point!"

Nor is that all. In 1817, one of the German translators of Shakespeare, Ludwig Tieck, began directing attention to various documents and texts which pointed to the performances of English actors in Germany in the 1580s, 1590s, and beyond.[112] These texts included German language versions of *Two Gentlemen of Verona, Titus Andronicus*, and *Romeo and Juliet*, as well as a *Hamlet* text similar to the 1603 quarto, but with an additional opening chorus, as well as two plays by the German playwright, Jacob Ayrer of Nuremberg (1543–1605). One of these, *The Beautiful Phaenicia*, has a plot similar to *Much Ado About Nothing*, while the other, *The Beautiful Sidea*, has a plot very similar to *The Tempest*. Both plays must have been written before Ayrer's death, but Malone had dated *The Tempest* to 1610, because he was convinced that that play was written after a particular voyage to Bermuda. So the discovery of these German texts not only raises questions about *Hamlet* but also potentially creates two new "Ur" plays.

---

[112] Tieck's activity refers to the publication of his "Old German Theater" as referenced by Cohn in the preface to *Shakespeare in Germany*.

Most orthodox Shakespeareans accept the general shape of Malone's chronology, while the chronology creates problems for most anti-Stratfordians. This is to be expected; the chronology was cut to fit Shakespeare. But that points to the biggest problem with the chronology: compiled on the basis of quarto publications, random references, and inspired guesswork, it seeks to map out the creative life of a writer about whose life as a writer we know essentially nothing. Thus, chronology implies biography, feeding the irresistible temptation to construct the latter on the basis of the former.

One of the problems with Malone's chronology is that henceforth there would be a strong tendency to forcibly bracket all of Shakespeare's productivity into the 20-year period from 1592 (when Greene referenced the "upstart crow" in *Groatsworth*) to 1613 (when the Globe burned during a performance of *Henry VIII*). Along with other factors this would compel the regular assignment of two plays a year to Shakespeare's already busy schedule. But it would also be necessary to provide some kind of intelligible arc to the plays themselves. Because of publication dates, and because of Meres, all the great tragedies would come in rapid succession after 1600; thus according to the standard chronology *Hamlet*, *Lear*, *Macbeth*, and *Othello* would all be written in close proximity, with no explanation for the change in Shakespeare's mentality.

In the same way, most of the other plays, not mentioned by Meres, or unpublished before 1600, would be assigned to the reign of King James (1603–1625); and these often display a marked decline in artistry.

Yet a further problem with the chronological bracketing is that a number of the plays seem concerned with issues (the status of the theaters, the role of drama, the proper performance of drama) which were current in the 1580s but not later. Finally, as we shall see, the analysis of the quarto versus the folio versions of the plays suggests priority to the folio versions, which in turn suggests intense activity before the typical chronology. This, in turn, leads to the notion of an "early start" for Shakespeare's literary career,[113] even when such proposals run afoul of the known biographical facts and standard chronology.

---

113 The idea that Shakespeare wrote some of the canonical plays before his London appearance in 1592 connotes the "early start" and has been championed mostly by EAJ Honigmann (*Shakespeare's Impact on his Contemporaries*) and Eric Sams (*The Real Shakespeare*). Under this heading, and for various reasons, *Hamlet*, *Lear*, *King John*, *Taming of the Shrew* and perhaps others have been assigned to the 1580s. Arguments about when the plays were written, and, by extension, what they were about (when they were not simply narratives) are the most important to emerge from the authorship controversy. It is fair to ask whether insisting on assigning these plays to one author or another does not distort the answers to these questions.

9 | Blood Is a Beggar

Sources for the Plays ~ Philosophical Sources ~ Montaigne ~ The Panchatantra ~ Milkmaid and Bucket ~ Aesop ~ Hellenist Philosophy ~ Epicurus, Zeno, Pyrrho ~ Dennis McCarthy, Sir Thomas North ~ Marcus Aurelius ~ Logos ~ Stoicism ~ Seneca

While Malone was working up his synthesis, more discoveries were being made about Shakespeare and his plays. One of these was the finding by Edward Capell in 1767 that Shakespeare had lifted a sentence from the *Essays of Montaigne*. Here is the passage in question, from *The Tempest*:

> I' the commonwealth I would by contraries
> Execute all things; for no kind of traffic
> Would I admit; no name of magistrate;
> Letters should not be known; riches, poverty,
> And use of service, none; contract, succession,
> Bourn, bound of land, tilth, vineyard, none;
> No use of metal, corn, or wine, or oil;
> No occupation; all men idle, all;
> And women too, but innocent and pure;
> No sovereignty;—
> [...]
> All things in common nature should produce
> Without sweat or endeavour: treason, felony,
> Sword, pike, knife, gun, or need of any engine,
> Would I not have; but nature should bring forth,
> Of its own kind, all foison, all abundance,
> To feed my innocent people. (2.1.23)

Here is the passage from Montaigne, from his essay *On Cannibals*:[114]

> [Brazilian Indians have] no kind of traffic, no knowledge of letters, no intelligence of numbers, no name of magistrate or politic superiority, no use of service, of riches or of poverty, no contracts, no successions…no occupation but idle, no respect of kindred but common, no apparel but natural, no manuring of lands, no use of wine, corn, or metal.

The plagiarism from Montaigne raises the larger issue of the sources for the plays, so let's pause briefly to consider these—not only the literary sources but also the philosophical sources. This will also help frame the entire issue of Shakespeare's "philosophy."

The first main source is the *Chronicles* of Rafael Holinshed (1529–1580), which is a large folio chronicle of English monarchs and the events of their reigns. The *Chronicles* were published in two versions, in 1577 and 1587, and formed the source material for most of the history plays, but also *Macbeth*, *King Lear*, and *Cymbeline*. It would be incorrect to believe that Holinshed was the sole author; in fact there is a lack of clarity as to who wrote what, and by the same token it would be wrong to assume that the use of the *Chronicles* was unique to Shakespeare: indeed, most of the history plays written in this time frame were so indebted. And not just history plays: a notorious murder during the brief reign of Edward VI was described in detail in Holinshed, and formed the backdrop for the anonymous *Arden of Faversham*.

Another source that was commonly used was Thomas North's 1579 translation of *Plutarch's Lives*. It provides the basis for paraphrase or plagiarism for all of the Roman or Greek plays. Again, this would not have been unique to Shakespeare.

The other comedies and tragedies are all traceable to prior texts in English, or in French and Italian, many of these coming from short story collections along the lines of the *Decameron*. Some of the plays were fairly direct copies of texts written by other English authors, such as Lodge or Greene. With only two exceptions—*Love's Labour's Lost* and *Midsummer Night's Dream*—all of the plays are derivative in terms of plot, characters, and action. And, depending on how strict one wants to be, most of the plays are plagiaristic. This is why, on the one hand, most Stratfordians tend to stress Shakespeare's brilliant

---

114 Montaigne, "On Cannibals" in the *Essays*.

"shaping power" or his ability to "turn others' dross into gold."[115] Anti-Stratfordians on the other hand tend to back up further and make their candidate not only the author of the plays in question but also the original source that it copies from, thus relieving their favored author from the charge of plagiarism.

The philosophy of the plays is usually compared to that of Montaigne. Montaigne's essays were first published in France in 1582, but they were not translated into English until 1603 (the first translation was by John Florio, whose father had migrated to Britain from Italy, and who we have previously met as the possible in-law of Samuel Daniel). In fact, one of the reasons Francis Bacon has been a perennial authorship candidate is because of the similarity of ideas and approach among Bacon, Shakespeare, and Montaigne.

At this point I would like to introduce two influences that are anterior to all three authors. These are Asian—and particularly Indian—animal fables, and Hellenistic philosophy.

As far as I know there is only one author who has drawn attention to the Indian background to Elizabethan intellectual life, and that is Dennis McCarthy, who recently wrote a book contending that Thomas North wrote the plays.[116] McCarthy's argument hinges on translations: North translated Plutarch; he also translated a version of Indian animal tales in the *The Morall Philosophy of Doni* (1570) as well as (from the Spanish) *The Diall of Princes* (1559). By McCarthy's reckoning, all three affect the verbiage of the Shakespeare plays. But the roots go significantly deeper.

The Morall Philosophy of Doni was itself a translation of *The Fables of Bidpai*, which in turn was an Italian version of the Indian folklore epic, *The Panchatantra,* which is a compilation of animal stories that are probably thousands of years old. In order to connect the stories, a stacked or framed narrative structure—such as we have already encountered in *Groatsworth,* and which was arguably employed by Homer—was used. Another Asian collection of animal tales, *The*

---

115 The "turn others' dross into gold" line seems to trace back to a prologue Theobald wrote for his version of *Richard II* in 1719, with the lines, "On his rich Fund our Author builds his Play, / Keeps all his Gold, and throws his Dross away," and has been used in innumerable permutations since (Vickers, *Critical Heritage*, II:357). The fundamental idea is that regardless of his dependence on, or even plagiarism of, prior sources, Shakespeare's artistry invariably made such indebtedness irrelevant. Brian Vickers, *Appropriating Shakespeare*, has also used this argument of Shakespeare's creative intentionality ("shaping power," 151) to transcend postmodern "death of the author" arguments as discussed in Chapter 25. (Vickers' entire discussion in *Appropriating*, in the section "Shakespeare at Work: The Author Transforms his Sources" (144–162) is relevant.)

116 McCarthy, *North by Shakespeare*; actually McCarthy does not explore the Indian angle at all, but does emphasize North's translation of *Doni* and emphasizes the moral and courtly dimension of beast fables.

Jatakas, is similar, but in that case the unifying principle is that each story is supposed to reflect the activities of the Buddha in one of his pre-human animal incarnations. Although of course animal stories need no justification, the point of the stories usually involves a moral of some kind, meant to inculcate virtue and self-possession (*nitti*) in the listener.[117] The influence of the *Panchatantra* is vast. It has migrated widely, with many of its stories turning up in other collections, including *The Arabian Nights* and *Aesop's Fables*.

A typical *Panchatantra* story goes something like this: A man leaves a mongoose to babysit his infant son. Upon his return, he sees the mongoose with blood on its jaws. Furious, he attacks the animal. Upon entry into his son's bedroom, he learns the truth: the blood on the mongoose's jaws was due to the deadly snake it had killed, and which is lying on the floor next to his son's bed. The ethical teaching for this story involves avoiding rash behavior.

Other stories include the story of the Brahmin who was tricked into buying an unclean beast for sacrifice on the recommendation of three thieves. We have already seen variations of that story with Macaulay and with George Peele, and there are other versions in the West, including a German version featuring Till Eulenspiegel.[118]

Another story involves a Brahmin and a pot of flour; this one is rather well known in the West through Aesop, where it is called "The Milkmaid and Her Bucket," and features a milkmaid and bucketful of cow's milk. In both cases, the imaginings of the characters lead to an unfortunate accident. Rather than recap one of those versions I will quote yet another version of the story, this one told by Ambrose Bierce in the 1880s:[119]

The Milkmaid and Her Bucket

A Senator fell to musing as follows: "With the money which I shall get for my vote in favor of the bill to subsidise cat-ranches, I can buy a kit of burglar's tools and open a bank. The profit of that enterprise will enable me to obtain a long, low, black schooner, raise

---

117 *Panchatantra*, Sarma; Rajan, eds., introduction xv–lv, on *niti*, xxv, xxvii–xxviii, moral concepts, xxxi and passim.

118 The Eulenspiegel version concerns a peasant carrying a bolt of green cloth, which Till and a confederate convince him is blue; the peasant having wagered the cloth, Till uses the green cloth to make his costume, Bote, Hermann, ed., *Till Eulenspiegel*, Tale #66.

119 Bierce, *Collected Works*, 6:369–370. Usually classed among the "Fantastic Fables" in Bierce compilations. The "cat ranches" derive from an actual newspaper hoax from the 1870s concerning a get-rich-quick scheme involving cats eating rats, and then rats eating cats, thus yielding an easy profit in presumably marketable cat pelts.

a death's-head flag and engage in commerce on the high seas. From my gains in that business I can pay for the Presidency, which at $50,000 a year will give me in four years—" but it took him so long to make the calculation that the bill to subsidise cat-ranches passed without his vote, and he was compelled to return to his constituents an honest man, tormented with a clean conscience.

The moral of this story is usually given as something along the lines of "don't count your chickens," but we will want to remember that story because it helps describe a kind of mental pathology that is commonly encountered in the authorship Controversy, by which I mean the tendency to argue on the basis of serial assumptions, none of which are adequately proved.

A typical example goes something like this:

1. at the time of his famous soliloquy, Hamlet is reading a book;
2. one of the images in that soliloquy is very similar to one found in a book called *Cardanus Comforte* which was an English translation of an Italian work;
3. *Cardanus Comforte* was published in England with some front matter written by the Earl of Oxford;
4. Therefore, the book that Hamlet is reading is *Cardanus Comforte*;
5. Since Hamlet is reading a book containing front matter provided by the Earl of Oxford, it follows that the Earl of Oxford wrote *Hamlet*; and
6. Since Oxford wrote *Hamlet*, he wrote all of the plays in the First Folio.

This may sound like a parody but that is how the argument runs. The "Milkmaid and her Bucket" stories are useful because they help us grasp what frequently passes for reason in this field, and on both sides. Harold Love, the Australian literature professor, would call this a "chain of deduction" as opposed to a "skein of deduction," the latter being characterized by multiple threads of reasoning which all arrive at a positive proof.[120] In the "skein of deduction" we can recognize a

---

120 Love, *Attributing*, 203–207 covering circumstantial evidence in detail.

concept similar to the "convergence of evidence" that Michael Shermer tirelessly proclaims. In practice, while this species of circumstantial evidence is superior to Milkmaid and Bucket reasoning, it frequently involves aggregating a number of partial proofs and calling it a proof. That is also fundamentally illogical.

Returning to Montaigne, Bacon, and Shakespeare, an influence that tends to be overlooked is Hellenistic philosophy, which is generally dated from the death of Alexander in 323 BCE and terminating 31 BCE.[121] Under this umbrella are included such philosophical schools as Epicureanism, Skepticism, and Stoicism (along with the three founders of these schools, respectively Epicurus, Pyrrho, and Zeno). Of course, we know little about the founders themselves, as our understanding of their thinking comes through their descendants, who —notwithstanding some maxims of Epicurus—include Lucretius, Epictetus, and Marcus Aurelius, as well as Roman philosophers like Seneca.

The schools were not identical but they shared many qualities. They rejected doctrines of ideas, did not accept the existence of the Gods (or, when they were agnostic, maintained that the Gods had no ability to interfere in human affairs), and all three schools were empirical and rational in disposition. They doubted the permanence or authority of most conventional wisdom, teachings, beliefs, and social arrangements of their times. On the other hand, all three had a strong tendency toward introspection, so their cultural critique never rose to the level of praxis. They were concerned with the best way for an individual to live his or her life; not with other matters. As might be expected, all three schools were concerned with questions surrounding the meaning of life and death.[122]

Epicureanism tended to focus on avoiding pain. This meant training the mind and living a life that would avoid suffering; that is why "Epicureanism" is often used as a synonym for hedonism or pleasure-seeking. Stoicism, on the other hand, argued that the individual mind (*logos*) should be trained to achieve harmony with the universal *logos* that expressed itself in nature. As a result it tended to preach an ethics of self-abnegation. The reasoning is not hard to reconstruct. If

---

[121] Lang, A. A., *Hellenistic Philosophy* is the main source here; Oates, Whitney, ed. provides a convenient compendium of the main sources.

[122] T.S. Eliot provides a typical crotchety Christian rejoinder: "The ethic of Seneca is a matter of postures. The posture which gives the greatest opportunity for effect, hence for the Senecan morality, is the posture of dying: death gives his characters the opportunity for their most sententious aphorisms—a hint which Elizabethan dramatists were only too ready to follow." in "Seneca in Elizabethan Translation" (1927) in *Essays on Elizabethan Drama* (Kindle).

the annihilation of the ego is inevitable, then we should reconcile our minds to that reality, and live accordingly; this implies forbearance, simplicity, and acceptance. Violent passions must therefore represent a failure to align one's mind with nature. The similarity of these kinds of ethical teaching with Hinduism, Buddhism, and Taoism, as well as Christian ethics, should be clear: I do not think it is an accident that this kind of introspective teaching arose after Alexander's death—that is, after Alexander had further opened the East to Ancient Greece.[123]

Montaigne is usually described as a "Skeptic" in a general sense; other salient characteristics of his work include his constant return to the meaning of human mortality, his introspection, and his sort of observational philosophy whereby ordinary occurrences lead him into speculations about the workings of human nature and nature itself. In fact, the ancient philosopher who I think mirrors Montaigne best is Seneca, who wrote several books of letters on moral and philosophical themes.[124] (This sort of philosophizing is also common to later German philosophers like Schopenhauer and Nietzsche.)

Turning to Elizabethan times, there is no question that, along with Montaigne, many of the Hellenistic philosophers were widely read. Nashe, for example, quotes Sextus Empiricus, and Lodge continually references Seneca. Indeed, in 1614 Lodge would publish a folio of his translations of all of Seneca's writings. Some excerpts from Lodge's translation of Seneca's *Epistle LXXXII* are typical:[125]

> Retyrement without studie is a death, and the Sepulcher of a living man. Finally, what profiteth it us to be retired, as if the causes and cares and troubles followed us not beyond the Seas? What hidden place is there, whereinto the fear of death entereth not? [....] There is in every man a certaine love of himselfe, and an engrafted will of abiding and preserving himselfe, and a shunning of dissolution, because it seemeth to take away many good things, and to leade us out of the abundance of this, whereunto wee have accustomed ourselves. That thing also alienateth us from death, because we have already

---

123 Lang, *Hellenistic Philosophy*; on Epicureanism and hedonism, 65; on Stoicism, logos, 107, 108.

124 On Montaigne and Shakespeare, see Robertson. Ben R. Schneider, Jr. at his website stoics.com, which is devoted to attempting to reconstruct "Shakespeare's Moral" in terms of the "Stoic Legacy," also concurs that Montaigne resembles Seneca and has transcriptions on his site of many relevant texts from Stoicism as well as a number of books that would fall under the classification of "self help" or "moral guidance" (e.g., Cicero, Castiglione) but not Balthazar de Grazian or *Diall of Princes*. The technical name for this kind of literature is "eudaimonic," that is, aiming for a good life. Schopenhauer's *Wisdom of Life* fits the same mold, and psychological insights, if not moral instruction, are rampant in Nietzsche's aphoristic works.

125 Lodge translation of Seneca, 1614, 340–344. Unfortunately, the Senecan transcripts at stoics.com use the Loeb Library translation, which is too modern for our purposes and completely different from Elizabethan translations.

knowne these things: those things whereunto we are about to goe; wee know not of what sort they may bee, and we feare things that be unknown. Furthermore, there is a natural feare of darknesse, into which it is supposed that death will conduct us. [....] Vertue doth nothing upon necessitie. [....] Great Monsters are stricken with great weapons. In vaine with Arrowes and Slings did they shoot at that great cruell Serpent in *Africa*, and more terrible to the Legions of *Rome* then Warre itself. Not *Python* indeed was to be wounded, sith huge greatnesse according to the solide vastnesse of his body, cast backe again Weapons, and whatsoever the hands of men had darted against him; at length was hee broken with Millstones. And against death dost thou dart so petty things? With a Bodkin encountrest thou a Lyon? These things are sharpe which thou speakest of. Nothing is more sharpe than the Beard of an Eare of Corn. Smallnesse it selfe maketh somethings unprofitable and without effect.

The main linkage of Eastern philosophy and Hellenistic philosophy derives from their emphasis on virtue and self-sufficiency. In this respect the *Panchatantra* and the Hellenists are pointing in the same direction. But at the same time these are philosophical teachings that point to self-possession for its own sake: there is no God, there is no redemption. So when Shakespeare says "The fault dear Brutus is not in our stars, but in ourselves" or "All men are ready if their minds be so" or "Men must endure their going hence, even as their coming hither. Ripeness is all" or "There is nothing either good or bad, but thinking makes it so," he is not being original nor is he engaging in the kind of mutant shape-shifting that impresses the apologists for his plagiarism, nor is he even "inventing the human." He is simply repeating the precepts of Hellenistic philosophy.[126]

---

126 This is in reference to Harold Bloom's *Shakespeare: The Invention of the Human*, which claims, *inter alia*, that Shakespeare should be credited with the invention of "personality" and "human inwardness" (4, 5) as well as the "invention of the human" (403) and the "internalization of the self" (409).

10 | FRAUDS AND FORGERIES

William Henry Ireland ~ John Payne Collier ~ Permanent Damage to Primary Sources ~ Thomas Carlyle ~ Of Heroes and Hero Worship ~ Disraeli's Venetia

Shakespeare's popularity continued to grow after the Jubilee in 1769. Stratford-on-Avon became the new mecca for the Shakespeare religion, and visitors were taken on tours and sold trinkets to remember their trip. Such reverence created the demand for yet more information about Shakespeare, which, in the late 18th and early 19th centuries, led to some well-known incidents of forgery and fraud. At the same time, reverence can inspire an oppressive climate of orthodoxy and taboo, censure and even the censor; so reverence also inspires its opposite in the form of irreverence. Let's examine some examples of both.

The Ireland forgeries are probably the best known example of fraudulence in Shakespearean studies. The story goes that the father of William Henry Ireland visited Stratford in order to do some research. No doubt he visited the Church of the Holy Trinity, where Shakespeare, among others, is buried in the chancel along with his monument, the floor before the monument bearing one of the absolutely undisputed poems by the Bard:[127]

> Good friend for Jesus sake forbeare,
> To dig the dust enclosed here.
> Blessed be the man that spares these stones,
> And cursed be he that moves my bones.

However, Samuel Ireland was unable to find anything else: no records, no letters, no literary remains of any kind. At this point, his son

---
127 Chambers, *WS*, II:181, the notorious epitaph on his grave; modernized.

William, who worked in a law office with access to ancient parchments, and who was inspired by the tragic career of the young forger Thomas Chatterton,[128] began forging Shakespearean documents on his own. Soon there was a flood of documents, certified as authentic by some authorities, questioned by others. The most important new discoveries were the manuscripts of two hitherto unknown Shakespeare plays: *Vortigern and Rowena* and *Henry II*.[129]

The forgeries began in late 1794 and continued into 1795. Finally, in early 1796, Edmund Malone published a book exposing the forgeries. When *Vortigern and Rowena* was put on stage later that year, it was a complete failure. Both father and son were ruined as a result of the exposure of the hoax, although there is no evidence that Samuel Ireland understood what his son was doing.

The Ireland forgeries probably helped create the scenario for what became, in the early 20th century, the founding text of the anti-Stratfordians: the story of James Wilmot. According to this story, the Reverend Wilmot went all over Warwickshire looking for artifacts on the life of Shakespeare in the late 18th century. He investigated every library within 50 miles, and found no books or other records. He learned much of local folklore but found none of it in the Shakespeare plays. His conclusion after a hasty milkmaid and bucket calculation: the plays must have been written by Francis Bacon. The reverend wrote nothing down, but he did communicate his views to a friend. This friend—again, according to the story—then presented the theory to a local scientific society, as witnessed by the handwritten lectures from the occasion.[130]

The story makes little sense, but it was highly suggestive. Throughout the 20th century, Wilmot's investigation would be alluded to as the beginning of not only anti-Stratfordianism but also the Baconian theory. But in the 2010 the document on which the story was based was exposed as a forgery. The conclusion was obtained by a number of investigators independently, among them the prominent Shakespeare scholar James Shapiro of Columbia University.[131]

---

128 Thomas Chatterton (1752–1770) was a brilliant young English boy who beginning at about age 12 began writing under various pseudonyms, sometimes in archaic style. He committed suicide by drinking poison in a London garret at the age of 17. He was remembered because the quality of some of his anachronistic poetry was admired posthumously; on further review, fraudulence was revealed.

129 Schoenbaum, *Shakespeare's Lives*, new edition, 132–136, 143–150.

130 On Wilmot, see, e.g., Michell, *Who Wrote Shakespeare?*, 62, 103–104.

131 Shapiro, *Contested*, 3, 11–13, also 283–284 for bibliographic detail.

The Ireland forgeries were relatively innocuous, and so was the faked story of Reverend Wilmot. The Collier forgeries were a much more serious affair. John Payne Collier (1789–1883) was a talented student who followed in his father's footsteps as a journalist. In the 1820s he began to publish books on the Shakespearean era, focusing on long-neglected plays, poems, and primary source texts. After gaining access to some of the repositories of primary source information, he began editing and publishing those materials as well. These included the diary of Philip Henslowe and the description by the occultist Simon Forman (1552–1611) of performances of three Shakespeare plays: *Macbeth*, *Winter's Tale*, and *Cymbeline*.

The problem was that Collier, while doing invaluable work in bringing primary sources to light, was also disfiguring the raw materials with forgeries, usually in the form of additions to existing manuscripts. Chambers itemized dozens of possible forgeries in Colliers' publications, ranging from 1831 to 1865.[132] Most of them appear to be of little account, but bearing in mind the kind of milkmaid and bucket reasoning so prominent in this field, even the smallest change to a primary source can have far-reaching consequences. Moreover, by altering documents Collier, however inadvertently, cast doubt on all of his primary source discoveries. For example, the Forman manuscript describing the performance of three Shakespeare plays is very valuable because it is the main source for dating them, but it has been questioned because Collier discovered it. The notation on another play, *Locrine*, which ascribes authorship to Charles Tilney, has also been questioned, and for the same reason.

However, the problem is bigger than Collier: the lackadaisical treatment of Shakespearean primary sources before modern times has led to priceless archival losses. For example, Shakespeare's son-in-law, Dr. John Hall, is supposed to have left two volumes of notes pertaining to his medical practice—the source from which we know that he treated Michael Drayton in his dotage. But while the volumes were supposedly transcribed, one of them—the one that would have covered the lifetime, illness, and death of his father-in-law—is missing.

The most spectacular failure in terms of document destruction concerns John Warburton (1682–1759), an Englishman who collected old texts. The standard account is that Warburton left a heap of over 50

---

132 Chambers, *WS*, II:377–393, itemizes all the apparent forgeries pertaining to Shakespeare only: Freeman and Freeman's biography of Collier covers the many attributed forgeries involving other authors in detail.

old play manuscripts in his kitchen, and when he inquired as to their whereabouts a year later he was informed by his cook that she had used them in the baking of pies. Thus "Warburton's pies" has become a watchword for document destruction.[133]

So far we have discussed forgery and fraud in the name of reverence. But there was also irreverence—and skepticism—at play. One of the first expressions of skepticism concerning Shakespeare's overarching genius comes from a slim pamphlet entitled *An Essay Against Too Much Reading* (1728) by a probably pseudonymous "Captain Goulding." The pamphlet argued that Shakespeare made up for his lack of education by hiring a "chuckle-pated historian" to give him the details for his plays, further employing this character to go back and correct grammatical errors. The Captain claimed to have received this information from an "intimate acquaintance" of the playwright. In 1769, another book, *The Life and Adventures of Common Sense: An Historical Allegory*, was published. It described a young man who came upon a special book containing "an Infinite Variety of Modes and Forms, to express all the different Sentiments of the human Mind," along with the rules for using them in drama. Needless to say, the young man's name was Shakespeare.[134]

Yet another example of this kind of tongue-in-cheek authorship controversy emerged in *The Story of the Learned Pig*, which was published in 1786, at a time when England was undergoing one of those fits concerning sentient mammals that crops up from time to time. The story, by an "Officer of the Royal Navy," was another framed narrative worthy of the *Panchatantra*. It described the transmigration of a soul that was at this point a performing pig, but who in a previous incarnation (under the name "Pimping Billy") was a horse holder and procurer who met William Shakespeare and wrote his plays for him, with Shakespeare taking all the credit and the profits.[135]

Stories like these survive as amusing ephemera, but they also indicate that doubts about Shakespeare were fairly widespread during the time of his ascendancy. On the other hand, the use of humor and fable suggests that public expressions of such skepticism were likely to be met with social disapproval. Regardless, within a few decades the expression of

---

133 Apparently, the scripts were used as pie pans, i.e., on the bottom of the pies to prevent them from burning. Matus, Irvin Leigh, *Shakespeare in Fact*, 49; also Freeman and Freeman, *John Payne Collier*, II:180, which registers contemporary doubts about the accuracy of Warburton's lament.

134 Michell, *Who Wrote Shakespeare?*, 61; also Friedman, William & Elizebeth, *The Shakespearean Ciphers Examined*, 1–2; also see *The Life and Adventures of Common Sense: An Historical Allegory* (1761).

135 Michell, *Who Wrote Shakespeare?*, 61; Friedman, *Ciphers*, 2–3; also see *The Story of the Learned Pig* (1786).

such doubts would become much more casual and unguarded. In 1837, Benjamin Disraeli published *Venetia*. That novel, in five books, mixed chapters of period-typical romance with lengthy discussions between two characters about art, philosophy, and literature. One such discussion concerns English literature as compared to the Greek:[136]

> "The Greeks excelled in every species of poetry. [....] As for the epic, I confess myself a heretic as to Homer: I look upon the Iliad as a remnant of national songs; the wise ones agree that the Odyssey is the work of a later age. My instinct agrees with the result of their researches. I credit their conclusion. [....] And now for the drama. You will adduce Shakspeare?"
>
> [....] "Shakspeare I esteem of ineffable merit."
>
> "And who is Shakspeare?" said Cadurcis. "We know of him as much as we do of Homer. Did he write half the plays attributed to him? Did he ever write a single whole play? I doubt it. He appears to me to have been an inspired adapter for the theatres, which was then not as good as barns. I take him to have been a botcher of old plays. His popularity is of modern date, and it may not last; it would have surprised him marvelously. Heaven knows, at present, all that bears his name is alike admired, and a regular Shakspearian falls into ecstacies with trash which deserves a niche in the Dunciad. For my part, I abhor your irregular geniuses, and I love to listen to the little nightingale of Twickenham."[137]

But the point of view of Disraeli, among others, was largely drowned out by the Bard-adulating chorus. The elevation of Shakespeare, not only the level of National Poet, but to a kind of demigod, was momentous. Thomas Carlyle's *On Heroes, Hero-Worship, and the Heroic in History* (1841) thus provides some relevant quotes to end this part of our narrative. Carlyle hits all the appropriate notes: that Shakespeare was the greatest poet of all time, that he required no learning but was the simple expression of Nature, and that he was compelled to write his immortal dramas to keep from starving:[138]

> Of this Shakspeare of ours, perhaps the opinion one sometimes hears a little idolatrously expressed is, in fact, the right one; I think

---

136 Disraeli, *Venetia*, 306.

137 The "little nightingale of Twickenham" is a reference to Alexander Pope.

138 Carlyle, *On Heroes and Hero Worship*, Chapter 2, Gutenberg.org.

> the best judgment not of this country only, but of Europe at large, is slowly pointing to the conclusion, that Shakspeare is the chief of all Poets hitherto; the greatest intellect who, in our recorded world, has left record of himself in the way of Literature. On the whole, I know not such a power of vision, such a faculty of thought, if we take all the characters of it, in any other man. [....]
>
> If I say, therefore, that Shakspeare is the greatest of Intellects, I have said all concerning him. But there is more in Shakspeare's intellect than we have yet seen. It is what I call an unconscious intellect; there is more virtue in it than he himself is aware of. Novalis beautifully remarks of him, that those Dramas of his are Products of Nature too, deep as Nature herself. I find a great truth in this saying. Shakspeare's Art is not Artifice; the noblest worth of it is not there by plan or precontrivance. It grows up from the deeps of Nature, through this noble sincere soul, who is a voice of Nature. [....]
>
> Well: this is our poor Warwickshire Peasant, who rose to be Manager of a Playhouse, so that he could live without begging [....]

The veneration of Shakespeare that one finds in Carlyle, which had been building for a hundred years (following a hundred prior years of relative incuriosity) creates a number of historical problems for the understanding of the plays and poems. In the first place, because of the august status of the works themselves, the revelation of biographical detail (e.g., the Will) are bound to introduce discordancy in need of explanation—or apology—but never by changing the fundamental assumptions of authorship or influence.

Deifying Shakespeare also has the effect of negating the historical context in which the man lived and wrote. Many of the popularly dispensed portrayals of Shakespeare would make one think that his many peers were talentless hacks, rather than true or near equals. In turn, taking Shakespeare and his plays and poems out of their historical context makes it impossible to understand them other than by reference to some possible but ultimately trivial biographical facts.

We will speak later of the Death of the Author. But the worship of Shakespeare flirts with the Death of Historical Understanding as far as our subject is concerned.

11 | HENSLOWE AND HIS CREW

The Diary of Philip Henslowe ~ Edward Alleyn ~ Anthony Munday ~ Henry Chettle ~ Thomas Dekker ~ Thomas Heywood ~ John Webster ~ Sir Thomas More Manuscript

In the 1840s, two new documents were published, both providing primary source information about how Elizabethan plays were written, financed, and produced. The first, the manuscript to the play *Sir Thomas More*, was published soon after its discovery by Alexander Dyce in 1841. The second, the diary of Philip Henslowe, had been known among a small circle of Shakespeareans since the 1780s, but was not published until 1846. We will discuss the documents in reverse order, with due attention to Henslowe and some of the writers he employed.

Philip Henslowe was an Elizabethan businessman with a variety of interests: timber, real estate (including brothels), and blood sports. However he is mainly remembered for his role as manager of the Rose Theater, where several theater companies performed over the ten or so years covered by his diary. The chief theatrical tenant of the Rose was The Admiral's Men, probably the most successful rival to Shakespeare's own company, the Lord Chamberlain's Men (so much so that the Admiral's Men are sometimes referred to as "Shakespeare's Opposites").

It should be noted that Henslowe's "diary" is not an actual diary but rather a book of accounts, reflecting income and expenses. Its survival is directly related to the career of Edward Alleyn, perhaps the greatest of Elizabethan actors. Alleyn married Henslowe's stepdaughter in October 1592, and Henslowe and Alleyn remained close thereafter. It appears that Alleyn took up some of Henslowe's interests (Henslowe himself died in 1616) but focused more on bear-baiting than drama.

Even so, Alleyn made a small fortune as an actor and he used some of his wealth to found Dulwich College, where the diary—and many other primary source documents, e.g., letters from Henslowe to his wife—were found toward the end of the 18th century. Malone made use of the diary in his Shakespearean studies.

There are two types of entries in the diary that are particularly relevant. One is a list of performances, with the amount of the gate listed. Here is an example from June 1594:[139]

The 3 of June 1594	Rcd at heaster & asheweros	viij s
The 4 of June 1594	Rcd at the Jewe of malta	x s
The 5 of June 1594	Rcd at andronicous	xij s
The 6 of June 1594	Rcd at cutlacke	xj s
The 8 of June 1594 ne	Rcd at bellendon	xvij s
The 9 of June 1594	Rcd at Hamlet	viij s
The 10 of June 1594	Rcd at heaster	v s
The 11 of June 1594	Rcd at the tamynge of A shrowe	ix s
The 12 of June 1594	Rcd at andronicous	vij s
The 13 of June 1594	Rcd at the Jewe	iiij s

Note that there are no less than seven different plays performed in a ten-day period, indicating that plays were normally performed in a repertory format. Note the performance of three plays that sound a lot like Shakespeare, namely, *Hamlet*, *Taming of the Shrew*, and *Titus Andronicus*. Note that *Hamlet* only brought in eight shillings: since normal admittance to a performance was a penny, and since there are twelve pennies in a shilling, it follows that only about 96 people attended that performance of *Hamlet*. Some commentators have taken this to mean that it could not possibly be the *Hamlet* we know.

The other kind of entry in the diary, starting a few years later, involves lists of disbursements. Here are a few such listings, with very slight changes to Henslowe's idiosyncratic spelling and interpolations.[140]

> Aprell 7 day 1599 – Lent unto Thomas downton to lend unto mr dickers and harey cheattle in earnest of ther boocke called Troyeles & crease day the some of iij L
>
> Lent unto harey cheattle & mr dickers in pte of payment of ther boocke Troyelles & cresseda the 16 of Aprell 1599 xx s

---

139 *Henslowe's Diary*, W.W. Greg, ed., I:17.

140 *Henslowe's Diary*, W.W. Greg, ed., I:104, 109, 138, 166.

> Lent unto mr dickers and mr chettell the 26 of May 1599 in earnest of a Boocke called [troylles & creseda] the tragede of Agamemnon the some of xxx s
>
> Lent unto William Borne & Jewbey the 21 of June 1599 to lend unto mr chapman upon his Boock called the world Ronnes a whelles the some of xxxx s
>
> Lent unto Samwell Rowlye 1601 to pay unto harye [S] chettell for writtinge the Boocke of carnalle wolseye life the 5 of June some of xx s
>
> Lent unto the company the 22 of maij 1602 to geve unto antoney Monday & mihell drayton webester & the Rest (mydelton) in earneste of a Boocke called sesers falle the some of v L

Some of the names will be familiar by now. The "mr chapman" is the same George Chapman previously discussed; "harey cheattle" is the same Henry Chettle who published *Groatsworth*; and we have likewise already been introduced to the poet "mihell drayton." Most of the other names are new, so we should pause in order to identify some of them.

Anthony Munday (1553–1633) was born in London. He was the son of a draper (cloth merchant), and he was apprenticed to a printer in 1576. He then traveled with a companion to Italy. Munday's adventures among expatriate English Catholics in Rome would form the backdrop for his *English Romayne Life* (1582), which was probably his most popular work.

Munday wrote extensively in all genres over several decades. Based on a dedication to the Earl of Oxford in 1579, he is usually considered—along with Lyly, Greene, and Nashe—as one of Oxford's writers. He was also involved in the writing of a number of plays, dating back to the 1580s. These included several plays referenced by Henslowe but which are now considered lost. The most famous plays attributed to Munday are *John a Kent and John a Cumber* and *The Downfall of Robert Earl of Huntingdon*. Munday also appears to have played both sides of the street: while active in the theater, and even as an actor, he also penned one of the early attacks on the theater, *A Second and Third Blast of Retrait from Plaies and Theaters* in 1580, although the tract was published anonymously.

Munday's reputation is blackened by his work for Richard Topcliffe, who was Elizabeth's Grand Inquisitor and persecutor of Catholics. His participation in the execution of Edmund Campion (1540–1581), which involved the ritual castration and disembowelment of the still-living victim ("drawing and quartering") is, in a word, revolting.[141] The best that can be said is that Munday was a man who was to some extent driven by his hatred of religious schismatics; his association with Catholics, including recusants, defies credulity.

Another member of Henslowe's crew was Henry Chettle (1560–1607), who we have already encountered in our discussion of Greene's *Groatsworth* (Chettle also wrote the response, *Kind-Heart's Dream*). The diary finds Chettle involved in the writing of thirty-six plays. A Londoner, Chettle apparently moved from his status as a stationer's apprentice in the 1570s to a writing career. Based on Henslowe's disbursements, Chettle was chronically short of funds; he was imprisoned at least once for non-payment of debts.

Among Chettle's writings was *England's Mourning Garment* (1603), which centers on memorials for the passing of Queen Elizabeth. In one memorial, Chettle appears to entreat Shakespeare to provide verses on her death; but neither here nor anywhere else did Shakespeare ever contribute any commendatory verse or occasional piece that was signed or printed under his name.

Thomas Dekker (1571–1641) was probably the most productive writer on Henslowe's payroll. Another Londoner (but perhaps of Dutch background), his early life and education remain mysterious. The first reference to Dekker comes in Henslowe's diary in January 1597. Over the course of the next five years he appears to have collaborated on as many as forty plays, the vast majority now lost.

Among the plays Dekker is known to have worked on are *The Spanish Moor's Tragedy* and *Troilus and Cressida*, but these are supposed to be lost and are assumed not to bear any relationship to Shakespeare's two seemingly analogous plays, *Othello* and *Troilus and Cressida*. Two plays that are usually attributed to Dekker in whole or in part are *Shoemaker's Holiday* (1600), a populist comedy drama in the Frank Capra mode, and *Patient Grissel* (1603), a lullaby from which would later be immortalized on the Beatles' album *Abbey Road*. Both of these plays were originally published anonymously. Another of Dekker's plays, *Satiro-mastix*, will be discussed later.

Like most of the writers of this time, Dekker suffered from debts. In 1599, suit was brought against both Dekker and Chettle for unpaid

---

141 Nicholl, *The Reckoning*, goes into this aspect of Munday in terms of his spying activity, and matches this assessment, 175.

debts to the Lord Chamberlain's company—that is, Shakespeare's company. Henslowe ultimately paid the several pounds owed, but this episode suggests that both men were under some kind of contract to Shakespeare's company. Dekker's debts eventually caught up with him; during the early reign of King James he spent several years in the King's Bench debtors' prison.

Despite his dramatic endeavors, Dekker is best known for several books and pamphlets, of which the *Gull's Hornbook* is the most celebrated. Here is an excerpt that gives a good sense of his style and his sense of humor:[142]

> For doe but consider what an excellent thing sleepe is: It is so inestimable a Jewel, that, if a Tyrant would give his crowne for an hours slumber, it cannot be bought: of so beautifull a shape is it, that though a man lye with an Empresse, his heart cannot be at quiet, till he leaves her embracements to be at rest with the other: yea, so greatly indebted are we to this kinseman of death, that we owe the better tributary, half of our life to him: and thers good cause why we should do so: for sleep is that golden chaine that ties health and our bodies together. Who complains of want? Of woundes? Of cares? Of great mens oppressions, of captivity? Whilest he sleepeth? Beggers in their beds take as much pleasure as Kings: can we therefore surfet on this delicate Ambrosia? Can we drink too much of that whereof to tast too little tumbles us into a church-yard, and to use it but indifferently, throwes us into Bedlam? [....] Can lying abedde till noone then [....] be hurtful?
>
> Besides, by the opinion of all Phylosophers and Physitians, it is not good to trust the aire with our bodies till the Sun with his flame-colored wings, hath sand away the mistie smoake of the morning, and refind that thick tobacco-breath which the rheumaticke night throwes abroad of purpose to put out the eye of the Element: which worke questionlesse cannot be perfectly finished, til the sunnes Car-horses stand prancing on the verytop of highest noon: so that then (and not till then) is the most healthfull houre to be stirring.

Thomas Heywood (1565–1641) was first mentioned in Henslowe's Diary in 1596, and appears to have been the most prolific writer of the lot. In the chatty preface to one of his plays in 1633, he claimed to have had "an entire hand or at least a maine finger" in no less than 200 plays.

---

142 Dekker, *Gull's Hornbook* in *The Non-Dramatic Works of Thomas Dekker* (5 vols, Alexander Grosart, ed.), II:216–217.

A friend claimed that Heywood acted every day and then went home and wrote a page of text every day for several years.

Heywood has some relevance to other playwrights as well as to Shakespeare. For example, in a book in 1612 he supplies the only reference to Thomas Kyd as the author of the *Spanish Tragedy*; otherwise that play would be unattributed. In 1612, a printer sought to reissue *The Passionate Pilgrim*, which, as we recall, included a few poems by Shakespeare along with a couple by Heywood (though most were by others). Heywood's subsequently published protest[143] is good evidence for Shakespeare's public reputation as playwright and poet.

The youngest member of Henslowe's crew was Thomas Middleton (1580–1627). It appears that he attended both Oxford and the law school at Gray's Inn, but he acquired no degree. He then turns up in Henslowe's Diary, contributing to several plays, and thereafter partnered with Thomas Dekker to write several others, *The Roaring Girl, or Moll Cutpurse* (1611), being probably the most famous of these collaborations. Middleton's greatest success was *A Game at Chess* (1624), which was understood to be a political allegory over a proposed marriage between the ruling houses of England and Spain.

Middleton's reputation today is much enhanced due to the painstaking work of the American scholar Gary Taylor, whose decades-long effort culminated in the 2007 publication of what was in effect a Middleton Folio, containing over 34 plays and numerous miscellaneous writings. Many of the plays were collaborations. More noteworthy is that Taylor assigned Middleton a role in three Shakespeare plays, *Macbeth, Measure for Measure,* and *Timon of Athens,* as well as three plays of the Shakespeare apocrypha, *The Yorkshire Tragedy, The Puritan,* and the *Second Maiden's Tragedy*.[144]

Other playwrights in Henslowe's crew included Samuel Rowley (no dates) who was perhaps mentioned earlier in Meres' *Palladis Tamia*, where there is a reference to "Master Rowley who was once a rare scholar at Pembroke Hall at Cambridge," John Day (1674–1638), another

---

143 On the very last page of his *Apology for Actors* (1612, the same book that mentioned Kyd), Heywood referenced the unauthorized publication of two of his poems, which are known to have been published under the name "Shakespeare" in a re-printing of *The Passionate Pilgrim* in that year. On that page Heywood speaks of the poems printed "under the name of another, which may put the world in the opinion that I might steale them from him, and hee, to doe himselfe right, hath since published them in his owne name: but as I must acknowledge my lines not worthy his patronage under whom he hath publisht them, so the author, I know, much offended with M. Jaggard [....] presumed to make so bold with his name." This is considered a reference to Shakespeare, and his assumed anger. To be fair, however, I think Heywood is affecting a subjunctive mood throughout—not that Shakespeare was angry, but would have been, since, after all, there is no record of Shakespearean outrage over the original publication of *Pilgrim*. (See Heywood, *Apology*, last page). Chambers, ES, IV:250–254 dates the *Apology* to 1608 (?) on his assumption that it was mostly written earlier.

144 Taylor, Gary; Lavagnino, John, eds., *Thomas Middleton: The Collected Works* (Oxford, Oxford UP: 2007).

student at Cambridge, and John Webster (1580–1625). Webster, a tailor's son, embarked on a literary career with Henslowe in 1602. He was associated with both Munday and Dekker early in his career, but he didn't really come into his own until he published *The White Devil* (1612) and *The Duchess of Malfi* (1616). These were enormously popular plays, but they belong to a later age.

The enumeration of these various members of Henslowe's crew helps us set the stage for the manuscript of *Sir Thomas More*.

The manuscript for *Sir Thomas More* is 20 folio leaves in length. Almost all of the leaves have writing on both sides (with a few paste-ins). Seven hands have been identified, and are listed below, with the typical identifications:

- Edmund Tilney—Master of the Revels – This hand does not involve the play itself outside of numerous cross-outs (particularly at the beginning of the manuscript), along with a written advisory as to how the play should be constituted.
- Hand S – So-called because it was the main scribal hand in the manuscript, it is now generally accepted to be Anthony Munday's. Put another way, Munday either wrote the basic text or copied it.
- Hand A – Identified as belonging to Henry Chettle, and involving one addition. Some see Chettle's voice in Munday's hand as well.
- Hand B – Thomas Heywood; two additions.
- Hand C – Unknown scribe, the text of which, as with Hand D, has been assigned by some to Shakespeare. One addition.
- Hand D – Argued by some since 1871 as being in Shakespeare's hand. One scene, about 160 lines.
- Hand E – Thomas Dekker.

The first thing we should note about the manuscript is that all of the identified collaborators (except Shakespeare) wrote collaboratively for Henslowe. We know this from Henslowe's Diary (Shakespeare appears nowhere in the diary). Thus the document shows us exactly how such playwriting collaborations were done. Based on this evidence, there should be little doubt that this is a Henslowe play; that it is not listed or identified in the diary should not be an issue since the diary has gaps and doesn't cover the full extent of Henslowe's activities. Nevertheless, this has not stopped advocates from arguing that both Hand C and Hand D reflect the hand, or voice, of Shakespeare.

The identification of Shakespeare in *Sir Thomas More* began in 1871 and reached its apogee in 1923. Some skeptics believe the argument is meant as a riposte to the advocates of alternative candidates. The argument for Shakespeare is made on two grounds: first, paleography—that is, the claim is advanced that Hand D is discernible in the half dozen samples of Shakespeare we possess (namely, the six ragged signatures), and second, stylistically, in that the voices of Hand D and Hand C "sound like" Shakespeare. In the end, however, the argument comes down to the stylistic "sounds like" business, since Hand C is not claimed to be Shakespeare's actual handwriting. Thus the paleographic argument is essentially superfluous.

In my opinion, the attempts to link Shakespeare to this manuscript fail. At the same time, I respect the scholarship that has gone into the argument, as well as the realization among the more serious advocates (e.g., Jowett[145]) that such an attribution opens wide the door to the discussion of general collaboration in the creation of Elizabethan drama.

The *Sir Thomas More* manuscript and the diary of Philip Henslowe are, in my estimation, the two most important documents to have emerged about the history of the Elizabethan stage. These documents had, and still have, the potential to revolutionize how we view the products of that stage as well as the Shakespearean canon itself. In a general sense, they did no such thing; but in a way, they did, because they led to the authorship controversy as we know it today.

---

145 John Jowett, ed., *Sir Thomas More* (Third Series of Arden Shakespeare), 459–460.

12 | The First Dissidents

Joseph C. Hart ~ Chambers' Edinburgh Review ~ William Henry Smith ~ Francis Bacon ~ Delia Bacon

The first open skeptics about Shakespearean authorship emerged in the late 1840s and early 1850s, and their arrival may be considered a natural consequence of the publication of Henslowe's Diary and Collier's various books. There are four early skeptics that are particularly worthy of note: Joseph C. Hart, William Henry Smith, an anonymous contributor to *Chambers Edinburgh Review*, and Delia Bacon (no relation to Francis Bacon).

Joseph C. Hart was an American lawyer and also a yachtsman: that is the background to his *Romance of Yachting* (1848), which described a trip across the Atlantic to the Mediterranean. During the voyage, Hart frequently engaged in desultory monologues about whatever was on his mind, and about halfway through the book he suddenly takes up the case of Shakespeare authorship.

Hart begins with the observation, "How prone the English people are to kill their own great men!" This is reminiscent of a human fault Thomas Lodge described in *Wit's Misery* in 1596:[146]

> The first by Sathan (his grandsire) was called HATE-VERTUE or (in words of more circumstance) Sorrow for another mans good success) who after had had learnt to lie of LUCIAN, to flatter with ARISTIPPUS, & conjure of ZOROASTES, wandred a while in France, Germanie, & Italy, to learn languages & fashions, & and now of late daies is stoln into England to deprave all good deserving. And though this fiend be begotten of his fathers own blood, yet is he different from his nature, & were he not sure that JEALOUSIE

---
146 Lodge, *Complete Works*, E. W. Gosse, ed., IV:56.

could not make him a cuckold, he had long since published him for a bastard; you shall know him by this, he is a foule lubber, his tongue tipt with lying, his heart steeld against charity, he walks for the most part in black under cover of gravity, & looks as pale as the Vizard of the ghost which cried so miserably at the Theator like an oister wife, Hamlet, revenge: he is full of infamy & slander, [....]

Hart makes no reference to this quote in his book, but the underlying idea is a favorite of the Stratfordians: those that question Shakespearean authorship are motivated by hatred, resentment, or "Hate Virtue." Hart at least agrees that such a phenomenon exists: "They first raise them up to the loftiest pinnacle of fame, and then, [....] dash their victims 'all to pieces' on the rocks below."[147]

Hart then proceeds to take apart the Shakespeare narrative, not by way of original investigation but simply on the basis of what scholarly research had revealed—that Shakespeare came from a humble background, that he had no formal education, that he was accused of plagiarism by Greene, that he was involved in various financial affairs, that he left behind no manuscripts or other writings. In this part of his exposition Hart clearly relies on one of the spurious passages created by Collier, which tended to make Shakespeare more financially active than other records indicate.

Hart moves on to deconstruct the canon of plays, based on two hundred years of previous Shakespeare scholarship. Thus he points out that *Comedy of Errors* may be the same as the play *History of Error* from 1576, or that *Love's Labour's Lost* may refer back to a play called *Holofernes* from 1556. Hart mentions that *The Merchant of Venice* contains a plot that was referenced in Gosson's *School of Abuse* in 1579, and also points to the background texts for many of the plays.

Sometimes Hart overreaches: for example, he claims that the "to be or not to be" soliloquy is "taken almost verbatim" from Plato, which is an exaggeration, though it is true that the sentiments expressed were common in the ancient world.[148] More important is Hart's clear reliance on Henslowe's Diary, which is invoked no less than four times to explain the origin of individual plays. However, the part of Hart's analysis that later commentators have chosen to focus on was his rather tightly buttoned Victorian morality, which looks quaint in retrospect.

---

147 Hart, *Romance of Yachting*, 209.

148 Hart, *Romance*, 232. The sentiments are similar to those expressed by Socrates in the last four dialogs of Plato.

Thus, Hart's remarks that the plays are "full of gross impurities" and are "vulgar and impure" generate bemused derision today, while the fact that his remarks are a fairly consistent summary of scholarship to that point is ignored.[149]

Hart also hurts himself a little with his rather whimsical dismissal of the entire Shakespeare story. He concludes that Shakespeare's reputation was simply invented in the early 18th century, and that the only play that Shakespeare could have possibly written was *Merry Wives of Windsor*, because it was the worst, and the most "vulgar ... impure ... revolting piece of trash."[150]

The next two authors are less important for substance than for traditional issues of priority, as well as recapitulating some concepts that we have already encountered.

In August 1852 an issue of *Chambers' Edinburgh Journal* featured an article entitled "Who Wrote Shakspeare?" It began:[151]

> Thus asks Mrs Kitty in High Life Below Stairs, to which his Grace my Lord Duke gravely replies: 'Ben Jonson.' 'O no,' quoth my Lady Bab: 'Shakspeare was written by one Mr Finis, for I saw his name at the end of the book!' and this passes off as an excellent joke, and never fails to elicit the applause of the audience; but still the question remains unanswered: Who wrote Shakspeare? a question, we humbly think, which might be made the theme for as much critical sagacity, pertinacity, and pugnacity, as the almost equally interesting question, who wrote Homer? In the former case, the question is certainly in one respect more simple, for the recognised plays and poems that go by Shakspeare's name are—at least by far the larger portion—unquestionably from one and the same pen; while Homer, poor, dear, awful, august, much-abused shade! has been torn by a pack of German wolves into fragments, which it puzzles the lore and research of Grote and Muir to patch together again.

Noting the reference to Homer, we can infer that the anonymous author was familiar with Disraeli's arguments in *Venetia*, which appears to reflect a common way of thinking of the time.

The author then offers an interesting alternative, while rehearsing standard anti-Stratfordian arguments:

---

149 Schoenbaum's reaction to Hart is typical, *Shakespeare's Lives*, first edition, 548–549.

150 Hart, *Romance*, 228, 233–234.

151 *Edinburgh Journal*, August 7, 1852. Quoting is extensive because of the rarity of the summary quality of the remarks and the rarity of the source, e-text gutenberg.org.

> May not William Shakspeare—the cautious, calculating man, careless of fame, and intent only on money-making—have found, in some furthest garret overlooking the 'silent highway' of the Thames, some pale, wasted student, with a brow as ample and lofty as his own, who had written the *Wars of the Roses*, and who, with eyes of genius gleaming through despair, was about, like Chatterton, to spend his last copper coin upon some cheap and speedy means of death? What was to hinder William Shakspeare from reading, appreciating, and purchasing these dramas, and thereafter keeping his poet, as Mrs Packwood did?
>
> [....]
>
> This assumption, we are sorry to say, smooths away many of the difficulties that have hitherto baffled the critics. How could Shakspeare, say they, have been able to write at all, while obviously and laboriously employed in the active business of his profession? Where did he acquire that all-comprehensive knowledge of nature, men, and books? How could he paint with such exact fidelity the peculiar scenery pertaining exclusively to the subject in question, when he can be proved never to have left London?
>
> [....]
>
> Again, not one single manuscript of Shakspeare's plays or poems has ever been discovered; and certainly the search has been as rigorous and continuous as that for the Philosopher's Stone; while even Scott, when owning to the Novels, found it necessary to say that almost all the manuscripts were holograph; nor, if we do not very much mistake, is there among all the records and traditions which have been handed to us, any statement of Shakspeare having been seen writing, or having delivered his manuscript.

This is followed by a clear reference back to Henslowe's Diary:

> Take, besides, the custom of the age, the helter-skelter way in which dramas were got up, sometimes by half-a-dozen authors at once, of whom one occasionally monopolised the fame; and the unscrupulous manner in which booksellers appropriated any popular name of the day, and affixed it to their publications; and who so popular with all playgoers of the period as the gentle, well-living Shakspeare? And his name would better suit his friends and the then public, than any mere recluse, unknown poet, until his name, like other myths, acquired sanctity by age. Indeed, we fear it is not necessary to go back to Shakspeare's time to find the practice of assumed authorship

of purchased plays, without either the reasons or the excuses which apply to Shakspeare. Unfortunately, however, for those who claim Shakspeare for Shakspeare, the secret was not wholly kept. Robert Greene, a well-known contemporary, a writer of reputation, but one who led the skeldering life peculiar to most of his class, addressed, on his death-bed, in 1592, a warning to his co-mates not to trust to the puppets 'that speak from our mouths.' He then goes on in these remarkable words, which we believe every critic thinks were intended for Shakspeare: 'Yes, trust them not; for there is an upstart crow beautified with our feathers, that, with his tiger's heart wrapt in a player's hide, supposes he is as well able to bombast out a blank verse as the best of you; and, being an absolute *Johannes Factotum*, is in his own conceit the only *Shake-scene* in a country.' Again: with this view, the disputed passages—those in which critics have agreed that the genius is found wanting—the meretricious ornaments sometimes crowded in—the occasional bad taste displayed—in short, all the imperfections discernible and disputable in these mighty dramas, are reconcilable with their being the interpolations of Shakspeare himself on his poet's works.

The author of the article, later revealed to be Dr. R. W. Jameson, ultimately backs down, accepting Shakespeare as the author of the plays. Yet we note the mischief in the final paragraph that is consistent with Hart: Shakespeare had a hand in the plays, but only in the bad parts.

William Henry Smith (1825–1891) was involved in his father's newspaper business and in September 1856 published a twenty-page letter entitled "Was Lord Bacon the Author of Shakespeare's Plays?" The argument turns on two substantive points: the inarguable presence of sizable legal terminology in some of the plays (Bacon was a lawyer), combined with the much more arguable assertion that the plays in the First Folio are "the productions of one mind" (revealing Smith as a unitarian).

Recall that within decades of Shakespeare's death, seven other plays were published in later versions of the Folio, and to these can be added another half-dozen or more as being by Shakespeare, at least in part. And we shall see that that number continues to increase. Therefore a basic assumption on both sides in the debate is that the 36 plays in the First Folio represent a deliberate selection of the creative output of one person. On the other hand, one could also consider this an illusion fostered by the physical fact of the Folio and the centuries-old tradition of reading it as a unity.

Smith's greatest legacy, which would later be extended into book form, was that he was the first person to claim in print that Francis Bacon wrote the Shakespeare plays (he further claimed that he had been of that opinion for twenty years). A problem arises, however, in that his letter, published in September 1856, had been preceded by an article written about the authorship of the plays by an American woman in January of the same year. The woman's name was actually Bacon—Delia Bacon (no relation to Francis). To avoid any confusion, I shall refer to her by her full name or simply as "Ms. Bacon."

Delia Bacon (1811–1859) was born on the Ohio frontier, to a minister who returned his family to the Northeast in her childhood. She acquired a good education, and in her twenties had already established herself as an author, lecturer, and playwright. She was known and appreciated by many of the authors of her time, including Poe, Emerson, and Hawthorne.

In early 1845 she began working on her theory of Shakespearean authorship. She published a twenty-page article in *Putnam's Magazine* in January 1856, which was followed in 1857 by her massive (600 page) treatise, *Philosophy of the Plays of Shakespeare Unfolded*. Both the article and the book make for tortured reading. In the article, Ms. Bacon invokes the Homeric model we have discussed, mentions *Groatsworth*, and references Shakespeare's humble origins; but for all such intimations, the article is a triumph of No Antecedent: Delia Bacon continually refers to a "he" as the author of the plays, but never names him.[152]

Her book is no improvement. Early on, she identifies Sir Walter Raleigh and Sir Francis Bacon as patrons of Ben Jonson, suggesting their involvement in the plays. But then she moves on to long chapters on Raleigh, Montaigne, and Bacon, with long undigested extracts and paragraph-long sentences that serve no clear subject or conclusion and frequently end in rhetorical questions. Further on in the book she appears to propose that the plays comprise a unity meant to set forth a new moral and political teaching, which rings bells with Bacon's *Advancement of Learning* among other projects, but aside from long and tedious readings of selected plays, none of Ms. Bacon's speculations ever seem tied to any external facts; the reader is soon and again lost in the exposition.

---

152 Bacon, D., "William Shakespeare and his Plays: An Inquiry Concerning Them," *Putnam's Monthly*, v. VII, N XXXVII, Jan., 1856, 1–19: the lead article. The book followed: Bacon, Delia, *The Philosophy of the Plays of Shakspere Unfolded* (London, Groombridge: 1857).

The fact that Delia Bacon was already, however obliquely, articulating problems of Shakespearean authorship as early as 1845 would seem to give her intellectual priority among all the individuals discussed here. But that attitude, I believe, misunderstands the extent to which anti-Stratfordian ideas had gained currency (witness Disraeli) as well as the fact that the four dissidents discussed here are not identical in their views. Hart, for example, simply connected the dots from previous scholarship; Jameson's analysis did the same, but stressed the Homeric model. Smith referenced neither Henslowe nor Homer but selected Bacon because he was the best well-known fit that came to mind in terms of legal training, literary talent, and general education. Delia Bacon, on the other hand, was simply a unitarian who could not reconcile her faith in the deep meaning of the plays with the modest facts of Shakespeare's biography. Her work exemplified a tendency that one finds on both sides of the authorship debate: seeing something that isn't there.

It is possible to view the first dissidents as encapsulating the entire spectrum of Shakespearean positions, from "extreme analyst" to "monolithic unitarian." The emerging biographical evidence in the second half of the 18th century provided little support for pure Shakespearean authorship, and in fact introduced considerable equivocation. The discovered historical evidence in the early 19th century likewise provided no support for Shakespearean authorship, but instead evidence for collaboration and revision. In turn, these trends fed Joseph C. Hart's analytical tendencies even as Shakespeare was being raised to the level of creator-god by Carlyle and others. Delia Bacon's writings, on the other hand, represented an attempt to maintain monotheistic fidelity by putting the plays and poems on a firmer biographical and historical foundation—even when that foundation relied on conjecture, hypothesis, and assertion, and even when such an approach required ignoring the emerging biographical and historical evidence. It has been the same for all unitarians ever since.

13 | BACON AND CIPHERS

Ignatius Donnelly ~ Standard Anti-Shakespeare Arguments ~ Parallelisms ~ The Cipher ~ Vedic Expansions ~ Elaboration of Ciphers and Baconism

Delia Bacon's book presented an argument for group authorship under a unitarian umbrella, in which Francis Bacon played only a part. Along with other writings that emerged at about the same time, her study nevertheless fueled the idea that Francis Bacon was the true author of the plays and poems attributed to William Shakespeare. The fullest statement of the "Baconian" position would not be realized for some thirty years, when the famously eccentric Ignatius Donnelly would publish *The Great Cryptogram*.

The son of Irish immigrants, Donnelly was born in Philadelphia in 1831. He moved to Minnesota when he was in his twenties and got involved in local business and politics. For his writings on Shakespeare and other subjects Donelly would later be called the "Prince of Cranks."[153] He might as easily have been dubbed the "Emperor of Esoterica," since, before tackling Shakespeare, he wrote *Atlantis: The Antediluvian Empire*, which is still a basic text in Atlantology, and *Ragnarok: The Age of Fire and Gravel*, which, among other things, sought to explain the moraines of his adopted state as the result of a comet impact on Earth, thus anticipating Velikovsky by over fifty years.[154]

A massive tome of some 1,000 pages, *The Great Cryptogram* was published in 1887 in a deluxe leather and buckram edition with a gold leaf medallion of Francis Bacon embossed on the cover.[155] The book

---

153 Michell, *Eccentric Lives and Peculiar Notions*, 192.

154 Michell, *Eccentric*, includes three chapters on the authorship controversy and one exclusively devoted to Donnelly. Both *Atlantis* and *Ragnarok* have remained in print for many decades by Dover publications.

155 Donnelly, *The Great Cryptogram* (1888).

is broken into three parts: the first part covers a general argument against Shakespeare (and for Bacon); the second presents a couple hundred pages of parallelisms, that is, passages that are similar between Shakespeare, Bacon, and others; and finally, there are about five hundred pages detailing a cipher which, according to Donnelly, had left messages in the First Folio.

The first part of the book is actually a fairly good summary of the arguments that have been made against Shakespeare throughout the controversy, so we can summarize those arguments here; the arguments for Bacon will be discussed later. The parallelisms will also be given some attention, since they become a recurrent feature of internal evidence arguments hereafter. The cipher will receive only provisional attention; while Donnelly's esoteric textual analysis spawned many offspring, it is intrinsically implausible. Finally, I will attempt to draw attention to another trick of the mind involved in this controversy—something I call a Vedic Expansion.

The arguments against Shakespeare have to do with the absence of evidence and also a kind of continuation of the arguments of "nature versus art." Recall that in the first century of Shakespeare criticism, a standard point of contention concerned whether Shakespeare's excellence was due to great learning or precisely the absence of it. Arguments have circled around this problem ever since. It can be instructive to consider how these arguments resemble the "nature versus nurture" arguments that persist in our own time. This perspective helps explain why we encounter an endless procession of usually noble candidates for Shakespearian authorship, as well as why those who question Shakespearean authorship are so often accused of snobbery or classism.

The known facts of Shakespeare's life are not promising. He was born the son of John Shakespeare, a glover and small-time trader in Stratford-on-Avon, and Mary Arden. Both families appear to have had deep roots in Warwickshire with no distinguished ancestors. Stratford itself had a population of about 1,500, in about 250 homes. The backwardness of the town is indicated by the fact that the first reference to John Shakespeare in the town records, from 1552, concerns a citation for having an unlicensed dung-heap in front of his house.[156]

John Shakespeare and his entire family were almost certainly illiterate, as can be deduced from extant signed documents where marks

---
[156] Donnelly, *Cryptogram*, 28–29.

were used in lieu of a proper signature. The town had a school and it is generally assumed that young Shakespeare went there, but no records have survived.[157] The question of Shakespeare's early education has naturally been the focus of longstanding discussion and dispute, with Stratfordians insisting the quality of schools from the era was such that Shakespeare would have learned a great deal, and with anti-Strats arguing that he could not have learned much.[158] I think it is fair to say that if Shakespeare grew up in an illiterate home, it is unlikely that he grew up among books or in a household that valued learning.

Another point worth making about Shakespeare's education is that he was never identified as a promising student. Stratfordians like to fall back on the legend that William was compelled to leave school at fourteen in order to help his father. But we know, at least from the case of Christopher Marlowe, that a bright child would often be singled out early, and given every opportunity to advance his education. It is also true, as several previously cited examples illustrate,[159] that a lack of funds would not debar a promising student from attending university. So again we are left to make sense of a situation in which an undistinguished student with no apparent intellectual ambitions was allowed to abandon his education, let alone the prospect of any higher education, at an early age.

The discussion of Shakespeare's undeniably humble origins naturally raises the issue of the considerable erudition on display in some of the plays. There are essentially two explanations, tied to notions of nature, nurture (and, as a sort of trump card, genius).

Arguments for nature are especially divisive. Nature-driven arguments tend to imply not only genetic determinism, but a kind of political quietism with regard to social inequalities. This was as true in the 19th century as it is today. Donnelly quotes Herbert Spencer

---

157 Shapiro, *Contested*, 276.

158 There is a large literature in what we might call the "All Shakespeare Ever Needed to Know He Learned in Kindergarten" genre, the most exhaustive being T. W. Baldwin's *William Shakspere's Small Latine & Lesse Greeke*, 2 vols. Urbana, IL, 1944 (The entire text is available online at http://durer.press.illinois.edu/baldwin/index.html). Donnelly also quotes some speculations as to what a student might learn in an English grammar school, but it is unlikely that a great command of Latin would be a feature, since it is precisely that which was the main course of study for a BA (while Greek was reserved for MA aspirants). Shapiro, *Contested*, 277, 321, relies on Baldwin, and prefers to follow the line of reasoning that Shakespeare learned all he needed to learn during his "lost years" (the period ca. 1585–1592 for which we have no record), but he does not suggest, as do those attempting to reconstruct the "lost years" of Jesus Christ or Sherlock Holmes, that he visited the lamas in Tibet.

159 In addition to Marlowe, both Greene and Nashe were sizars (students with a combination of scholarship or work-study arrangments) at Cambridge, Daniel also came from a humble background and attended Oxford.

approvingly in this regard,[160] but he might as well have quoted Arthur Schopenhauer, who once averred: "...no man will write *Iliads* whose mother was a goose and whose father was a dullard, even if he has studied at six universities."[161]

Of course the strict nature argument is flawed; we need look no further than Marlowe to find an exception. At the same time, most of the alternative candidates—and all of the noble candidates—come from bookish or educated backgrounds, so it is hard to tell where the line should be drawn between presumed aristocratic excellence and simply an educated milieu which valued learning.

But the nurture argument doesn't support Shakespeare, either. His environment was unlearned, and mostly illiterate. Even James Halliwell-Phillipps, a leading Shakespearean of his day (quoted frequently by Donnelly) concedes as much.[162] This line of argument can be expanded in various ways to align with modern psychological studies. For example, Shakespeare meets none of the requirements for intellectual giftedness in sociological terms (birth order, life conditions, exposure to learning, travel, and so on).[163] Yet the erudition, and therefore presumably high intelligence, that is conspicuous in some of the plays could not have emerged spontaneously; it must have been cultivated from childhood. Donnelly notes as much, albeit somewhat crudely, when he writes:[164]

> Genius is a powerful predisposition, so strong it overrules a man's whole life, from boyhood to the grave. The greatness of a mind is in proportion to its receptivity, its capacity to assimilate a great mass of food; it is an intellectual stomach that eliminates not muscle but thought. Its power holds a due relation to its greed—it is an eternal and insatiable hunger. In itself it is but an instrument. It can work only on external material.

The usual way Stratfordians respond to these arguments is by recourse to their own concept of genius, by which they mean not the predisposition that Donnelly describes, but rather that Shakespeare

---

160 Donnelly, *Cryptogram*, 32. Spencer's argument features fashionable 19th century racist concepts, but to be fair, he references not only physical differences but also cultural differences, and the latter point holds.

161 Schopenhauer, *Parerga and Paralipomena*, (EFJ Payne, trans.) Oxford, Oxford UP:1974, I:197.

162 Halliwell-Phillipps, quoted by Donnelly, *Cryptogram*, 31, 34.

163 Steve McClarran, *I Come to Bury Shakespeare*, 57–123, esp. 67-90.

164 Donnelly, *Cryptogram*, 37.

somehow managed to write the plays and poems despite his lack of background or education. Thus we are told that Shakespeare's parents must have taught him to read and write (even though they themselves could not), that his teachers at the Stratford school must have made available to him all the books he would have needed to gather the learning he possessed (even though there is no evidence of large numbers of books in Stratford),[165] and that the rest was filled in by reading books here and there and having intense conversations in which he learned many things. While that kind of explanation has the appeal of a legend, it simply doesn't fit well with what we know about the studious inclinations of most gifted people, which is what Donnelly had in mind. Furthermore, it is essentially an argument that apprehends genius a *causa sui* (self-generating cause); in other words, it is not an explanation at all.

Here we come to a certain paradox in moral and ideological positions. Defenders of the orthodox Shakespeare narrative tend to be conventional and liberal in their approaches to the world around them, and they accuse anti-Stratfordians of harboring snobbish, classist, and even reactionary political and social views.[166] Upon examination, however, their case for Shakespeare is even more status quo oriented than their opponents' contrary stance, since it is the essence of political quietism to argue that the power of genius or imagination can, and will, overcome all obstacles, or that 10,000 hours of practice will make anyone an expert in a field.[167] While such assertions may be expected in response to arguments that savor of genetic determinism, simple-minded bromides about the human spirit bear little relation to reality as it is actually lived; no one believes that a child born to an illiterate family has good odds for even becoming successful in life, let alone becoming a leading intellectual; and no academician would seriously argue that university education is not important for intellectual advancement, or that great learning can simply be absorbed, as it were, by a process of osmosis. Certainly, there may be exceptions, but precisely insofar as

---

165 Donnelly references sources suggesting that there would have been no more than half a dozen books in Stratford and cites other wills, including those of Shakespeare's matrilineal line, which also make no reference to books. *Cryptogram*, 36, 31.

166 E.g., Alan Massie, "Only Foolish Snobs Don't Believe in William Shakespeare" (Telegraph Online, 25 Oct 2011); the notion of reaction is an important part of Shapiro's evaluation of Looney, *Contested*, 188–189 (he also links Oxfordians with conspiracists, 211). Other articles to be sought online: David Womersley, "The Zombie Argument that Refuses to Die," *Standpoint*, July/August 2013; Amanda Marcotte, "Barders and Birthers", *Raw Story*, 9 May 2011 (Marcotte self-identifies as an English major); Adam Serwer, "Friday Nerdblogging: The "Barders" and Their Classism," *The American Prospect*, 6 May 2011.

167 The idea that "10,000 hours" of practice would make someone an expert was popularized in Malcolm Gladwell's *Outliers: The Story of Success* (2008).

we are already dealing with a profound exception, the probability of the accuracy of the standard Shakespeare narrative must be low—unless it is trumped by other facts.

However, the other facts do not help. The next thing we know about William Shakespeare is that he married at the age of 18, to Anne Hathaway, who was 25 or 26 at the time. Their first child was born about six months later. Two years later, in early 1585, twins were born. Thus before his 21st birthday, William Shakespeare was married with three children. At this point, the record falls silent for about seven years, until references to Shakespeare begin to appear in London. There are a few facts that we have about his time in London; we know that by 1597 he had purchased a large home in Stratford, and that at some point in the early 1600s—perhaps around 1607—he returned to Stratford for good. We also know that his wife and two surviving children, both daughters, were illiterate. And then, of course, there is the Will.

If these comprise the facts of William Shakespeare's life, what about his literary remains? Excepting the contentious excerpts in the *Sir Thomas More* manuscript, there are none. We already know from the Will that he left no books, and made no comment about any books, manuscripts, or other literary effects. There are no other records of his life that can be associated with the plays—no correspondence, no receipts, no legal documents. There are no manuscripts, no letters, not even a discarded or scribbled-on leaf of paper survives. Summarizing this absence of evidence in her 2001 book, *Shakespeare's Unorthodox Biography*, Diana Price compared Shakespeare to two dozen of his contemporaries, noting that he was the only one who left behind no paper trail.[168]

Indeed, it is even worse than that: Shakespeare died a well-to-do and successful man—he did not die under impoverished circumstances like many of his peers. Precisely for this reason the stark absence of any literary remains must be the source of consternation. In a recent book Shakespeare scholar James Shapiro insists that none of this matters.[169] That is nonsense. The situation has been the frank source of considerable wonder and speculation among Shakespeareans—the vast majority of whom are Stratfordians—for hundreds of years. It is one thing to say that the absence of evidence proves nothing. It is another thing

---

[168] Diana Price, in her *Shakespeare's Unorthodox Biography* (2001), pioneered the approach of contextualizing Shakespeare's lack of remains or even notice with his contemporaries.

[169] Shapiro, *Contested*, references Price, 243–44, and then moves on, but later insists that any lack of evidence for education, reading, or life experience is trumped by Shakespeare's "imagination"; in other words, the "Genius self-caused" argument.

to say that the absence of evidence is irrelevant to the question under review: namely, that Shakespeare wrote the plays and poems under his name.

After providing his case for Shakespeare not writing the plays, Donnelly then moves on to parallelisms, in which he provides 200 pages of literary passages from Shakespeare and Bacon in which they used almost the same words or expressed almost the same thoughts. Thus, for example, Shakespeare wrote, in the *Tempest* (all italics are Donnelly's), "There is a divinity that shapes our ends, *rough-hew* them how we will," while Bacon once wrote "a *rough-hewn* seaman"; or Bacon wrote, "The particular remedies that learning doth *minister* to all the *diseases of the mind*" while Shakespeare wrote, in *Macbeth*, "Canst thou not *minister* to a *mind diseased?*" Of course, these are not particularly good examples of parallelisms, but they are of the kind that Donnelly uses.[170]

A more convincing case for parallelisms was made by Constance Potts, the head of the Francis Bacon Society, who in 1883 published the *Promus*, a notebook of Bacon's which contained numerous aphorisms and sayings. Here the comparisons in expression are much more striking: [171]

> Promus: "A fool's bolt is soon shot"
> *Henry V*: "A fool's bolt is soon shot"
>
> Promus: "To slay with a leaden sword"
> *Love's Labour's Lost*: "Wounds like a leaden sword"
>
> Promus: "Thought is free"
> *Twelfth Night, Tempest*: "Thought is free"

I will have more to add about this approach later, but suffice it to say that in most cases parallelisms, like other internal evidence tests (such as rare words or idioms), fail to distinguish between common speech or even the simple borrowing of expressions in currency. This is not in itself a strong way of advancing an argument for authorial identity.

One unique document that Donnelly describes is the "Northumberland Manuscript," which is actually a collection of documents that was found in 1867.[172] The main interest concerns the folder in which the documents were kept, because it is scribbled on in all directions. Among other

---

170 Donnelly, *Cryptogram*, 298.

171 Quote from McClinton, *Shakespeare Conspiracies*, 225–226. Donnelly was aware of Potts' work independent of his own, cited it, and even provided her portrait in his book.

172 Donnelly, *Cryptogram*, 281–282

things, the contents list two Shakespeare plays, *Richard II* and *Richard III*, a fragment from *The Isle of Dogs*, and some other materials, including some essays by Francis Bacon. In addition, the names "Shakespeare" and "Bacon" are written several times on the folder cover. It is a bizarre document that is still not adequately explained.

The entire second half of Donnelly's book is taken up by the "Great Cryptogram," which Donnelly claimed was a numerical cipher embedded in the actual text of the First Folio. Donnelly got the idea from the fact that Bacon had in fact created a cipher, and that if he had authored the plays nothing would have been more natural than to put one in the First Folio.[173] Following lengthy experiments, Donnelly came to believe he had hit upon a meaningful result by counting the words on one column—sometimes from the top, and sometimes from the bottom—subtracting or adding the number of words from some larger total number of words, determining the difference, and then identifying the one word that resulted. Repeating the computation several times, and stringing all the words so derived together, would yield a coded message. For example, here is the narrative that Donnelly extracted by bouncing back and forth between pages 74 and 76 of the Folio (Donnelly showed his work—all addition and subtraction, but still incomprehensible):[174]

> These plays are put abroad at first upon the stage in the name of more low [Marlowe] a woe-begone sullen fellow. He had engaged in a quarrel with one arch or [Archer] a servant about a wanton ending in a bloody hand to hand fight in which he was slain the point of his own sword struck against his head and eye making fearful wounds

Through this method of word-by-word extraction Donnelly was thus able to present the conventional narrative of Christopher Marlowe's death, while incidentally implying that whoever planted the cipher in the Shakespeare plays also wrote Marlowe's plays! But Donnelly does not stop there; he goes on to propose that not only did Bacon write the plays of Shakespeare and Marlowe, he also wrote many of the anonymous plays from the era, as well as the plays of a half-dozen other playwrights of the period (Marston, Massinger, Middleton, etc.), and also the *Essays* of Montaigne (in

---

173 The cipher Bacon created was the binary five bit A/B cipher, which allows for almost the entire alphabet due to the twenty five permutations. Since the cipher employed two letters, it could be transposed to any other two state format.

174 Donnelly, *Cryptogram*, 690–692.

his youth), and Robert Burton's *Anatomy of Melancholy* (in his old age).[175]

There really is no substance to these claims, unless one accepts the notion that if Bacon thought a thing, and someone else shared the sentiment, then Bacon must have written it; or unless one is willing to believe that any reference to bacon—a fairly common food, after all—is a coded message revealing Baconian authorship.

I call this form of escalating authorship a Vedic Expansion, in honor of a famous poem from the *Rig Veda* that describes the effects of drinking soma, a ritual drink from early Hinduism.[176] The poem, with the constantly interjected refrain of "Have I not drunk the soma juice?" reads as follows:[177]

> This, even this was my resolve, to win a cow, to win a steed:
> Like violent gusts of wind the draughts that I have drunk have lifted me
> The draughts I drank have borne me up, as fleet-foot horses draw a car:
> The hymn hath reached me, like a cow who lows to meet her darling calf:
> As a wright bends a chariot-seat so round my heart I bend the hymn:
> Not as a mote within the eye count the Five Tribes of men with me:
> The heavens and earth themselves have not grown equal to one half of me
> I in my grandeur have surpassed the heavens and all this spacious earth
> Aha! this spacious earth will I deposit either here or there
> In one short moment will I smite the earth in fury here or there:
> One of my flanks is in the sky; I let the other trail below:
> I, greatest of the Mighty Ones, am lifted to the firmament:
> I seek the worshipper's abode; oblation-bearer to the Gods:

The poem perfectly captures the escalation of intent, culminating in the exhilaration and intoxication of power and mastery which knows no limits. The cause might be simply psychological, yet it is a phenomenon not uncommon in the authorship controversy. As we shall see.

---

175 Donnelly, *Cryptogram*, 954, 955, 969.

176 Soma has never been identified, and should not in any case be confused with the opioid in Huxley's *Brave New World*. Many substances have been suggested including mushrooms and hashish. Based on its effects, I would say that soma was probably a kind of tea made from ephedra, which is native to the region. If so, that would make Donnelly the "Prince of Cranks" in more ways than one.

177 *Rig Veda*, Book X, 119, translated by Ralph J. H. Griffith, in Yutang, Lin, ed.; *The Wisdom of China and India*, 14–15.

14 | Turn-of-the-Century Skeptics

New Shakespeare Society ~ Frederick Fleay ~ J. M. Robertson ~ George Greenwood ~ Walt Whitman, Henry James, Mark Twain ~ Marlowe (Zeigler, Mendenhall) ~ William Stanley, Earl of Derby ~ Roger Manners, Earl of Rutland ~ John Aubrey

From the latter part of the 19th century through the First World War, orthodox Shakespearean study was dominated by the biographies of James Halliwell-Phillipps and Sidney Lee, but analysts such as Frederick Fleay and J.M. Robertson also made significant contributions. In the 1890s the case would be made for two new candidates, and in the early 20th century, two literary heavyweights—Mark Twain and Leo Tolstoy—would enter the fray with sharply critical works on Shakespeare. As this period came to a close, yet another authorial candidate would be advanced, and invested scholars would meanwhile be left to contemplate the publication of more sources contemporary, or nearly contemporary, to Shakespeare's time.

The analysts were tied to the founding in 1873 of the New Shakespeare Society, and its leading member was Frederick Fleay. Over the course of several books Fleay sought to periodize and attribute not only Shakespeare's plays but also the large volume of anonymous plays that were left over from the Elizabethan and Jacobean theater. His method largely depended on metrical tests applied to the poetic structure of the plays, emphasizing the use of one kind of line (say, masculine lines versus feminine lines), as well as the use of specific vocabularies, and so forth. With perhaps overweening confidence, Fleay was thereby able to assign a large volume of plays to Marlowe, Kyd, Peele, or Lodge. Whatever his faults, Fleay's analyses were always very clear and his books are still very readable and informative today.

After Fleay's death in the early 20th century, his place was largely taken by J.M. Robertson. Before becoming a Shakespeare critic, Robertson was probably best known as an economist and atheist. He wrote numerous books (well into the 1930s) disputing the canonicity of the Folio and the attribution of several plays.

It is important to note that while both Fleay and Robertson concluded that a significant part of the Shakespeare canon was written by others, neither questioned Shakespeare's authorship of the bulk of the plays. This, however, did not spare them the enmity of more orthodox scholars, who called them "Disintegrators."

Robertson's style is prolix and leaden, lacking the directness of Fleay. But to his credit, he was an equal-opportunity arguer: when he wasn't attacking orthodox Shakespeareans, he was attacking dissidents—particularly Baconians. His most frequent sparring partner was George Greenwood.

George Greenwood was a barrister and a member of Parliament (as was Robertson—perhaps this explains their verbosity). He was adamant that the author of Shakespeare must have had legal training, and was convinced that the arguments concerning Shakespeare's signatures and the manuscript of *Sir Thomas More* were vacuous.

One of Greenwood's readers was the American author, Mark Twain. Twain had been exposed to the authorship controversy as a teenager while working on a steamboat on the Mississippi, and Greenwood's *The Shakespeare Problem Restated* (1908) inspired him to write his own semi-autobiographical study, *Is Shakespeare Dead?* (1909). Twain's main problem appears to have been the rigidity and speculative biographical approach of the Shakespeareans; calling to mind the reconstruction of the brontosaurus specimen at the Museum of Natural History, he memorably compared Sidney Lee's biography to "nine bones and six hundred barrels of plaster of paris."[178] He also appears to have been persuaded by Greenwood's argument that whoever wrote the plays must have been a lawyer. Twain even quoted a chapter from Greenwood's book, before summarizing the Shakespeare-Bacon debate in inimitable fashion:[179]

> Let me try to illustrate the two systems in a simple and homely way calculated to bring the idea within the grasp of the ignorant and

---

[178] Twain, *Is Shakespeare Dead?*, 49.

[179] Twain, *Is Shakespeare Dead?*, 52; 26 years before Erwin Schrödinger.

unintelligent. We will suppose a case: take a lap-bred, house-fed, uneducated, inexperienced kitten; take a rugged old Tom that's scarred from stem to rudder-post with the memorials of strenuous experience, and is so cultured, so educated, so limitlessly erudite that one may say of him "all cat-knowledge is his province"; also, take a mouse. Lock the three up in a holeless, crackless, exitless prison-cell. Wait half an hour, then open the cell, introduce a Shakespearite and a Baconian, and let them cipher and assume. The mouse is missing: the question to be decided is, where is it? You can guess both verdicts beforehand. One verdict will say the kitten contains the mouse; the other will as certainly say the mouse is in the tomcat.

Twain was not the only American author to raise questions about Shakespeare. Emerson, back when Delia Bacon was active, confessed that he "could not marry the man with the verse"; both Henry James and his brother William James expressed their doubts; Walt Whitman expressed doubts on two occasions, and was convinced that only one of the "wolfish earls" of the time could have written the plays. (Whitman's dig is notably "classist" in arguing that the real Shakespeare must have been a nobleman—yet the argument is to bury, not to praise.[180])

More or less concurrent with Twain's book, the author of *War and Peace* and *Anna Karenina* weighed in on the subject of Shakespeare's legacy. Leo Tolstoy's essay, *On Shakespeare and Drama*, did not question the authorship of the plays, and was originally written in support of another essay, *Shakespeare and the Working Class*, criticizing (in the wake of Whitman) Shakespeare's lack of empathy for the lower classes. Instead, Tolstoy used the opportunity to engage in a very sharp critique of Shakespeare's style, which included a scene by scene dissection of *King Lear*. Perhaps the most interesting part of Tolstoy's analysis was his conclusions that while *King Lear* failed as drama, the related play, *King Leir*, was a comparative success.[181]

While Tolstoy did not question Shakespeare's authorship, and Twain was somewhat equivocal about Bacon's, three new authorship candidates emerged during this period.

The first of these was William Stanley, the 5th Earl of Derby (1564–1642). Unlike most of the other alternative candidates, Stanley has specific documentary evidence supporting him. In 1891, James H. Greenstreet found two letters written by French spies that indicated

---

180 Various expressions of Shakespeare skepticism at doubtaboutwill.org/past_doubters

181 Tolstoy, *Tolstoy on Shakespeare, O Shekspir i o drame*, 445–446 provides the bibliographic details.

that Stanley was "engaged in writing comedies for the common players." Greenstreet died shortly thereafter and was unable to complete his studies but Sidney Lee made reference to the letters in the early 20th century and the theme was taken up by the American Robert Frazer in his *Silent Shakespeare* (1912), where it was argued that Stanley wrote the best parts of Shakespeare but that Shakespeare and many others were involved. Frazer was what would be called a "groupist," that is, someone who believes that the plays were variously written by others but with an overarching intelligence guiding the final product. Frazer had been anticipated by T.H. White, whose *Our English Homer* (1892) took the Homeric analyst position to its logical conclusion (indeed, the main difference between White and Frazer is that White installed Francis Bacon as the superogatory mind, while Frazer elected Stanley). The capstone to the Derbyite edifice was provided by the French professor Abel Lefranc, whose two-volume *Sous le masque de William Shakespeare* was published in 1918–1919.

The Derbyite position has never been very popular but it has figured in a number of other groupist theories. The strongest points in its favor involve the possible influence of Stanley in individual plays, such as *Love's Labour's Lost*. The main problem with the theory is that it doesn't provide sufficient scope to sustain a unitarian thesis, and that is what most anti-Stratfordians want.[182]

Another candidate nominated in the 20th century was Roger Manners, the Duke of Rutland (1576–1612). A number of writers advanced his candidacy, most notably the Belgian Celestine Demblon. The main factors in his favor were his reputation as a polymath, the fact that he had actually been to Denmark, and the fact that he had attended the University of Padua. While the Rutland school had long existed on the outer fringes of the authorship controversy, it received strong support in 1997 when Ilya Gililov published *Igra Shekspira* (*The Shakespeare Game*) in Russia, where it became a bestseller.[183]

The final candidate to emerge in this period was Christopher Marlowe, who is possibly the best alternative of them all. By virtue of his education, travels, poetical skill, and several published plays, Marlowe would seem to be the ideal replacement for Shakespeare. The problem,

---

[182] John M. Rollet's *William Stanley as Shakespeare: Evidence of Authorship by the Sixth Earl of Derby* (2015), is the most recent book on the Derbyite position.

[183] Gililov (in either Russian or English) summarizes the Rutland arguments and also touches on much of the more obscure evidence used by anti-Stratfordians. Part of the reason for the success of Gililov's book is that it not only repeats the Rutland candidacy, but also recapitulates the entire controversy and the alternative candidates in a lively style for an audience that had long been parched for such a presentation.

as attentive readers will have surmised, rests in the inconvenient fact that contemporary records indicate that he had been killed in 1593. On the other hand, many have noted that Marlowe was in trouble at the time of his presumed death—and it is true that Shakespeare's first publication followed not long after the obituary was filed.

In his 1894 novel *It Was Marlowe*, a San Francisco attorney named Wilber G. Zeigler added a layer of intrigue to Marlovian speculation. As imagined by Zeigler, Marlowe was not slain on the fateful date in 1593; rather, he was caught wooing the wife of Francis Frizier, whereupon a sword-fight between the two men ensued. When Marlowe issued the fatal thrust, he then changed clothes with the dead man (they conveniently resembled each other) and ran to Bankside where he consulted with George Peele and William Shakespeare. They in turn agreed that Marlowe would continue his writing career incognito, using Shakespeare as a front man. (Marlowe and Frizier's widow would be reunited at the end of the story.) Zeigler supported his story with numerous footnotes.[184]

Swashbuckling embellishments aside, one line of surprising support for the Marlowe thesis was presented around the same time—and from an unlikely source. Dr. Thomas Mendenhall, an American physicist, had a theory that authors could be identified by word length, that is, the comparative frequency of letter clusters could be used to identify and distinguish an individual's writing. Mendenhall was commissioned to do such a study comparing Shakespeare and Bacon, but as a control he employed his word counters on Marlowe as well. The result, published in 1901, obtained an exact match between Shakespeare and Marlowe.[185]

Following the initial spate of enthusiasm, Marlovian theory was moribund for several decades. Interest would be renewed in the early 1950s thanks to the efforts of Calvin Hoffman, an American publicist, whose *Murder of the Man Who Was Shakespeare* (1955) is a classic in authorship studies, partly because of its clear exposition but also because Hoffmann provided an extended appendix of parallelisms (many of which are quite impressive[186]). To be sure, the popularity of Hoffman's treatment probably owed something to the fortuitous discovery (during the remodeling of a dining hall at Cambridge University in the early 1950s) of two pieces of wood, which, when pieced together,

---

184 Zeigler, *It Was Marlowe: The Story of the Secret of Three Centuries*.

185 Michell, *Who Wrote Shakespeare?*, 228–229, Pinksen also covers Mendelhall in detail.

186 Hoffman, *Murder of the Man Who Was Shakespeare*.

provided a portrait of a young man who would have been 21 in 1585—a datum that would match Marlowe's birth year. Reassembled and refurbished, the discovery has since been christened the portrait of Marlowe, and is now ubiquitous. The identification is by no means certain, but the portrait was discovered at the right time. Without a proper icon, hero worship is difficult.

In the potpourri of developments dating from late 19th and early 20th century, the final event to be noted concerns the publication of John Aubrey's *Brief Lives*. We have already encountered Aubrey in his archaeological aspect, and we know that his brief narrative of Shakespeare's life was consulted by Rowe; but it was not until 1898 that his notebooks were finally gone over and published. On one page of his notes was found a brief entry on Shakespeare which did not make it into the biographical sketch. It reads as follows:[187]

> the more to be admired q [*quia*] he was not a company keeper
> lived in Shoreditch, wouldnt be debauched, & if invited to writ;
> he was in paine.
>   W. Shakespeare.

The plain meaning of the passage is that Shakespeare kept to himself and did not socialize with his colleagues. In one sense, this weakens the popular idea that Shakespeare acquired his vast knowledge over drinks at one of London's taverns. On the other hand, Shakespeare's solitary ways would also explain why there are no memoirs of him actually writing any plays or poetry. Yet another implication of the passage is that Shakespeare had difficulty writing; since he "was in pain" when asked to do so. This conclusion accords well with Donnelly's critique of Shakespeare's signatures and with the impression of everyone who has found fault with them since. However, Stratfordians never concede the point. Instead, they argue that when Shakespeare was asked to go debauching, he would simply write a note begging off. Needless to say, an exemplar of such a note would be invaluable evidence—if such a note ever existed.

---

[187] Chambers, *WS* 2, 252; Chambers also provides a photograph of the document. Wells, *Shakespeare and Co.*, quotes the text but repunctuates; Brooks, on the other hand, insisted the text had to do with William Beeston (ca. 1606–1682, an actor and son of Christopher Beeston (a contemporary of Shakespeare), who was one of Aubrey's sources.

15 | Topical Allusions and Generation J

The Parnassus Plays ~ The "War of the Theaters" ~ Satiromastix ~ Ben Jonson ~ John Marston ~ Thomas Middleton ~ John Ford ~ Philip Massinger ~ Beaumont and Fletcher ~ Essex Rebellion ~ Gunpowder Plot ~ Shakespeare's Absence

One of the things that tends to be overlooked when discussing Shakespeare's theatrical career is the fact that it spanned two generations. Shakespeare, who was born in 1564, was active at the tail end of a generation that would for the most part abandon the stage in the 1590s to be supplanted by a younger generation, born in the 1570s and 1580s, that would carry on the development of stage drama into the 17th century and well beyond Shakespeare's life. I propose calling this later group "Generation J." This serves to distinguish it from the previous group while honoring of its most famous member, Ben Jonson (along with the monarch, King James, under whose reign they would achieve their greatest success). A discussion of this later generation also allows us to review some of the topical allusions found in the theater of the time, as well as the political activities that may or may not have been dissected in specific plays.

We have already encountered Ben Jonson (1572–1637), whose 1616 folio created the model for the First Folio.[188] Jonson's father was a Scottish minister (named "Johnson"—Ben deliberately dropped the "h") who died before his son was born. Jonson's widowed mother remarried a master bricklayer when he was still an infant. He attended a modest grammar school, but then was brought, unhappily, into his

---

[188] Donaldson, *Ben Jonson*, is a recent and thorough biography. Otherwise, for Jonson and the rest the sources are the same as for the others: Chambers, *ES*, 3; Bentley, *JCS*, 3–4; *DNB* entries.

stepfather's business. He soon escaped, enlisting in military service in the Netherlands where he fought and killed a Spaniard in single combat, taking his armor. Jonson was active in the theater from about the mid-90s, working for Philip Henslowe, but none of his (presumably collaborative) work from that period has survived. In 1598, he fought a duel with a fellow actor, Gabriel Spencer, killing him. For this he was imprisoned, escaping the death penalty by "benefit of clergy," which is to say, by showing that he could read. Before this, Jonson had collaborated with Thomas Nashe (and perhaps others) on *The Isle of Dogs* (1597). That play was considered so seditious that all copies were destroyed; to this day there is no clear idea as to why it caused such offense.

In 1598 Jonson got his first big break with the play, *Every Man in His Humour*. It was originally written for Henslowe, but due to the circumstances surrounding the duel with Spencer, it ended up being staged by Shakespeare's company. In the 1600s Jonson went on to write the plays which made his reputation, including *Cynthia's Revels*, *Poetaster*, *Volpone*, *Epicoene*, *The Alchemist* and *Bartholomew Fair*, but it would appear that Jonson secured most of his income from noble patronage as well as from writing masques (including the *Masque of Blackness*) for the court of King James.

Other playwrights from Ben Jonson's cohort that we have already encountered include Thomas Heywood, Thomas Dekker, and Thomas Middleton—all of whom, along with Jonson, worked for Philip Henslowe.

There are a half-dozen other playwrights who deserve mention but whose main output belongs to a later age. Chief among these were John Fletcher (1579-1625) and Francis Beaumont (1584-1616), both of whom would become the titular playwrights for the King's Men after Shakespeare's retirement. Fletcher was the son of a bishop and attended Cambridge. Beaumont, the son of a judge, had to leave Oxford after the death of his father; he then attended law school. The two became friends and entered into a playwriting partnership that flourished for about ten years (1606-1616). Beaumont died in 1616, the same year as Shakespeare. Unlike Shakespeare, he was widely mourned in public.

The first (1647) folio of the works of Fletcher and Beaumont was modeled on the folios of Jonson and Shakespeare. It contained 34 plays. Their second folio (1679) contained 53, but it was acknowledged that many of the plays included the participation of Philip

Massinger. (1583-1640). Massinger's family were servants to William Herbert, one of the dedicatees of the First Folio, but their position did not prevent their education; Massinger's father eventually became a fellow at Oxford and Massinger himself was educated at Oxford. Philip Massinger eventually turned up in London, where over a period of decades, he would write over a dozen plays, collaborating on many more.

John Ford (1586-ca. 1640) was yet another poet and playwright. He attended law school at the Middle Temple from 1602, and began publishing his poetry in 1606. Though he authored about a dozen plays, his most famous piece was *'Tis Pity She's A Whore* (1633),[189] a frank play about brother-sister incest that culminates in a series of onstage murders, including one sequence where the sister's heart is carried about impaled on a dagger.

Our final playwright from Generation J is John Marston (1576-1634). Marston was the son of a lecturer at Middle Temple and his mother was the daughter of an Italian surgeon living in London. He received a BA from Oxford in 1593-94. It appears that he was originally intended to become a lawyer, but like Lodge before him, he soon abandoned law for a career as an author and playwright. He published several satires in 1598, including his most famous, *The Scourge of Villainy*, which, along with another play, was ordered burned by the Archbishop of Canterbury the following year (presumably under the same line of reasoning that had enjoined the burning of the writings of Thomas Nashe and Gabriel Harvey—though the poetry of *The Scourge* is so obscure and allusive that it is difficult to determine who exactly Marston was seeking to offend).

Marston later had a hand in a group of plays dating to about 1597 that are traditionally associated with the "War of the Theaters" (also known as the "Poets' War") in which he was at odds with Ben Jonson.[190] As a result of their public dispute, Jonson and Marston apparently had

---

189 So titled because of the verse that ends the play; delivered by the Cardinal:

> We shall have time
> To talk at large of all; but never yet
> Incest and murder have so strangely met.
> Of one so young, so rich in nature's store,
> Who could not say, 'Tis Pity She's A Whore?

A far cry from *Romeo and Juliet*:

> Go hence, to have more talk of these sad things;
> Some shall be pardon'd, and some punished:
> For never was a story of more woe
> Than this of Juliet and her Romeo

190 Sources for the "War" include Sharpe, *The Real War of the Theaters*, Bednarz, *Shakespeare and the Poets' War*, and Zbierski, *Shakespeare and the 'War of the Theaters': A Reinterpretation*.

several confrontations (Jonson even claimed to have disarmed Marton of his weapons on one occasion), but in later years they became friends. When Marston and Chapman wrote *Eastward Ho!* in 1605, they were imprisoned for making fun of Scots when a Scotsman was the King of England. Jonson, who had also contributed to the play, accompanied them to prison. After a brief ten-year career, John Marston abandoned his literary career and became a reverend. He died in 1634.

The so-called "War of the Theaters" revolved around a series of plays in which theaters and acting troupes made fun of each other and of various poets and playwrights. The objects of ridicule are not explicit, but there has emerged a broad consensus about the major personalities being satirized. In his 1937 study, R. Boies Sharpe listed ten plays:[191]

- *The Case is Altered* (Ben Jonson, 1597) – satirizing Munday and the Admiral's Men;
- *Every Man in his own Humour* (Jonson, 1598) – satirizing Munday and the Admiral's Men;
- *Histriomastix* (John Marston, 1599) – satirizing Munday, Jonson, and both the Admiral's and Lord Chamberlain's Men;
- *Jack Drum* (Marston, 1600) – satirizing Jonson and Drayton, the Admiral's Men and perhaps the Chamberlain's Men;
- *Cynthia's Revels* (Jonson, 1600) – satirizing Dekker, Marston, and Paul's Boys;
- *What You Will* (Marston, 1601) – satirizing Jonson and the Chapel Boys;
- *The Poetaster* (Jonson, 1601) – satirizing Dekker, Marston, also the Chamberlain's Men;
- *Satiro-mastix* (Dekker, 1601) – satirizing Jonson and Marston, also the Chapel Boys (and see discussion below);
- *Hamlet* (Shakespeare, 1601?) – satirizing the Boys companies (but this explanation can only be partial; see below);
- *Return from Parnassus* (Anon, 1601?) – the last of the Parnassus plays, written about 1601 at Cambridge.

---

191 Sharpe, *Real War*, 192. The plays are listed here to facilitate further study. *Eastward Ho!* is not on the list but it is another highly topical play deserving investigation. Zbierski would also add *Julius Caesar* to the list, since he thinks the comment "this side Tiber" in the Funeral Oration alludes to the conflict.

One of the Parnassus plays had been known for centuries, but it wasn't until 1896 that all three plays were published. Then, in 1899, G.L. Kittredge brought out a monograph by the recently deceased R.A. Small, covering the "War of the Theaters."[192] Together, these documents opened the door for much wider speculation about the personalities of the London stage.

The Parnassus plays are memorable for a variety of reasons, not just for their topicality. A recurring theme that may resonate with modern readers concerns the false promise of higher education. Characters express frustration over what to do with the university degrees they have acquired.[193] Options were limited: one could accept a position as a country parson (and live in poverty), or one could become a tutor for the children of the wealthy (and live in frustration), or one could strike out on his own, shooting for the romance and prestige of a career in writing. These are precisely the kinds of circumstances that created the Elizabethan Beats.

The plays also offer brief characterizations of a number of writers we have already met, thus Samuel Daniel:[194]

> Sweete hony dropping Daniell doth wage
> Warre with the proudest big Italian,
> That melts his heart in sugred sonneting.
> Onely let him more sparingly make use
> Of others wit, and use his own the more:
> That well may scorne base imitation.

And here is a summary of Thomas Lodge:

> For Lodge and Watson, men of some desert,
> Yet subject to a Critticks marginall.
> Lodge for his oare in every paper boate,
> He that turns over Galen every day,
> To sit and simper Euphues legacy.

Michael Drayton also makes an appearance:

> Drayton's sweet muse is like a sanguine dye,

---

192 The Parnassus plays comprised three short plays that were performed at Cambridge at the end of the 16th century; Small, Roscoe Addison, *The Stage-Quarrel between Ben Jonson and the So-Called Poetasters* (1899).

193 *Pilgrimage to Parnassus*, 3, 4, 10, 19, 29, 34–37, 40–42, 46, 49–50.

194 *Pilgrimage*, 85–87.

> Able to ravish the rash gazers eye.
> How ever he wants one true note of a Poet of our times,
> and that is this, hee cannot swagger it well in a Taverne,
> nor dominere in a hot house.

And so does Marlowe:

> Marlowe was happy in his buskind muse,
> Also unhappy in his life and end.
> Outty it is that wit so well should dwell,
> Wit lent from heaven, but vices sent from hell,
> Our Theater hath lost, Pluto hath got,
> A Tragick penman for a driery plot.

And as for Ben Jonson:

> The wittiest fellow of a Bricklayer in England.

There is also a sequence suggesting that the authorship controversy was already underway at this time. Two characters, Ingenio and Gullio, discuss their verbal techniques for the seduction of women:[195]

> Gull: Pardon, faire lady, thoughe sick-thoughted Gullio maks amaine unto thee, and like a bould-faced sutore 'gins to woo thee.
> Ingen: (We shall have nothing but pure Shakspere and shreds of poetrie that he hath gathered at the theators!)
> Gull: Pardon mee, moy mistressa ast am a gentleman the moone in comparison of thy bright hue a mere slutt, Anthonie's Cleopatra a black browde milkmaid, Helen a dowdie.
> Ingen: (Marke. Romeo and Juliet! O monstrous theft! I thinke he will runn through a whole book of Samuel Daniel!)

The humor of the passage derives from Gullio's casual misappropriation of verbiage from *Venus and Adonis* and *Romeo and Juliet*, but it is hard not to read the passage without coming to the conclusion that someone thought that Daniel had a hand in *Romeo and Juliet*.

The main point of contact in these plays, insofar as they touch on Shakespeare, comes from the quotation in the *Return from Parnassus, Part II, The Scourge of Simony*. In that play, written about 1601, the character Kempe says:[196]

---

195 *Pilgrimage*, 56–57.

196 *Pilgrimage*, 138.

Few of the university men pen plays well, they smell too much of that writer Ovid, and that writer Metamorphosis, and talk too much of Proserpina & Jupiter. Why here's our fellow Shakespeare puts them all down, Aye, and Ben Jonson, too. O that Ben Jonson is a pestilent fellow, he brought up Horace giving the Poets a pill, but our fellow Shakespeare hath given him a purge that made him bewray his credit.

The last quotation is valuable inasmuch as it identifies Shakespeare as a real person, assumed as a poet and playwright and active on the London stage. Naturally, Shakespeareans have expended great effort attempting to identify the occasion when Shakespeare "gave Ben Jonson a purge." The usual candidate put forward is in the characterization of Ajax in *Troilus and Cressida*, but a more immediate likely source is Thomas Dekker's *Satiro-mastix*. There are several reasons, the first being that the attempts to derive such a satire of Jonson in *Troilus* seem strained.[197] In addition, *Satiro-mastix* was performed by Shakespeare's company, the Lord Chamberlain's Men, and it does contain a hard to miss characterization of Ben Jonson as the character "Horace," who is humiliated twice in the play. Finally, the play features a character named Sir Adam Prickshaft, which appears to be a parody of Shakespeare's name.[198]

Shakespeare scholar Jonathan Bate has followed the general reasoning presented here, further observing the baldness of the Prickshaft character (which coincides with the balding Shakespeare in the Droeshout engraving) as well as the fact that Prickshaft makes a plausible reference back to *Henry IV*.[199] However, it should be pointed out that, according to Small, the entire Prickshaft subplot derives from an earlier play that Dekker had been working on, which may account for most of the references (including the baldness).[200] Even so, a possible explanation is that the author of the *Parnassus* play understood that Prickshaft was a doppelgänger for Shakespeare, and knew also that the play was performed by Shakespeare's company—that it was, therefore, a Shakespeare play, and referenced accordingly.

[197] "Shakespeare's Purge of Jonson" in Bednarz, 19–52. The key element is that there is a character named "Ajax" in *Troilus* (as indeed in the *Iliad*), and as we already know from Nashe's dispute with Gabriel Harvey, "Ajax" was Elizabethan slang for a commode.

[198] Dekker, *Satiro-mastix, Or The Untrussing of the Humourous Poet*.

[199] Bate, *Soul of the Age*, 355–357. This is apparently a rare interpretation; the only other one Bate could find goes back to a German publication in 1856. However, Bate then goes on to suggest that Shakespeare wrote the purge scene in *Satiro-mastix* anyway, 450–451.

[200] Small, *Stage-Quarrel*, 124.

There is also a passing reference to *Hamlet* in *Satiro-mastix*, though the context has nothing to do with Shakespeare (or Prickshaft); it is in reference to "Paris Garden," a bear-baiting facility near Henslowe's The Rose, which was also apparently used for putting on plays. Boies Sharpe adds *Hamlet* to the list of plays primarily because of some notorious lines in the 1604 quarto of *Hamlet*, which are supposed to refer to the boys companies:

> Nay, their endeavour keeps in the wonted pace: but
> there is, sir, an aery of children, little eyases,
> that cry out on the top of question, and are most
> tyrannically clapped for't: these are now the
> fashion, and so berattle the common stages—so they
> call them—that many wearing rapiers are afraid of
> goose-quills and dare scarce come thither.[201]

The problem is that play companies of boys had been common for twenty years, so there seems to be no reason to consider this a reference to the War of the Theaters—especially since there is no attempted satire of any of the other playwrights, a fundamental characteristic of the quarrel.

So far we have tended to scant other things that were going on in Elizabethan times. Let's reconstruct that chronology now, partly to further contextualize the plays and playwrights, but also because some contemporaneous events generated large amounts of text, often featuring many of our Elizabethan writers.

The first thing we need to keep in mind is that Elizabeth I, who took the throne in 1558, followed a very violent period in English history that involved shifting allegiances, religious martyrdoms, and numerous political killings. Elizabeth was the sixth Tudor monarch in less than 70 years. The previous century had been marked by a decades-long struggle between the Lancastrians (from which the Tudor dynasty derived) and the Yorkists (which line ended with the death of Richard III in 1485). Subsequently, Henry VII reigned for some 25 years, during which time many former Yorkist sympathizers were conveniently done away with. He was followed in 1509 by Henry VIII, who as we know, was married six times and had three of his wives executed. But that was not the only difficulty in Henry's reign; he had also

---

[201] It is important to note that this text is in the Folio *Hamlet* as well as the 1604 *Hamlet*, but it is not in the 1603 *Hamlet*. Depending on the time-frame for the Folio *Hamlet*, the lines may have no direct relevance.

taken the opportunity to disestablish the Catholic Church in England, thereby allowing himself to accrue the Church's wealth, which was then dispensed to loyalists; he also authorized the secularization or destruction of many Catholic monasteries. Predictably, this led to numerous martyrdoms of prominent Catholics, the most famous of these being Sir Thomas More.

Henry died in 1547. He was succeeded by his nine-year-old son, Edward, who reigned for five and half years and died in 1553. After the ten-day interregnum of his cousin, Lady Jane Grey, Edward was succeeded by his sister, Mary, known to history as Bloody Mary. She reinstituted a Catholic reign, and protestant martyrdoms followed. Mary reigned for five years, before Elizabeth took the throne and re-instituted a protestant regime.

The point of this condensed history is that England had been riven by political and religious strife for a hundred years prior to Elizabeth, with some predictable consequences. One was that the kingdom had many characteristics of a surveillance state, and was, in fact, awash with spies—spies for the government, for foreign governments, and for sectarians of all stripes.[202] And this was not just a matter of Yorkist or Catholic sympathizers;[203] there were problems with non-English immigrant communities, usually Dutch or German, who had a long history in London insofar as they had been targeted during the Wat Tyler rebellion in the 14th century. There were also problems with an emerging religious sect called the Puritans, who felt that the disestablishment of the Catholic Church had not gone far enough, and who sought a more decentralized religious establishment (as well as a more severe social order). All of these elements would contribute to an atmosphere favoring not only strict control of any public gathering—for example, a stage performance—but also a tendency to look for hidden messages or hidden meanings in any public speech.

And the prevailing political landscape provided ample material for writers. Consider, for example, the literary reverberations of the Babington Plot of 1586. This was a plot to assassinate Elizabeth, which

---

202 There were further problems in the case of Catholic spies, whether from France, Italy, or Spain, which brings up the issue of foreign policy. Of course, we know that this was something of a cat and mouse game, insofar as both Marlowe and Munday (and perhaps some others) had traveled to the continent in order to spy on English Catholics.

203 This is the proper context for the biographies of Marlowe cited earlier that stressed his involvement with spying; it is a connection that includes Anthony Munday, and also Giordano Bruno. See John Bossy's *Giordano Bruno and the Embassy Affair* (1991).

led directly to the trial and execution of Mary Queen of Scots. In response to a pamphlet containing the frequently anthologized poem by Babington conspirator Chidiock Tichborne, a contrary pamphlet was soon published, bearing a parody of the Tichborne poem signed with the telltale initials "T. K." —Thomas Kyd.[204]

Or consider the Martin Marprelate tracts, referenced earlier in our discussion of Thomas Nashe's career. The original Marprelate tracts constituted a violent verbal assault on the established church from a Puritan (Presbyterian) perspective. While the tracts elicited the usual denunciations from officialdom, they also inspired a series of pamphlets with colorful titles like *Pap with a Hatchet* and *An Almond for a Parrat*. No one knows for sure (since the pamphleteers were anonymous or pseudonymous), but the general consensus is that Lyly, Nashe, Greene, and even Munday may have had a hand. It is difficult, in any case, to imagine that these four authors—all of whom had either worked for or publicly defended the Earl of Oxford—came together purely by coincidence.[205]

We discussed earlier Henry Chettle's apparent request for Shakespeare to contribute lines in tribute at the death of Elizabeth in 1603. Shakespeare was silent then, and he would remain conspicuously silent during the Essex Revolt in 1601, the Gunpowder Plot in 1605, or any number of other political events or executions that marked his lifetime during the reigns of Elizabeth I or James I.[206]

Shakespeare's failure to contribute anything specific to the political or even theatrical topics of his time could, of course, be explained by his businesslike demeanor and general prudence. But therein lies the rub; given the prolificity and resourcefulness of his peers,

---

204 Boas, ed., *Works of Thomas Kyd*, xxv.

205 Black, Joseph L., *The Martin Marprelate Tracts: A Modernized and Annotated Edition* (Cambridge, Cambridge UP: 2008) is the only recent reprinting of the tracts and provides valuable contextual information, such as the belief at the time that the tracts were written by John Penry and Job Throckmorton, as well as details about the suggested participation of Lyly, Nashe, and others in the responses. Nina Greene, on the other hand, believes that Edward de Vere, the Earl of Oxford, not only wrote the *Martin* tracts but the various other tracts in response. See oxford-shakespeare.com.

206 The Essex Rebellion was led by Robert Devereaux (1565-1601), the second Earl of Essex, against Elizabeth as a result of her rescinding his political and economic powers as punishment for his failures on military campaign in Ireland. Near ruin, he plotted a rebellion, and Shakespeare's company was hired to perform *Richard II* (because the unexpurgated version features a deposition scene) to seed the ground. However, the government sought his arrest, which precipitated a group of some 200 marching on the palace on February 8, 1601. They were quickly dispersed. Essex was found guilty of treason, and was beheaded two weeks later. The relevance to Shakespeare studies comes from the fact that among the conspirators were the Earl of Southampton, Henry Wriothesley (the dedicatee of *Venus and Lucrece*), Sir Henry Neville (a proposed author of Shakespeare), as well as from the usage of *Richard II*, and, I would argue, because the campaign of Essex to the Azores coincided with the premiere of *The Isle of Dogs*.
As for *Macbeth*, Garry Wills' *Witches & Jesuits: Shakespeare's Macbeth* (1996), is a successful but not unique attempt to tie that play into the Gunpowder Plot.

Shakespeare's curious silence would have placed him at a disadvantage. Unlike Shakespeare, his contemporaries were ready, willing, and able to write on any topic, in any style, at any time.

16 | BLACK IRON PRISON

Philip K. Dick ~ "Black Iron Prison" ~ "Bad Quartos" ~ Sir Thomas More Attribution ~ Stipulations About Parallelisms ~ The "Disintegration" Speech ~ The Clayton Loan

In the first act of Wagner's *Parsifal*, there's a point when the old hermit says to the young hero, "You see, my son, that here space becomes time," at which point a musical interlude ensues, moving the action from the forest to the castle of Montsalvat where the Holy Grail is held. The line may seem a bit pretentious, and one might suspect that Wagner was being a little tongue-in-cheek as well: after all, in a theatrical performance a change of scene requires *time*; that's why there are interludes, intermezzos, and so on. Of course, the linking of space and time also fits very well within the German philosophical tradition. Kant decreed that space and time were preconditions for sensory perception—an idea that Schopenhauer would elaborate voluminously (in works that would have been familiar to Wagner). Tracing the line forward, the linkage of space and time in German philosophy carries into 20th century mathematical developments, ensuring that the concept of a four dimensional space-time continuum is now very familiar.

But one of the mysteries of aesthetics is that different people respond to stimuli in different ways. One person who took Wagner's utterance very seriously was the American science fiction writer Philip K. Dick.

Dick (1928–1982) was born in the Midwest and grew up in the San Francisco Bay Area, graduating from Berkeley High School in 1947. After dropping out from Cal Berkeley in his first semester, he settled into a prolific writing career that would span more than three decades until his death in 1982. Dick's science fiction was distinguished by his abiding interest in metaphysical questions, alternative realities, and the experience of ordinary people cast into fantastic situations. Dick would have been perfectly situated, by the way, to observe—and absorb—the emergence of Beat culture during his formative years as a writer; Ginsburg's *Howl* was supposedly typed on the machines in the basement of the Berkeley Public Library, just up the street from the high school.

In one of his last novels, *VALIS* (1981)[207] Dick elaborated on a concept which he called the "Black Iron Prison." The notion derived from Dick's own (often drug-enhanced) experiences and was typical of the cheerful paranoia endemic to Northern California at the time. The basic idea centers around a pink light that transmits premonitory signals; after encountering the light repeatedly, the protagonist, Horselover Fat, comes to the conclusion that it is extraterrestrial in nature. Normal empirical reality, he further concludes, is simply one of three holograms being projected by pink lasers onto planet Earth—one dated to 70 BCE Rome, one to contemporary California (in 1974), and one far in the future. But since the holograms were all-encompassing, one didn't even know they were there. This predicament was the "Black Iron Prison."

Beneath the novel's hallucinogenic and paranoid trappings, Dick appears to have been arguing—decades before *The Matrix*—that there are constraints within our consciousness that prevent us from seeing reality as it truly is. This kind of thinking would pass muster with Kant, whose epistemological system it rather resembles. It is also compatible with more recent ideas holding that the structures determining our view of the world are more elastic—for example, in hermeneutics (where the process of our thinking determines the structures), or in structuralism (where the variability of language accomplishes the same purpose).

In any case, I want to appropriate Dick's notion of an all-encompassing prison of thought to describe the limitations—or "mind forg'd manacles"—of the Shakespearean establishment in the 20th century. I will focus on five manifestations of this phenomenon from the first decades of the century:

1. the arguments about the Bad Quartos;
2. the stipulations for parallelisms;

---

[207] VALIS stands for "Vast Active Living Information System." In the novel, Dick interchanges with the titular protagonist, Horselover Fat, whose name is simply Dick's taken to its Greek and German roots.

3. the promotion of the "Hand D" in the *Sir Thomas More* manuscript;
4. the Clayton loan; and
5. the *ex cathedra* nature of Chambers' "Disintegration" speech.

The notion of "bad quartos" is usually dated to 1909, the date of Alfred Pollard's survey of Shakespearean publications.[208] But there was more than one person working on the idea, which developed further throughout the century. The original idea had to do with the discrepancies between the First Folio texts of several plays, which were usually longer than the previous quarto versions. *Henry the Sixth*, Parts 2 and 3, *Romeo and Juliet*, and *Hamlet* were typical examples. One reaction would be to follow the lead of multiple authorship. Or, following *Groatsworth*, one might consider plagiarism or revision of other works. But that explanation didn't really work—not only because of assumed Shakespearean authorship, but also because of the nature of the discrepancies.

Consider for example *Henry the Sixth* Parts 2 and 3. Both had previous quarto versions under different titles. These versions were recognizably the same plays, more or less, except that the earlier versions were shorter and of lesser literary quality. If these earlier plays, published anonymously, were in fact by other authors, then we would have a situation in which Shakespeare rewrote them later, scene by scene. That already seems unlikely, and so does the explanation that would have Shakespeare revising these old plays (assuming they were his) into their Folio form. So, in short, the "bad quarto" hypothesis held that the earlier, shorter, and inferior quarto versions of several plays were in fact memorial reconstructions by actors; that is, that an actor who had been in the play would sit down with a scribe and recite

---

208 Pollard, Alfred W., *Shakespeare's Fight with the Pirates and the Problems of the Transmission of his Text* (Cambridge, Cambridge UP: 1920) is the main text introducing the concept of bad quartos. Kirschbaum, Leo, *Shakespeare and the Stationers* (Columbus, OH, Ohio State UP: 1955), extends the concept. Two recent studies, Maguire, Laurie E., *Shakespearean Suspect Texts: The 'Bad Quartos' and Their Contexts* (Cambridge, Cambridge UP: 1996) and Werstine, Paul, *Early Modern Playhouse Manuscripts and the Editing of Shakespeare* (Cambridge, Cambridge UP: 2012) are critical of the concept—in Maguire's case because she finds little evidence that the "bad quartos" (which concern many plays, not just those by Shakespeare) are "memorial reconstructions," in Werstine's case, because the evidence does not support the notion that one version or another represents a stage version as opposed to an abstract authorial holograph.

as much of the play as he could.[209] Over time this argument gathered adherents. Ultimately a situation evolved in which, based on the difference in lines for different characters, or whether a character was on stage, a studious reader could presume to figure out exactly what role in the play was performed by the hypothetical memorialist.

Of course, other alternatives were offered to explain "bad quartos." For example, it was argued that they simply represented cut-down or edited versions of the plays in question for provincial touring parties. The net effect of the competing explanations was, in any event, to solidify the notion of sole authorship by Shakespeare.

The next development involved the authoritative analyses of "Hand D" in the *Sir Thomas More* manuscript. Recall that the manuscript was discovered in 1841 and was quickly put into print. Beginning in 1871 the argument emerged that one of the six hands—the so-called "Hand D"—was Shakespeare's. The identification rested on the known Shakespeare signatures, but this was empirically difficult since the extant signatures, being crabbed and shaky, differ even among themselves. Thus the ultimate justification for assigning "Hand D" to Shakespeare came down to the formation of a single letter, with supporting evidence drawn from parallelisms and stylistic similarities. The argument, renewed in 1916 and fully expressed in 1923, eventually appealed to paleographic analysis to support the claim that the signatures were in fact adequate to confirm that "Hand D" was William Shakespeare's. At the same time, a stylistic analysis was leveraged to support the conclusion that Shakespeare wrote not only "Hand D" but dictated "Hand C"—thereby extending Shakespeare's credit while also rendering the paleographic analyses irrelevant.

There are obvious problems with this kind of argument. First, the six remaining signatures are such a sparse source of evidence that it seems imprudent to derive any attribution from them at all. But a more important problem is internal; the contextual evidence does not fit the interpretation. Four of the other hands have been identified, or tentatively identified, as belonging to Munday (the main text), Henry Chettle, Thomas Heywood, and Thomas Dekker: in other words, the manuscript was prepared by the same crew that worked up most of

---

[209] We note that the concept of bad quartos essentially inverts the criticism of Pope, who felt that the Folio plays were too long and had been corrupted by the players; the bad quarto thesis is that the quartos are corrupt and too short, because of the faulty memories of the players. We may state this as a general maxim: *the actors are always to blame.*

Philip Henslowe's plays. That leaves the question of how and why Shakespeare would have gotten involved in a Henslowe play completely unexplained.

Over the years, the attribution of "Hand D" to Shakespeare has fallen short of a scholarly consensus, but it is still used as leverage to advance other arguments. Just recently, for example, "Hand D" was invoked to anchor a "milkmaid and bucket" series of assumptions in support of the claim that Shakespeare was a co-author of Thomas Kyd's *Spanish Tragedy*.[210]

Dispensing with the pretense of forensic authority, the only real argument that makes "Hand D" the hand of William Shakespeare is that only William Shakespeare could have said the words that are written down in that hand. But that is an argument from internal evidence.

However, in 1932 further development would hamstring the use of internal evidence. Muriel St Clare Byrne's outline of "maxims" concerning the interpretation of parallelisms is often quoted and bears review:

1. Parallels may be susceptible to at least three explanations: (a) unsuspected identity of authorship, (b) plagiarism, either deliberate or unconscious, (c) coincidence;[211]

2. Quality is all-important, and parallels demand very careful grading [...]

3. Mere accumulation of ungraded parallels does not prove anything;

4. In accumulating parallels for the sake of cumulative effect we may logically proceed from the known to the collaborate, or from the known to the anonymous play, but not from the collaborate to the anonymous;[212]

5. In order to express ourselves as certain of attributions we must prove exhaustively that we cannot parallel words, images, and phrases as a body from other acknowledged plays

---

210 The attribution to Shakespeare of parts of *Spanish Tragedy* now has a bibliographic grounding in *William Shakespeare and Others: Collaborative Plays* (Palgrave MacMillan: 2013). For *Spanish Tragedy*, see 210–211, and consult the essays of Jonathan Bate and Will Sharpe in that volume.

211 Love, *Attributing*, 90–91, to which Love adds, quite rightly, a possible mother source for both parallels.

212 This rule appears somewhat opaque. I take it to mean that one cannot accumulate parallels on the basis of multiple assumptions; in other words, if you have a collaboration you have to assume first that X wrote a part, and then apply the parallels you are attributing to X to an unknown play. In short, I think of it as a safeguard against Milkmaid & Bucket sequences.

of the period; in other words, the negative check must always be applied.

Although the list is often referred to in a positive degree by Shakespeareans—probably because it tends to undercut the arguments of anti-Stratfordians, and of analysts like Fleay and Robertson—one cannot help but think that the maxims spell the end of internal evidence as a meaningful procedure in attributional research.[213]

The first maxim—concerning possible sources—opens the door to endless recursions to lost plays, Ur-plays, or missing manuscripts. This makes the entire internal evidence enterprise dubious, since all one would require is some reference to a hypothetical text that no longer exists. Indeed, if we take the full context seriously, a common source may be nothing more than a witticism delivered over dinner, or in the course of a conversation, that then made its way into oral folklore to be written down by two different hands.

The second through fourth maxims simply muddy the water (albeit with acceptable caution as to the utility of invoking parallels at all), while the fifth maxim—concerning negative tests—represents a hurdle that could probably never be overcome: even in such cases where one had confidently located a *hapax legomenon*, that is, the single usage of a word, the possibility for a prior text would always remain.

A simple example will suffice. We know that the ending of the XCIV (94th) sonnet reads: "Lilies that fester smell far worse than weeds." The very same text in the very same order occurs in the middle of a speech in Act II of *Edward III*. Indeed, that parallelism, among other verbiage, is the reason that Brian Vickers has argued that Shakespeare wrote Act II of *Edward III*. Aside from the fact that the attribution breaks Byrne's rules (going from a presumably known poem to an anonymous and probably collaborative text, and arguing on the basis of a parallelism when we do not know for sure which text came first), the attribution is close in words, and identical in thought, to a passage in Lodge's *Rosalynde* quoted earlier, from which one could then argue that Lodge wrote *Edward III*—and indeed that has been argued. But it does not mean as a positive fact that Lodge wrote *Edward III* or that Shakespearean sonnet. It simply means that this sort of thinking—about lilies and stench and beauty and ugliness combined—was

---

213 This is almost where Schoenbaum ended up. He also extended the rules in *Internal Evidence and Elizabethan Dramatic Authorship*, 191–193.

in the air. As to the actual formulation cited above, how do we know this wasn't a casual witticism directed toward John Lyly by the Earl of Oxford during their quarrel? We do not, and so caution is advised.

Although E.K. Chambers' famous "Disintegration" speech of 1924 antedated Byrne's maxims by eight years, he nevertheless managed to cover much of the same ground—with the substantive points being repeated in his authoritative two-volume biography of Shakespeare which appeared in 1930.[214] Chambers accepted, with some diffidence, the reading of "Hand D" in *Sir Thomas More*. He accepted the notion of "bad quartos" as developed by Pollard. Furthermore, he set aside all of the metrical tests of Fleay and Robertson, stressing instead the common vocabulary of the age and therefore the dubious nature of parallels. Chambers attributed the well-known unevenness of the canon to Shakespeare's fallibility and occasional lapses (although he did not call them "Shakespearean Nods"), and he insisted that Shakespeare was an experimenter, who could write like Marlowe one day and Chapman the next. Chambers also argued that parallel passages were not very useful, in the sense that a writer would be less likely, rather than more likely, to repeat himself.

All of which begs the question: how do we know a text is Shakespeare? We know, according to Chambers, because of the First Folio, because of title pages for quartos, because of Francis Meres, because of contemporary references to the plays, and finally, because of "such internal evidence as the plays themselves bear to the presence of a single 'shaping spirit of imagination.'" It is not hard to see the overwhelming hand of tradition and title-page ascriptions here. But such reasoning, as Erasmus noted, is unreliable. It necessitates a sizable leap of faith. If the purpose of attribution studies for the Elizabethan and Jacobean era is to identify who wrote what, the analysis will be heavily skewed if we must proceed on the assumption that the largest known single collection of such plays was written by one person.

Lastly, some mention must be made of the Clayton Loan. Halliwell-Phillipps referenced a suit Shakespeare brought against a man named Clayton in 1600 for the sum of seven pounds, blandly commenting that

---

[214] The "Disintegration Speech," Chambers, *Gleanings*, 1–21. According to Gililov (222 in the Russian edition, 216 in the translation) Chambers accused Roberson of the "Bolshevist nationalization of Shakespeare," which is a possible formula for a 1924 speech. For historical reasons that are not hard to adduce, however, the expression appears to be absent from the 1944 book, .

financial acumen was not incompatible with literary genius.[215] What Halliwell-Phillipps did not mention is that the loan of seven pounds was made on May 22, 1592, even before Greene's complaint in *Groatsworth*, suggesting in turn that Shakespeare was not only a successful man of the theater by this time, but was sufficiently successful to be lending relatively substantial sums of money.[216] For whatever reason, both Sidney Lee and E. K. Chambers subsequently rejected the applicability of the document to Shakespeare (even though neither had any problem accepting a document concerning a dowry suit discovered in the early 20th century[217]).

E. K. Chambers was the most important Shakespearean of the first half of the 20th century, and perhaps of the entire century. His histories of the medieval and Elizabethan stage (in two and four volumes respectively) and his two-volume biography of Shakespeare stand as treasure troves of citations and data that no student of the era can ignore. Chambers' judgments tend to be conservative, in both good and bad ways; while his assessments are stated modestly and never stray far from the evidence at hand, he cannot see clear of the Shakespearean canon being set in stone. And Chambers' work would cast a long shadow.[218]

But to the extent that Chambers' arguments are based on a leap of faith with regard to the Shakespearean canon, his views, which dominated Shakespearean criticism at least until the 1980s, have a certain hermetic and inviolate quality. Quartos which strayed from the authoritative texts in the First Folio must be "bad quartos," either reconstructed from memory or derived from unauthorized pirated texts prepared for other theaters or for traveling companies. Metrical tests are invalid because everyone spoke the same language in those days, rendering conclusions ambiguous at best. And parallelisms are not valid except in the case of a negative proof, which is an impossible standard both in theory (because it necessarily excludes common speech) and in practice (because it would require all texts). Taking an analytical perspective on any Shakespearean text constitutes "disintegration,"

---

215 Halliwell-Phillipps, *Outlines of the Life of Shakespeare*, 164.

216 Ros Barber, *Shakespeare: The Evidence*, 419 (A-25) has the text of the loan. Nina Green has substantial analysis at her website, oxford-shakespeare.com. Barber's book is an excellent assemblage of documentation on the controversy, however, as an online e-book it remains a work in progress.

217 Brooks takes strong issue with Chambers' ignoring the Clayton loan, *Dyer's Hand*, xii–xv.

218 Later scholars, like S. Schoenbaum, were largely epigones of Chambers' approach (although Schoenbaum carried it to extremes, virtually negating internal evidence as a meaningful category of investigation altogether).

inspired by idolators who could not accept the idea that Shakespeare was Shakespeare—a genius *sui generis* who could write like any of his contemporaries, but who, at the same time, had the supreme genius to write badly (which he was prone to do, partly because he was experimenting, and partly because he was Shakespeare). Meanwhile, the texts of both "Hand D" and "Hand C" just might be Shakespeare, even though such ascription violates all of the other rules laid down.

Thus in the early 20th century was articulated the self-contained universe, or the Black Iron Prison, of Shakespearean orthodoxy.

17 | Oxford and Marlowe

James Looney's Idea ~ The Life of Edward de Vere, the 17th Earl of Oxford ~ Prince Tudor Theory ~ Vedic Expansion ~ Christopher Marlowe (Hotson)

For most of the 20th century orthodox Shakespeare studies proceeded under the dictates established by E.K. Chambers. Until the slow process of self-destruction and dissipation began in the 1980s, most of the interesting work was done by anti-Stratfordians. A signal event was the advancement of the candidacy of Edward de Vere, the 17th Earl of Oxford. But there were other developments, notably the discovery by Leslie Hotson of the actual inquest of Christopher Marlowe in 1925.

The Oxford candidacy began with great solemnity when an English middle school teacher named J. Thomas Looney handed a sealed envelope to the Librarian of the British Museum in November, 1918, just as the Great War was coming to an end. The envelope contained a germinal outline of a thesis that, two years later, would be fully developed in Looney's book, *"Shakespeare" Identified in Edward de Vere the 17th Earl of Oxford.*[219]

In the first part of the book, Looney explains how he came to his theory. As a teacher, he had taught *The Merchant of Venice* for many years, but he could not relate the money troubles of the heroes of that comedy with the successful businessman who had emerged from the studies of Halliwell-Phillipps and others. Looney's suspicion led him first to read the plays with an eye toward constructing, at it were, a criminal profile of the author, comprising eighteen characteristics.

---

[219] Looney, J. Thomas, *"Shakespeare" Identified in Edward de Vere the Seventeenth Earl of Oxford* (NY: Frederick A. Stokes: 1920), v.

Here are the first nine:[220]

1. A mature man of recognized genius
2. Apparently eccentric and mysterious
3. Of intense sensibility—a man apart
4. Unconventional
5. Not adequately appreciated
6. Of pronounced and known literary tastes
7. An enthusiast in the world of drama
8. A lyric poet of recognized genius
9. Of superior education—classical—the habitual associate of educated people

Then, Looney set out a secondary set of nine characteristics:

1. A man with feudal connections
2. One of the higher aristocracy
3. Connected with Lancastrian supporters
4. An enthusiast for Italy
5. A follower of sport including falconry
6. Loose and improvident in money matters
7. A lover of music
8. Doubtful and somewhat conflicted in his attitude toward women
9. Of probable Catholic leanings but touched with skepticism

While Looney expands on his enumerated characteristics, he does not actually prove the adequacy of any of them, which makes the list look arbitrary on closer examination. Most of the first nine, in fact, simply flow deductively out of the premise that the author of the plays was a genius, with all the commonsensical conclusions that would follow perforce: that he would keep to himself, that he would be unappreciated, that he would be misunderstood, that he would be different, and so on.

---

220 Looney, *"Shakespeare" Identified*, 92, 103.

The second set of characteristics is also somewhat arbitrary. It is certainly true that the political sympathies in the historical plays align with the nobility, and not with the commoners. It is also true that commoners are often portrayed as simpletons, while the nobility are portrayed as deep and purpose-driven characters. But of course one does not have to be a member of the nobility to portray characters in this light: all one needs is to have a good sense of what one's audience wants to hear—and certainly many of the authors we have seen moved in noble circles. By the same token, "Lancastrian supporters" would simply mean someone who supported the current House of Tudor. It would be hard to imagine a playwright under Elizabeth who would dare to present himself as anything else.

Some of Looney's characteristics do make sense. This leads us back into the discussion of the special knowledge of a "nurtured" Shakespeare who cultivated expertise in law, noble lineage, music, medicine, tennis, falconry, plant lore, military matters, seamanship, and so on. Based on the number of references in the plays, some of these topics do warrant explanation. Others are so rare as to be meaningless. For example, a quick search yields only four references to falconry in the plays, and two of them are in *The Merchant of Venice*. This hardly qualifies Shakespeare as an expert on the subject.

At any rate, equipped with his list, Looney consulted poetry collections, and found a poem similar to one of Shakespeare's early efforts. It was written by Edward de Vere. He then consulted the *Dictionary of National Biography* and read the entry there. Being tentatively convinced, he began looking for connections between the life of Edward de Vere and the plays.

There is no question that Edward de Vere led a very interesting life. He was a brilliant and intellectually curious man, and he had a wide range of education and experience.[221] Born in 1550, he became, at age 12, the presumptive 17th Earl of Oxford, securing his position in an ancient line going back to the Norman Conquest. After his father's death, de Vere became a ward of William Cecil, Lord Burghley, a close adviser to the Queen. He was tutored by Arthur Golding, his uncle, who had translated Ovid's *Metamorphoses*, a key Shakespearean source. In 1564 and 1566, he received honorary MA's from Cambridge and Oxford. The following year he attended Gray's Inn to study law. In 1571, he

---

221 Adulatory biographies include Looney, the Ogburns, Charlton Ogburn, Mark Anderson, and presumably Ward (not consulted). A critical biography is Nelson's *Monstrous Adversary*.

married Cecil's 14-year-old daughter, Anne. In 1575, after an aborted trip the previous year, de Vere traveled to the continent and visited northern Italy. During his trip abroad, he became estranged from his pregnant wife. Returning home in 1576, he reconciled with her.

From 1576 until 1587, Oxford is actively involved in London literary affairs, and the production of plays. At this time he also maintains a large estate in London called Fisher's Folly, which we might imagine as a gathering place for his circle. In 1576, Oxford publishes some of his early poems—the only poems that we can directly attribute to him. In 1579, he has an argument with Philip Sidney at a tennis court. From 1580 onwards, Oxford is affiliated with many of the writers we have already discussed: Anthony Munday is his servant, John Lyly his private secretary, and by inference, Robert Greene and Thomas Nashe both receive some patronage from him. Numerous books are dedicated to him and his patronage is inferred. It is during this time that Oxford is offended by the supposed caricature of him by Gabriel Harvey.

Like King Lear, Oxford had three daughters. One of them was a proposed match for Henry Wriothesley, the Earl of Southampton, who was the dedicatee of Shakespeare's first published work. However, that daughter, Elizabeth, later went on to marry William Stanley, the Earl of Derby (and another authorship candidate). The last daughter, Susan, would marry one of Mary Sidney's sons, Philip Herbert—the Earl of Montgomery and one of the "incomparable pair" dedicatees of the First Folio. In addition to these connections, Oxford also was a favorite of Queen Elizabeth's until he took up with one of Elizabeth's ladies-in-waiting, for which he was briefly confined in the Tower, and subsequently banished from court. But even this offense did not suspend the thousand-pound annuity which Oxford received from the Crown for the rest of his life.

From a purely contextual point of view, it is clear that Oxford is a perfect candidate for the authorship of the Shakespeare plays. He knew everyone, he was highly educated, and he was trained in law. He was also involved in the theater for many years. However, we do not have any documentary or literary evidence to support his candidacy. Oxford's poetry comes from the late 1560s and early 1570s and bears little relationship to any of the writing in the Shakespeare canon. There are few other literary remains; such that exist consist chiefly of letters in which Oxford requests various favors, payments, and so on. No literary spirit shines forth from these, and the diction in many of the letters almost suggests that they were written by someone who was translating from a foreign tongue into English—not all that surprising for someone like Oxford, who was a master of multiple languages; but they do not resemble the language of Shakespeare.

The usual response from Oxfordians is that de Vere wrote the plays, but kept his identity secret, because it would have been considered *infra dig* for a nobleman to publish under his own name. Bearing in mind that Philip Sidney died without publishing, the argument makes some sense. But Sidney's manuscripts circulated privately for many years and there was never any doubt who wrote them. In addition, his sister Mary Sidney did publish, and did not appear to suffer any loss of standing as a result. The arguments for anonymity are therefore weak.

One way that Looney attempts to work around this is by arguing that Oxford used the writers at his disposal as fronts for his own creativity. For example, Looney argues that Lyly's style while working for Oxford was at a higher level than it was later, from which he inferred that Lyly's style from this period betrayed the working of Oxford's hand. It goes without saying that a patron of the arts will use the artist as a vehicle for his own aesthetic inclinations, but the nature of such influence is impossible to gauge—especially in a case like this where we have hardly any literary remains from Oxford except for the same small group of poems. Looney's hypothetical attributions to Oxford of some of Lyly's comedies also lead to Vedic expansions: thus later Oxfordians attribute to de Vere larger and larger chunks of Elizabethan literature.[222]

Another way in which Looney, and later Oxfordians, sought to prove his case was by associating Oxford's life with the plays. For example, in *All's Well that Ends Well* a reconciliation between a couple is achieved by means of the "bed trick," where a man is tricked into sleeping with a woman who turns out to be someone other than he intended, love is re-kindled, and everyone lives happily ever after. Everyone realizes that this is an archetypal story. It comes up in Boccacio, and, indeed, in the Bible as well; thus, simply because someone told the same story about Oxford, and the trope is part of the plot of a Shakespeare play, it does not follow that Oxford wrote this play, much less all of Shakespeare.[223]

Remember that stories of this kind were constantly being told about prominent individuals. While such stories might contain a kernel of

---

[222] Looney, *"Shakespeare" Identified*, 268–273. The argument concerning Lyly gives a good sense of Looney's style.

[223] The story is in *The Decameron*, as well as Genesis 29; even *Groatsworth* has a version of the story.

truth about a personality or about events, they were clearly just good, albeit ancient, yarns waiting for an opportunity to be retold (compare the story about George Peele and the sheep, recounted earlier, which turns out to be derived from the *Panchatantra*). In this respect Oxford's supporters can easily be accused of being naïve. We know that Oxford was banished from court because of his affair with Anne Vavasour, but there is a fanciful narrative of this as well. According to this account—which was, by the way, the only story about Oxford that John Aubrey bothered to write down—Oxford performed a curtsy for Elizabeth, broke wind, and fled from court in embarrassment. Upon his return, some years later, Elizabeth greeted Oxford by saying, "I had quite forgot the fart." This is the kind of story that Oxford's opponents liked to tell, but it is not only factually false; it can easily be derived from a vignette in the *Arabian Nights*.[224]

Since there is no direct documentary evidence connecting Oxford to the plays, and since the evidence in the plays is sketchy at best, the core argument for the Oxfordians ultimately rests on the contention that de Vere makes a better Shakespeare than Shakespeare. That much is true: Oxford has all the qualifications in education, learning, and leisure that Shakespeare lacks. But there were dozens of individuals who had such qualifications. Furthermore, both the Oxford and Shakespeare arguments hinge on the unitarian presumption of single authorship. That presumption itself has scant evidence in its favor.

There is a further permutation of the Oxford theory that deserves mention. This is known as the Prince Tudor variant.[225] According to this scenario, Oxford was driven not only by a desire to avoid political repercussions, or by a desire to avoid the stigma of print, but also by an overriding imperative to conceal scandal. The theory is based on the idea that Oxford was the illegitimate son of Elizabeth herself. It goes that they then met later and began an incestuous relationship, unbeknownst to either party; that union produced a child, who was taken away and raised—again unbeknownst to both parties—as the Earl of Southampton, who then in turn engaged in incestuous relations with both of his parents.[226]

---

[224] "How Abu Hasan Brake Wind" is in volume five of Richard Burton's translation, gutenberg.org.

[225] Rubinstein covers the Prince Tudor theory in *Who Wrote Shakespeare's Plays?* (Kindle). Rubinstein's book, along with Ros Barber's book, are both good, recent summaries of the authorship controversy, with a very clear, numbered, and point/counterpoint presentation.

[226] This was the theory underpinning Roland Emmerich's *Anonymous* (2011), although given the antics described the film might have been better titled *The Aristocrats*.

Looney's argument on behalf of Edward de Vere gained numerous converts. Probably as a direct result of his book, Henry Clay Folger obtained a Bible that had once belonged to Oxford in the 1920s (we will hear more about that Bible shortly). Sigmund Freud, who had long harbored doubts about the orthodox attribution, was won over to Oxford's candidacy, as were several other luminaries, including Orson Welles. As always happens when a new candidate is proposed, a minute examination of the record followed, culminating in the first full-length biography of Oxford in 1928. In 1952, Charlton and Dorothy Ogburn published a 1,200-page tome, *This Star of England*, attributing not only Shakespeare but much else to Oxford. Their work would be carried on relentlessly by their son, Charlton, Jr., in the later 20th century.

If Oxford was a better Shakespeare than Shakespeare, at least in theory, he was also a better candidate than Francis Bacon. The ascendancy of Bacon lasted sixty years, and involved every conceivable attempt at acquiring evidence, including séances.[227] But since Looney's book appeared almost a hundred years ago, Bacon and all other candidates have had to cede pride of place to Oxford. And yet, for all the circumstantial and contextual evidence, the absence of direct evidence suffices to hold back any positive attribution of the Shakespeare plays to Oxford. This doesn't mean that Shakespeare wrote them, or that Oxford did not: it means that in history one needs documents.

In the early 1920s, an American scholar named Leslie Hotson discovered some documents that helped clarify one of the greatest mysteries of Elizabethan times: the death of Christopher Marlowe.

Hotson had been working in the Public Records Office when he came across a reference to "Ingram Frizer." Since those two names had separately been associated with Marlowe's killer, he consulted the relevant roll, and found in Latin the text of Frizer's pardon. Following the trail, he then found not only the application for pardon, but the actual text of the inquest itself. This was an astonishing find. It was immediately published in 1925 to great acclaim.[228]

According to the testimony of the inquest, Marlowe had spent May 30, 1593, at a tavern with three other men, all of them in the employ

---

227 Schoenbaum, *Shakespeare's Lives*, new edition, 439–440. Under this heading we can also include the divinatory aspects of code decipherment, which Michell I believe properly connects to spiritualism (*Who Wrote Shakespeare?*, 152) as well as a detailed analysis of the cipher system of Elizabeth Gallup which particularly represents these tendencies, found in Friedman & Friedman, *Ciphers*. Shapiro also explores the telepathic aspect in his discussion of Percy Allen, *Contested*, 197–200.

228 Hotson, *The Death of Christopher Marlowe*.

of Sir Francis Walsingham, Elizabeth's chief spy. In the evening, while Marlowe was stretched out on a bed, and the other three were seated at a table to the side, an argument erupted about paying the bill (or "*le recknynge*"). In the course of the argument, Marlowe grabbed a dagger from Frizer's belt, and began hitting him in the head with the pommel of the weapon. Frizer, who had his back to Marlowe, swung back violently, driving the blade of the dagger two inches into Marlowe's right eye, causing his instantaneous death.[229] Frizer was therefore pardoned for killing Marlowe in self-defense.

Of course this does not end the matter. As Marlovians are quick to point out, John Penry, the Welsh protestant (and possible author of the *Martin Marprelate* tracts), had been hanged on short notice the day before, so a body substitution could have been arranged.[230] The attendance at Marlowe's death of three spies is also cause for some speculation; the testimony could have been at least self-serving, and at minimum Marlowe's death was convenient, given Marlowe's troubles. But these are all causes for speculation, not proof; it is quite possible that Marlowe's death was something other than self-defense. But to further argue that he was not killed is to again enter a speculative realm where there is no supporting evidence. We are left with the documents, and the documents provide a credible background to the claim that Christopher Marlowe was killed on May 30th, 1593, by Ingram Frizer in a fight over a bill.

---

[229] The inquest states that death was instantaneous. Others later claimed he lived and "blasphemed to the end" (Honan, 352–254, with extensive medical detail). His last words are the subject of some speculation, perhaps "Holla, ye tempered blades of Frizier!"

[230] It is commonly argued today that Marlowe was murdered (e.g., Riggs, Nicholl), and the circumstances of the death are still considered suspicious. Pinksen notes Penry's death nearby the day before, but does not explicitly argue for substitution, 32, 42.

18 | MODERN REINVENTIONS

Context of Discovery, Context of Justification ~ Kuhn's Paradigm Shift ~ Gary Taylor ~ "Shall I Die" ~ Donald Foster ~ "Funeral Elegy" ~ Brian Vickers

In the 1980s, orthodox Shakespearean scholarship began to change. First, there were two highly debatable attributions, which were, however, solidly grounded within traditional attribution parameters. Second, there was a general diffusion of the canon, as collaboration for some of the plays was again seriously considered (for the first time since Robertson's day). In addition, Shakespeare's involvement in plays which were hitherto anonymous or assigned to other authors was also argued. Finally, the methods of analysis became more sophisticated with the advent of computers and larger text databases.

We will discuss the sophistication of modern computer analysis first. This will require that we first dust off an old concept from the history of science: the context of discovery versus the context of justification.[231] The context of discovery is intuitively understood as the manner in which a scientist discovers something, whereas the method by which the discovery is proved is the context of justification. This dichotomy, which was first articulated in the late 1930s, can be very helpful in distinguishing the contingent nature of many scientific discoveries from the more rigorous proofs that must ensue afterward. Many examples come to mind: Archimedes discovering the principle of water displacement, Kekule discovering the benzene ring in a daydream, or Fleming discovering penicillin by accident.

---

231 The origin of the distinction goes back to the German analytical philosopher Hans Reichenbach, whose work sought to reconcile Kantian epistemology with Relativity; in his *Experience and Prediction*, "The objective relation from the given entities to the solution, and the subjective way of finding it, are clearly separated for problems of a deductive character; we must learn to make the same distinction for the problem of the inductive relation from facts to theories." plato.stanford.edu/entries/reichenbach/

Perhaps a better way of expressing the distinction is to focus on the accidental, contextual, and sequential nature of most discoveries, as opposed to the rational demonstration of such discoveries when they are presented to the public.

However, there are three problems with the discovery-justification context, just as expressed. The first is that, when the context of discovery-justification is normally brought into a discussion, it is often by way of biographical reductionism. Thus the context of discovery leads to the question, "Why was he asking that question?" while the context of justification becomes, "Why did he believe that to be true?"[232] The result is invariably a kind of *ad hominem* in which the value of a discovery is obscured by questioning the context in which the inquiry was initially mounted and resolved. A classic example with regard to the authorship controversy would be to question Delia Bacon's attempt to present a unified, rational Shakespeare by reference to her sad and troubled personal life.

A second problem with the contexts of discovery and justification is that, in fact, the context of justification is just as bound by circumstance as the discovery. In other words, if a discovery entails a series of descriptive events, then a justification is merely a logical summary of the discovery; it is not some kind of super-contextual confirmation.[233] To illustrate: Archimedes proved that the crown contained base metal by comparing its runoff to an equal amount of pure gold; yet no one would use that method of proof today. In the same way, if Joseph C. Hart questioned Shakespeare's authorship on the basis of Henslowe's Diary and Collier's fabrications (context of discovery), that does not impeach the rationality of Hart's conclusions (context of justification), even though we now know about Collier's forgeries.

A third problem is that the context of justification, when seen as some kind of super-contextual proof, cannot stand, precisely because the standards of justification change over time. This is why Thomas Kuhn referenced the distinction in his seminal text, *The Structure of Scientific Revolutions* (1962): the accumulation of knowledge over time

---

232 Gould, Stephen Jay, "Not in Our Genes: Biology, Ideology, and Human Nature," *New York Review of Books*, August 16, 1984

233 Monica Aufrecht has written convincingly on this aspect. I have introduced this perhaps arcane topic for several reasons: first, because of its typical use for reductive analysis; second, because Shapiro was specific in *Contested* that his aim was to explain why Shakespeare skeptics held their views (8–11), with the implication that the the justification contexts were contextual and not rational; third, because the sophistication of justification contexts has not been matched by any change in fundamental assumptions; fourth, to show that the discovery context does not subvert the justification context; and finally, because the discovery context can, depending on the information discovered, change the justification context, compare the Kuhn reference in the following note.

can change the fundamental assumptions of a particular field of study, but if that happens, the standards of proof must also change, simply because you are no longer trying to prove the presence of phlogiston, but rather, oxygen.[234] Think back to John Aubrey standing among the stones at Avebury. It is not as though no one had ever noticed them before; the "knowledge," as it were, stood ten feet tall. What was required was a model for discerning the pattern, and the source of these stones in human activity. That is what Aubrey provided, and it is that which enabled the development of a new way of inspecting, and preserving, Britain's pre-Roman past.

The way this distinction applies to Shakespeare studies is that there has been a long accumulation of evidence that, under a different set of assumptions, would probably lead to a different perception of what the Folio plays actually represent. But all techniques of proof or relatedness are based on the inherited assumption that Shakespeare was the sole author of the plays, even as the various stylometric tests have become vastly more sophisticated.

For hundreds of years Shakespearean scholars have attempted to assign texts on the basis of wide comparative readings, textual parallels, syllable counts, evolving metrics, and virtually every conceivable lexical test. Only in recent decades, however, could such tests be carried out—very rapidly and with great precision—against an ever-expanding database of Elizabethan-era texts. Prior to this technological development, one might simply aver that *Macbeth* "sounded like" Chapman or Middleton, and then quote parallel texts, and this would be considered sufficient to many. Today, one can reliably demonstrate that a figure of speech in *Macbeth* only occurs three times in the entire Elizabethan era (at least in terms of surviving printed texts). The standards of empirical proof have therefore greatly increased. But have the proofs become any more authoritative?

One way to test this is by reference to two texts that emerged in the 1980s and that were quickly, but not universally, attributed to Shakespeare.

The first of these was discovered by Gary Taylor, an American academic at Oxford. In November 1985 Taylor found a 90-line poem ("Shall I Die?") that was assigned in the manuscript to "William Shakespeare." Taylor took a couple of weeks to test the text against the

---

234 Thomas Kuhn, *The Structure of Scientific Revolutions* (Kindle). The last two paragraphs of Chapter I. I conclude therefore that Kuhn recognized how the discovery context can precipitate a change in the justification context.

Shakespeare canon, and conclude that it was a solid attribution. He then announced his discovery to the world.[235]

The second case involved Donald Foster, an American professor, who discovered a long poem entitled *A Funerall Elegye in memory of the late Vertuous Maister William Peeter*, with a reference to "W. S." While Taylor had been content to use standard lexical and metrical tests, Foster also used computer analysis, and came to the conclusion that the "Funeral Elegy" of 1612 was in fact a poem by William Shakespeare.[236]

Both attributions had problems, and neither received universal assent. Taylor's conclusion was hasty, and Foster failed to mobilize a consensus behind his verdict before going to print. A more serious problem, however, was that neither of the poems was very good. Just the same, it is not as though Taylor or Foster broke the rules; for four centuries, Shakespearean attribution had depended on title page attribution, and they could hardly be faulted for following that logic.

The dispute over Foster's attribution went on for over a decade, until in 2002 a French scholar named Gilles Monsarrat published a paper arguing that the author of the "Funeral Elegy" was John Ford. By this time, Foster had largely abandoned Shakespearean attribution studies for more sensational adventures in forensic linguistics, though he was gracious in acknowledging Monsarratt's contribution.[237]

The most detailed analysis using computer methodology was initiated in the early 1990s by Ward Elliott and Robert Valenza, in a rather clearcut attempt to dispute the Oxford candidacy. Their articles involved using text blocks from the Shakespearean canon—selected under the advice of Donald Foster—and then, after preliminary tests to ensure that the body of the selected canon more or less coheres, running the plays of other authors against it in order to test the rejection rate.

Oxford comes out poorly in the analysis, and so do all the other playwrights. Elliott and Valenza's technique has been subjected to criticism from all sides. This is not surprising since, while they put Oxford at a firm disadvantage for authorship, they also question the "Hand D" attribution for *Sir Thomas More*. The fact that their

---

235 Vickers, '*Counterfeiting*,' provides an extensive narrative on this.

236 Again, Vickers, '*Counterfeiting*,' provides extensive narrative. Consult Foster, *Elegy by WS*, for his version of events.

237 It is worth noting that Monsarrat was studying Ford's writings at the time of the connection; this is relevant to the context of discovery, but it is not relevant if the following justification is accepted as valid. Meanwhile, Vickers, '*Counterfeiting*,' provides a further narrative of Foster's career, including his attempted identification of the author of the JonBenét Ramsey ransom note, with an unfortunate outcome (456–462); and see Foster's own autobiography, *Author Unknown*, which includes a gracious acknowledgment of Monsarrat's work.

preliminary body of plays excludes several plays has also been a point of contention.

There are other problems with their analysis. One, immediately raised by the Oxfordians, is that the comparison of the Shakespearean canon to the slight body of Oxfordian poems fails to account for the assumption of authorial growth which underlies Oxfordian analysis. A further problem is that the body of texts for each author is simply too small to test against such a large database. Another problem is that the tests are too indiscriminate: Samuel Daniel, for example, is represented only by his *Cleopatra*, whereas a better test would be to run his *Civil Wars* against *Richard II*. This leads to yet another problem, the exclusion of non-dramatic poetry as well as prose (especially since Elizabethan prose often mimics pentameter). But the most basic problem is that the technique simply involves using the same well-known metrical tests that have been used for centuries against what is substantially the same assumed body of plays as always. The only real difference is that the method of demonstration, or proof, involves the use of computers and results are stated in numerical form. The assumption of the unitary authorship of the canon remains unchanged.[238]

Following the publication of the Monsarrat paper, a noted British academic named Brian Vickers[239] entered the fray with *'Counterfeiting' Shakespeare* (2002). Vickers' book issued a long and detailed assault on the Taylor and Foster attributions, using his own analysis and stylistic tests and incorporating the findings of Monsarrat. Rehearsing many of the strictures for attribution from Byrne, he found decisive fault with both attributions. But Vickers did not stop there. Using a large database, he then wrote *Shakespeare, Co-Author* (2004), supporting the long-held collaborative arguments concerning *Titus Andronicus*, *Pericles*, *Henry VIII*, *Two Noble Kinsmen*, and *Timon of Athens*.

Meanwhile, Gary Taylor embarked on a project to collect and assign the plays of Thomas Middleton into a kind of folio form. His final collection included *Timon of Athens*, *Macbeth*, and *Measure for Measure* as collaborations between Shakespeare and Middleton—as well as three plays from the Shakespeare apocrypha: *The Yorkshire Tragedy*,

---

238 One of the problems that would be involved in this approach is that eventually stylometric tests could be used to absorb an ever larger body of Elizabethan and Jacobean literature under the Shakespearean rubric. This has already begun: see Ilsemann, *William Shakespeare Dramen und Apokryphen*, who, on the basis of a new stylometric technique (rolling delta), has assigned a number of apocryphal Shakespeare plays to Shakespeare.

239 Vickers has taught in Switzerland for many years, and he has edited and written widely on the English Renaissance (with noteworthy attention to Bacon and Shakespeare).

The Puritan, and *The Second Maiden's Tragedy*.

Following the advent of forensic textual analysis, we may observe two recent trends that seem to be moving in opposite directions. While one trend has been expanding the circle of collaboration, another has been expanding the reach of Shakespeare's pen. Indeed, it appears that "Virtue Gluttony" or "Vedic Expansion," hitherto largely the sole province of anti-Stratfordians, has finally caught up to orthodox Shakespearean scholarship.

In 2008, Vickers was quoted in an article claiming that anti-plagiarism software made it possible to attribute part of the apocryphal play *Edward III* to Shakespeare. More recently, Shakespeare's hand has been discovered in the anonymous and apocryphal *Arden of Faversham*, and even in Kyd's *Spanish Tragedy* (though some of this is based on questionable extensions of the idea that Shakespeare wrote "Hand D" in *Sir Thomas More*). Soon we may see a situation in which all the good bits in Elizabethan drama will be attributed to Shakespeare. Perhaps some hundreds of years hence someone will dig up a copy of *Palgrave's Golden Treasury* and decide that Palgrave was the greatest poet in the English language, to be followed by someone else who will endeavor to trace Palgrave's biography, beginning with Mother Goose and ending with Philip Larkin's *Aubade*.[240]

For four hundred years, title pages were the gold standard in Shakespeare attributions. Beginning in the 1980s, this general rule has been discarded, mainly because of some uncomfortable attributions. Instead, previously questionable attributions, such as the "Hand D" of *Sir Thomas More*, have been used to relate the "internal evidence" of other plays to the Shakespeare corpus, even though the body of that corpus has been compromised by arguments for collaboration with other playwrights. On the one hand, arguments for collaboration have multiplied, both within the First Folio and outside of it. At the same time, the trace of Shakespeare's quill is now being found everywhere. The net effect has been a diffusion of Shakespeare's hand throughout the body of Elizabethan drama, even though we still do not have a reliable exemplar of his handwriting, and even though the entire project assumes Shakespearean authorship of most if not all of the First Folio, almost entirely on the basis of title page attributions.

---

[240] As a matter of fact, Palgrave begins with a lyric by Thomas Nashe.

19 | THE OXFORD REACTION

The Growth of Oxfordianism ~ Accusations of "Hate Virtue" ~ "Monstrous Adversary" or "Roaring Homo" ~ Shakespeare "Denialism" ~ Oxford's Bible (Strittmatter, Anderson) ~ Sackville, North, and other recent nominations

Concurrent with the simultaneous fragmentation and diffusion of the Shakespearean canon, the last few decades have seen steady growth among the unitarian revisionists—particularly the Oxfordians. This in turn has led to unprecedented, and at times acrimonious, scholarly engagement with anti-Stratfordian arguments.

After several decades of lying fallow, the renewal of the Oxfordian case owes largely to the work of Charlton Ogburn (1911–1998), an American author who began to represent Edward de Vere's candidacy in the mid-1970s. His main work, *The Mysterious William Shakespeare* (1984) led to television appearances, mock courts, and numerous articles in popular magazines. His example also encouraged many others to join the Oxford cause, or at any rate to publicly reject Shakespearean orthodoxy. For example, the American political columnist Joseph Sobran entered the fray in 1997 with *Alias Shakespeare*. Sobran was convinced that the bisexual de Vere was the only man who could have written the sonnets.

As Ogburn aged, his stature as the reigning Oxfordian was largely ceded to Roger Strittmatter and Mark Anderson. Strittmatter went back and analyzed the very same Oxford Bible that the Folger Library had obtained, and on the basis of his analysis received his PhD in literature; this was the first time a doctorate had been awarded in the field of authorship studies.[241] Around the same time, Mark Anderson, an American journalist, published *"Shakespeare" by Another Name*, buttressing the Oxford case with a detailed biography of the Earl including numerous tie-ins to the plays and poems.

There have been many others. Although not an explicit Oxfordian, Diana Price did important work in sifting through the historical record to establish a baseline for literary remains that applies to all of Shakespeare's contemporaries (but not to Shakespeare himself, since he left no literary remains). Meanwhile, Nina Green, whose approach to Oxford may be characterized as Vedic in the extreme, has nevertheless done very important work by laboriously transcribing the occasional writings of Robert Greene and Thomas Nashe, thus facilitating all future research.

The reaction of the orthodox Shakespeareans has at times been harsh. In previous decades, at least since mid-century, the opposition to anti-Stratfordians was generally urbane and non-confrontational, mainly because everyone realized—or should have realized—that engagement in the controversy was itself an indication of one's abiding involvement with Elizabethan literature. An example of this milder approach may be noted in Frank Wadsworth's *The Poacher from Stratford* (1961), which concluded:

> That is does matter [who wrote the plays], on purely emotional grounds, to a great many people who love the Shakespearean works, I do know. We believe these things, because, in the opinion of those best qualified to judge, the historical evidence says that they happened. [242]

The tone was matched in Harold Love's *Attributing Authorship* as recently as 2002. While speaking approvingly of the "outrage" directed toward John Michell for his notion of collective authorship in *Who Wrote Shakespeare* (1997), his summation was surprisingly similar to Wadsworth:

> This picture of the plays as Frankenstein's monsters put together from differently authored parts denies the possibility of a Shakespearean voice, and

---

241 Strittmatter's website includes the text of his dissertation: http://www.shake-speares-bible.com/dissertation/

242 Frank W. Wadsworth, *The Poacher from Stratford*, 163–164.

in so doing robs the plays of what is, for most of us, their main interest.[243]

Such displays of defensiveness (or hurt feelings) have even carried over to analysts. Thus when Gary Taylor explained to Ron Rosenbaum why he was attaching half a dozen plays to Thomas Middleton, rather than Shakespeare, he was compelled to assure Rosenbaum, "I don't hate Shakespeare"—as though any attempt to understand how and when the plays were created would be preemptively received as an unforgivable affront to the man from Stratford.[244]

Other reactions have been much less subdued. In recent years it has become commonplace for guardians of orthodoxy to compare anti-Stratfordians to "deniers" of various sorts. This tactic underscores not only the intellectual vapidity of the critics who deploy it, but also their willingness to pander. Thus Stephen Greenblatt wrote in 2005 to the *New York Times*:

> The idea that William Shakespeare's authorship of his plays and poems is a matter of conjecture and the idea that the "authorship controversy" be taught in the classroom are the exact equivalent of current arguments that "intelligent design" be taught alongside evolution.
>
> In both cases an overwhelming scholarly consensus, based on a serious assessment of hard evidence, is challenged by passionately held fantasies whose adherents demand equal time.
>
> The demand seems harmless enough until one reflects on its implications. Should claims that the Holocaust did not occur also be made part of the standard curriculum?[245]

While a recent book defending Shakespearean authorship made casual reference to "Shakespeare Denialists,"[246] it was left to Scott McCrae in his *The End of the Authorship Question* to put a tongue in every wound of Caesar with the following florid passage:

> What happens when the intelligentsia embrace a conspiracy theory? Doesn't a kind of thinking become legitimized? Reasoning like that

---

243 Harold Love, *Attributing*, 26. Outrage is the last thing that Michell's graceful and conciliatory volume could be said to evoke. The idea that the absence of a single voice "robs the plays" of "their main interest" might uncharitably be characterized as letting the cat out of the bag; at minimum, it helps explain the tenacity of unitarian theories.

244 Rosenbaum, *Shakespeare Wars*, 46, 52. At the time of Rosenbaum's book, Taylor included *Troilus* in the MIddleton group, but it was not included in the "Middleton Folio."

245 *New York Times*, September 4, 2005.

246 *Authorship Contested*, Robillard, Amy E., Fortune, Ron, eds., (Routledge, London: 2015); in the offering ,"'I Feel Like This Is Fake': Spontaneous Mediocrity and Studied Genius" by Val Perry Rendel.

of the Authorship theorists has led juries to believe in police conspiracies and thus to dismiss valid evidence and acquit murderers. Similar reasoning has led many Americans to believe that a government coverup prevents anyone from learning the truth about UFOs or the assassination of John F. Kennedy; their distrust has fueled the militia movement and made the 1995 Oklahoma City bombing seem almost inevitable. Today, Holocaust denial is ridiculous, but what about three hundred years from now, when the survivors are all dead and the original films of them are carefully preserved in vaults, the province only of scholars, as is the case with Shakespeare today? Will easily doctored computer images be trusted? Will the century's greatest atrocity be widely considered a hoax? I don't mean to be alarmist. Conspiracy thinking has been around a long time. In medieval France, lonely old women with pet cats and skin blemishes were routinely burned as witches. Assume a conspiracy and anything—or anyone—can be called into question. With the advent of the Internet, imaginary conspiracies can spread as never before, threatening our perception of the world in which we live. But we needn't resign ourselves to living with paranoia. We can start by disbelieving ideas—like the Authorship Question—that rest upon, are based on and require acceptance of unproven conspiracies.[247]

Such accusations may be considered false equivalences,[248] but I think it would be better to say that accusations of denial and denialism are simply imprecations hurled at anyone who disagrees with the reigning consensus about anything. The fact that "denial" and "denialist" have now been extended to a number of other topics—including climate change, vaccination research, and stem cell harvesting—seems to indicate little more than a poverty of thought as well as a poverty of tolerance. Mark Twain understood where this could lead: After noting the vociferous criticism that Shakespeareans directed toward their enemies, he wrote:

> This law [of irreverence], reduced to its simplest terms, is this: 1. Whatever is sacred to the Christian must be held in reverence by everybody else; 2, whatever is sacred to the Hindu must be held in reverence by everybody else; 3, therefore, by consequence, logically, and indisputably, whatever is sacred to *me* must be held in reverence by everybody else.

---

247 McCrae, *The Case for Shakespeare: The End of the Authorship Question*, 222.

248 Barber, *Shakespeare Examined*, 44.

> Now then, what aggravates me is, that these troglodytes and muscovites and bandoleers and buccaneers are *also* trying to crowd in and share the benefit of the law, and compel everybody to revere their Shakespeare and hold him sacred. We can't have that: there's enough of us already. If you go on widening and spreading and inflating the privilege, it will presently come to be conceded that each man's sacred things are the *only* ones, and the rest of the human race will have to be humbly reverent toward them or suffer for it. That can surely happen, and when it happens, the word Irreverence will be regarded as the most meaningless, and foolish, and self-conceited, and insolent, and impudent and dictatorial word in the language. And people will say, "Whose business is it, what gods I worship and what things hold sacred? Who has the right to dictate to my conscience, and where did he get that right?"[249]

The Oxfordian reaction has also featured a full-length biography of Edward de Vere by Alan Nelson of the University of California at Berkeley. Nelson's book is entitled *Monstrous Adversary* (2003), and it spends 500 pages attempting to hang that sign around de Vere's neck. (Nelson's hatchet job is at least more genteel than the imputation offered by A.L. Rowse, who, in the famous PBS special of 1992, proclaimed de Vere to be a "roaring homo"—an epithet he applied seconds later to both Christopher Marlowe and Francis Bacon.[250])

Despite Nelson's often petty tone, there are some merits to his work. For example, he compiled a large number of de Vere's letters and has gone to the trouble of making them available on the Internet. He also has kind things to say about some of de Vere's extant poetry (although, as we know, this comprises only a couple dozen items, mostly written in his early adulthood). On the other hand, Nelson's palpable animosity toward the Earl emboldens him to denigrate other writers of the age, apparently for no other reason than because they were patronized by de Vere. On one page he calls John Lyly, Robert Greene, George Peele, and Anthony Munday "second or third rank" authors;[251] on an-

---

249 Twain, *Is Shakespeare Dead?*, 135-137.

250 PBS, *Frontline*, April 18, 1989, at 38:03. Rowse also indicates a bit further on that Shakespeare was "abnormally heterosexual," the reaction shot at 38:45 is priceless. Available on YouTube as "Frontline: Shakespeare Authorship Controversy." It is a fascinating and amusing program; Shakespeare is represented by Schoenbaum and A. L. Rowse, and Oxford is represented by Charlton Ogburn and Enoch Powell. Rowse was himself gay and moreover an antinatalist *avant la lettre*; as he wrote in his journals, "I don't like other people; I particularly don't like their children; I deeply disapprove of their proliferation making the globe uninhabitable. The fucking idiots—I don't want to pay for their fucking." http://www.theguardian.com/books/2003/apr/13/biography.features1

251 Nelson, *Monstrous*, 287.

other page he soft-pedals the condemnation of Lyly but reinforces it for the others.[252] Nor does he miss any opportunity to impute guilt by association: Munday's involvement in the drawing and quartering of Campion works to his eternal disfavor, but Nelson brings up the episode merely to smear de Vere.[253] Even if this style of argument were persuasive, Nelson's conveniently selective approach betrays a more vindictive agenda. He neglects to rope in Thomas Nashe, for example, despite compelling evidence that Nashe was among the writers working under the Earl's patronage.[254] The omission is telling since Nashe's literary stature is not so easily dismissed (indeed, he was probably the greatest prose stylist of his time). To the extent that de Vere was "associated" with Nashe, such association would, by Nelson's dubious reasoning, only burnish his reputation. When one sets out to portray a monster, it's easy to overlook contrary evidence.

A more recent entry from the orthodox side is James Shapiro's *Contested Will* (2010). Oxfordians predictably denounced the book, but Shapiro is actually very receptive to the possibility of Shakespearean collaboration, and he fully grasps the implications of Henslowe's Diary. This more open-ended perspective is refreshing and keenly tuned to a scholarly environment that finds the Shakespearean corpus in a state of flux, with anonymous manuscripts being placed "either here or there." Shapiro is far more reasonable than the "Shakespearean fundamentalists" that have so irritated Brian Vickers. His concessions would have been rare in the days of Chambers and Schoenbaum.

Other parts of Shapiro's arguments are weak. He contends, for example, that Shakespeare must have had in mind a specific boy actor with a highly retentive memory when he wrote the 677 lines for Rosalind in *As You Like It*. Yet that speculation, implying that Shakespeare was tailoring parts for specific actors, begs questions—as to whether Shakespeare wrote the play, and whether it was ever actually performed.[255] The main point of irritation among Oxfordians is that Shapiro doesn't give them sufficient credit for unmasking the Wilmot

---

252 Nelson, *Monstrous*, 384, Greene and Munday were "regarded as hacks"; 393, Dekker characterized as a "hack writer." In fairness to Nelson, anti-Strats also engage in this sort of gratuitous name calling, thus, Mark Anderson, *"Shakespeare" By Another Name*, casually dismisses Robert Greene and Thomas Lodge as "hacks," while claiming that their precursor texts to *Winter's Tale* and *As You Like It* were copied from Edward de Vere's table talk at Fisher's Folly (Oxford's London estate) in the 1580s, 229, 515. The section at 229–235 and the notes, 514–516, are particularly relevant.

253 Nelson, *Monstrous*, 381. Munday, "a gutter journalist of the worst sort."

254 The reference in *Strange News*, quoted above ("the lord thou libellest") and from *Saffron Walden*, quoted above ("Lord Oxford") are two obvious indications.

255 Shapiro, *Contested*, 229.

forgeries. The complaint isn't meritless, but simultaneous or independent discoveries happen frequently. Disputes over intellectual priority, in the absence of evidence of fraud, are generally not worth the time.[256]

A further problem with Shapiro's treatment is that, as we have already discussed, he employs the idea of the context of discovery to disparage the validity of Shakespeare skeptics overall. Thus Twain's skepticism was rooted in the fact that he was a professional writer, while Freud's defense of de Vere was predicated on his fear of losing the idea of the Oedipal Complex, and so forth. (While there is much that could be said about the Shapiro's reading of the ostensible motives of prominent skeptics, there is a dulcet irony in the image of Freud being gainsaid by someone using the concepts of psychoanalysis to account for his Shakespeare denial.)

From this brief survey of recent scholarship, it is clear that the argument between the two main groups—Shakespeareans and Oxfordians—is ongoing. Unless and until some new documents are discovered, there is probably no end in sight. Meanwhile, a number of new and interesting candidates have emerged—each of whom will be discussed in course. First, due diligence demands that we pay some attention to the actual objects of the controversy: the plays and poems themselves.

---

256 Apparently neither party thought to register a sealed envelope with the British Museum.

20 | THE QUARTO PLAYS

A common fault in books about the authorship controversy is that they do not provide information about all of the individual plays in a centralized location. This can be especially frustrating for the reader who wants to follow up on a particular thesis. In this and the next two chapters, I will try to make things a bit easier for such readers. I will first discuss the Quarto plays (many of which were published in Shakespeare's lifetime, but not always with his name on the cover), then the Folio plays (which were never published until the First Folio in 1623), then some plays for which we have no reliable attribution outside of the Folio. Finally, due notice will be taken of the apocryphal plays and other assorted works.

In analyses of this kind, it is generally important to establish the earliest and latest dates at which a play could have been written.[257] For present purposes, however, dating parameters will be emphasized mainly to point out the most important sources that were used. The most important data about any of the plays will be: (1) the listing by the publisher in the Stationer's Register (in effect, the date of the requested copyright; hereinafter SR); (2) whether or not the play was listed by Meres in his *Palladis Tamia*, published in 1598 (because, if so, the play must have been in existence by that time); and (3) the actual date of publication. The manner in which any author is described will also be noted, along with the dates of subsequent Quarto versions and significant changes.

Although 18 plays—fully half of the First Folio—were published for the first time in 1623, our list contains 19 plays. This is because it includes *Henry V* (the Folio version of which is very different) and

---

257 This is known as *terminus ante quem* and *terminus ad quem* in the lingo, but we will not be concerned with these issues because we have no desire to fit the plays to a specific lifespan.

Pericles (which was published in quarto and attributed to Shakespeare but was not included in the Folio).[258]

1. *Titus Andronicus* (SR: 1594, February 6; Q1 published anonymously that year; Meres reference) Eighty years after the fact, Ravenscroft wrote that he had heard that someone else had written this play, and that Shakespeare had only added "master touches." Bullough lists five sources, including an anonymous narrative, Ovid's *Metamorphoses*, and Thomas North's translation of *Plutarch's Lives*. Collaboration has frequently been argued, and accepted; George Peele's name is usually mentioned.

2. *The second part of King Henry the Sixth* (SR: 1594, March 12; Q1 published anonymously that year; no Meres reference) We are using the Folio titles for this list, but at the time of publication the play was titled *The Contention of the Two Houses of York and Lancaster*. Thus, this is one of the plays that has been defined as a Bad Quarto. Bullough lists six sources, including Holinshed's *Chronicles*, Edward Hall's history, *The Union of the Two Noble and Illustre Famelies of Lancastre and York* (1548), Foxe's *Book of Martyrs* (1583 ed.), and *A Myrrour for Magistrates* (1559), a biographical miscellany. Alternative authors—just for this version of the play—include Marlowe, Kyd, Greene, Peele and Lodge.

3. *The third part of King Henry the Sixth* (SR: No entry; Q1 published anonymously in 1595; no Meres reference) Like *The Contention*, this play is considered a Bad Quarto. It was originally published under the title *The True Tragedy of Richarde Duke of Yorke*.[259] Alternative authors who are generally proposed are the same as for *Henry VI, Part 2*. This is the play that contains the line "tiger wrapped in a woman's hide," which was the reference point for Greene in *Groatsworth* in September, 1592. We can therefore be sure it was written (and performed) before that date.

---

258 Core source for the plays is Bullough, *Narrative and Dramatic Sources of Shakespeare*, in 8 volumes (1957-1975). Chambers, *WS*, and Gilvary (ed.), from an Oxfordian point of view are also very useful, as are studies by White, Frazer, and Sykes.

259 This is actually an abbreviation of the printed title; this play is also unique in having been originally published in octavo format, although Chambers still refers to it as a quarto in his table.

Bullough lists three sources, including Holinshed, Hall and *A Myrrour.*

4. *The Life & Death of Richard the Second* (SR: 1597, August 29; Q1 published anonymously in 1597; Meres reference) The Quarto version contains a reference to the play being performed by the Lord Chamberlain's Men, Shakespeare's company. Bullough lists seven sources, including Hall, Holinshed, *A Myrrour*, and Daniel's *Civil Warres.*

5. *The Life & Death of Richard the Third* (SR: 1597, October 20; Q1 published anonymously in 1597; Meres reference) The title mentions the Lord Chamberlain's Men. Q2 was published the next year, 1598, with "by William Shake-speare," the first such attribution.

6. *Romeo and Juliet* (SR: No entry; Q1 published anonymously in 1597; Meres reference) No reference to either Shakespeare or the Lord Chamberlain's Men; a reference to the latter comes with Q2, which was published in 1599. Q3 (1609) references a performance at the Globe, Shakespeare's theater. An undated late Quarto (before the Folio) lists "Written by W. Shake-speare" along with the phrase "newly corrected …" in some copies. Bullough lists only Arthur Brooke's *Tragicall History of Romeo and Juliet* (1562) as a source.

7. *The First Part of Henry the Fourth* (SR: 1598, February 25; Q1 published anonymously in 1598; Meres reference) Q2 was published in 1599, with the line "newly corrected by W. Shake-speare"—the same attribution for Qs 3 through 6 before the Folio. Bullough lists nine sources, including Holinshed, Daniel, and Lyly's *Endimion* (1591).

8. *The Merchant of Venice* (SR: 1598, July 22 and again 1600, October 28; Q1 published as "Written by W. Shake-speare" in 1600; Meres reference) This is the first play in our list to be attributed to Shakespeare on first publication; however, it is not the first play in actual chronology because of the delay of over two years in publication. Q2 is dated 1600, and is considered to be another one of the series of falsely dated ("Pavier") quartos. Bullough lists thirteen sources,

including a play entitled *The Three Ladies of London* by "R. W.," printed in 1584, a narrative by Munday from 1580, and Marlowe's *Jew of Malta*, written around 1590. He also references a lost play referenced by Stephen Gosson, called *The Jew*, which would have to have been from the 1570s. Fields makes an excellent point that in the two grand speeches ("Has not a Jew eyes" and "The quality of mercy is not strained") it is hard not to discern more than one hand—or more than one mind—in the text as it stands.[260]

9. *Love's Labour's Lost* (SR: No entry; Q1 "New corrected and augmented by W. Shakespeare" published in 1598, and not again until F1 [1623]; Meres reference) This would be the first play, in terms of chronology, assigned not only to Shakespeare but referenced by Meres as well. The Quarto is about the same as the Folio text. Bullough lists five possible sources, but none of them resonate directly with the text. Bullough also references both Lyly and Daniel as possible influences, further conceding (partly because of the way the title is given) the possible existence of a rather full precursor text. It is worth mentioning here that Meres listed not only this play but another entitled *Love's Labour's Won*. While there is much speculation on what he was referring to, no one has successfully proven what play that might be.

10. *Much Ado About Nothing* (SR: 1600, August 4 [and again, August 23]; Q1 "Written by William Shakespeare" published in 1600; no Meres reference.) This is one of four plays entered with an SR notation for August 4, all not to be published but to be "stayed."[261] The others are: *As You Like It, Henry the Fifth*, and *Every Man in His Humour*. No one disputes that *Every Man* is by Jonson. The Quarto is about the same as the Folio text. Bullough lists four sources including a play published in 1585 entitled *Fedele and Fortunio*, by "M. A." who is suggested as being Anthony Munday. It is a translation of an Italian play.

11. *The Life of King Henry the Fifth* (SR: 1600, August 4 [and

---

260 Fields, *Players*, 131-137, 241–242, 287-288.

261 The word "stayed" is usually construed to mean that the plays had been entered, not so much to publish them imminently, but to record what would be, in effect, copyright.

again, August 14]; Q1 published 1600 under the title *The Chronicle History of Henry the Fifth*, and anonymously; no Meres reference) The Lord Chamberlain's Men are named in the anonymous Quarto (another Bad Quarto). Bullough lists six sources, including Holinshed, Daniel, and *A Myrrour*.

12. *The Second Part of King Henry the Fourth* (SR: 1600, August 23 "by master Shakspere"; Q1 "Written by William Shakespeare" published in 1600; Meres reference) Note that this play was entered at the same time *Much Ado* was re-entered. Bullough lists eight sources, including Holinshed, Hall, Daniel, and a play from 1588 called *Famous Victories of Henry the Fifth*, which summarizes the action of the two *Henry IV* plays as well as *Henry V*. The relationship of this play to the others remains unclear.

13. *Midsummer Night's Dream* (SR: 1600, October 8; Q1 "Written by William Shakespeare" published in 1600; Q2 [1619]; F1 [1623]; Meres reference) Q2 is dated "1600" and this is one of a series of falsely dated "Pavier" quartos that appear to have inspired the printing of the First Folio. The Quartos are about the same as the Folio text. Bullough lists ten influences, including several from the 1584 version of Reginald Scot's *Discoverie of Witchcraft*, with respect to information about fairies, and also cites Lyly and Greene as other authors who had handled similar themes.

14. *The Merry Wives of Windsor* (SR: 1602, January 18; Q1 "By William Shakespeare" published in 1602; Q2 [1619], F1 [1623]; no Meres reference) There is a difference between the Quarto text and the Folio text; thus the earlier publication is considered a Bad Quarto. Bullough lists seven possible sources for the play, the latest being *Endimion*, a play by Lyly, published in 1591.

15. *The Tragedy of Hamlet* (SR: 1602, January 26; Q1 "By William Shake-speare" published in 1603; no Meres reference) This is the Bad Quarto of *Hamlet*. Q2 was published in 1604, with the following title attribution: "By William Shakespeare. Newly imprinted and enlarged to almost as

much againe as it was, according to the true and perfect Coppie." This is the augmented version, with 400 lines more than the Folio version. Bullough lists fifteen sources, including the *Historiae Danicae of Saxo-Grammaticus* and two tragedies by Seneca, but omitting Seneca's philosophical writings. For this play we have the *Ur-Hamlet* to contend with; that hypothetical play is usually attributed to Kyd—and there have been some claims for the hand of Kyd and Chapman in this play.

16. *King Lear* (SR: 1607, November 26 [the entry specifies "Master William Shakespeare"]; Q1 "Mr. William Shake-speare" published in 1608; no Meres reference) The play bears a marked resemblance to the anonymous *Leir* [sic!], which was entered with the SR 1594, May 14, but with no known quartos until 1605, when two quartos were issued—two years before Shakespeare's version. Bullough lists ten sources, including an actual court case from 1603 (the *Annesley* case) as well as Holinshed's *Chronicles* and of course the anonymous *King Leir*. The attributions for *Leir* include Lodge, Greene, and Peele. There are references to the performance of "king leare" as far back as 1594, but these are always assumed to pertain to the anonymous play, not the Shakespeare play, which is supposed to have been written about 1606. My inclination would be to assume that *Lear* preceded *Leir*; on that point Eric Sams at least agrees.[262]

17. *Pericles* (SR: 1608, May 20; Q1 "By William Shakespeare" published in 1609; no Meres reference) This is the only play in the present list of quartos that was not published in the First Folio but which has been generally ascribed to Shakespeare on the basis of the quarto and its inclusion in the Third Folio. It is now generally believed to have been written in collaboration with George Wilkins.

18. *Troilus and Cressida* (SR: 1609, January 28, with an actual earlier SR date of 1603, February 7; Q1 published in 1609 in two versions; no Meres reference) Bullough lists six sources, most prominently Chapman's *Homer*.

---

[262] This is argued in the second, posthumous, volume of Sams' *Real Shakespeare*, ("*Real Shakespeare II*") and exists only as a download on the Sams website, ericsams.com.

19. *Othello the Moor of Venice* (SR: 1621, October 6; Q1 "Written by William Shakespeare" published in 1622; no Meres reference) There is a recorded performance in 1604. This is the first play published after Shakespeare's death in 1616, and based on the dates, the publication of the First Folio of 1623 was already underway. Bullough lists three sources, the main one being a story in Cinthio's *Gli Hecatommithi* (1566).

In looking over the quarto plays there seems to be ample room for influence, either explicit or otherwise. The first seven plays were all published anonymously, and that is assuming that the two plays that tie into *Henry VI, 2* and *3*, are the same and by Shakespeare. The status of *Love's Labour's Lost* ("corrected" and "augmented"), the first published Shakespeare play, would seem to call for a prior play, although that is much disputed. The status of *Romeo* and *Troilus*, now published with a name, then not, is also rather hard to understand. Also hard to understand, if we assume a single author, are the stylistic and characterization differences between the *Henry VI* plays, *Richard III*, *Richard II*, and *Henry IV*.

21 | THE FOLIO PLAYS

The Folio plays were all entered with the Stationer's Register on November 8, 1623, with two exceptions: *Taming of the Shrew*, and *King John*. This was apparently due to the fact that those two plays were considered equivalent to earlier plays that were entered anonymously in the early 1590s. Only three of the Folio plays were mentioned by Meres in 1598: *Two Gentlemen of Verona*, *Comedy of Errors*, and *King John*. The contextual evidence for the others is not particularly strong, as three of the later plays (*Winter's Tale*, *Cymbeline*, and *Macbeth*) rest largely on the notes of Simon Forman, discovered by John Payne Collier.

1. *Two Gentlemen of Verona* (SR: 1623, November 8; Meres reference) Bullough lists six sources, including Lyly's *Euphues: The Anatomy of Wit*.

2. *The Taming of the Shrew* (SR: No entry; no Meres reference) The reason the play has no SR entry is assumed, as with *King John* below, to be the result of the printer considering the play to be more or less the same as the anonymous *Taming of a Shrew*, which was entered in the SR 1594, May 2 (but assumed by Chambers to date to the 1580s). Q1 was published in 1594, Q2 in 1596, and Q3 in 1607—all without attributions. The play (*A Shrew*) contains numerous plagiarisms from Marlowe, and therefore attributions are to the usual suspects, including Marlowe, Greene, Kyd, and Peele. Inter-group plagiarism strikes Chambers as odd. In effect, *A Shrew* is a Bad Quarto for *The Shrew*.

3. *The First Part of King Henry the Sixth* (SR: 1623, November

8; no Meres reference) Bullough lists four sources, including Hall and Holinshed. One point is the characterization of Joan of Arc (La Pucelle): it is inconceivable that a Catholic, recusant or otherwise, would have had a hand in this play. On the other hand, an embittered anti-Catholic like Munday might have. Because Nashe referenced Talbot in another place, he has sometimes been considered as a collaborator.

4. *The Comedy of Errors* (SR: 1623, November 8; Meres reference) Bullough lists three sources, the main ones being two comedies by Plautus. Many have attempted to tie this play into an early *History of Error* from the 1580s or earlier. There was also a performance of play with a similar name in December of 1594, but not by Shakespeare's company.

5. *The Life and Death of King John* (SR: No entry; Meres reference) The reason the play has no SR entry has been assumed to be because it was identical for registration purposes to the anonymous *Troublesome Raigne of John King of England*, published in two parts in 1591. However, the Q2 of *Troublesome Raigne* was published in 1611, with the ascription "Written by W. Sh.," and Q3, published in 1622, had "Written by W. Shakespeare." There is a textual relationship between the two plays, with *Troublesome Raigne* being a kind of Bad Quarto of *King John*, except that it was written before *King John*, which is usually assigned to about 1595. Keeping just to *Troublesome Raigne*, the attributions have included Marlowe, W. Rowley, Greene, Peele, and Lodge. Honigmann makes the case that *King John* came first, but following the logic of Shakespearean attribution, that can only mean that the play was written in the late 1580s, which is an argument for an "early start" to Shakespeare's dramatic career. In effect, *Troublesome Raigne* is a Bad Quarto of *King John*. Bullough lists six sources, including *Troublesome Raigne*, Holinshed, Hall, and Foxe's *Book of Martyrs*.

6. *The Life and Death of Julius Caesar* (SR: 1623, November 8; no Meres reference; Performance witnessed by Thomas Platter in 1599.) Bullough lists fourteen sources; North's

translation of *Plutarch's Lives* is prominent. Platter's brief description of the performance is in German, and describes how, at the end of the "Comodien," two men and two boys dressed as women came out and danced "wonderfully" (*wunderbahrlich*). Thus the testimony supports the idea that the performance of a Shakespeare play was not the same as its text.[263]

7. *As you Like it* (SR: 1623, November 8; no Meres reference) This is one of four plays that was "stayed" in August 1600, along with *Henry V*, *Much Ado About Nothing* and *Every Man in His Humour*. There is no confirmed record of performance in Shakespeare's time. It is directly based on Thomas Lodge's *Rosalynde*.

8. *All's Well that Ends Well* (SR: 1623, November 8; no Meres reference) Bullough lists only one source, from William Painter's *Palace of Pleasure* (1575).

9. *Twelfe-Night or What You Will* (SR: 1623, November 8; no Meres reference) A performance at Middle Temple in February 1602 is recorded. Bullough lists six sources, mostly Italian.

10. *Measure for Measure* (SR: 1623, November 8; no Meres reference) Bullough lists six sources, including a story by Cinthio.

11. *Timon of Athens* (SR: 1623, November 8; no Meres reference) Bullough lists eight sources, North's translation of *Plutarch's Lives* being the most prominent.

12. *The Tragedy of Macbeth* (SR: 1623, November 8; no Meres reference) Simon Forman recorded a performance in April, 1611. Bullough lists ten sources, including Holinshed's *Chronicles*, and two Senecan tragedies. Middleton has long been credited with certain passages. Chapman has been proposed as an authorial alternate.

13. *Anthony and Cleopatra* (SR: 1623, November 8; no Meres reference) Although the SR date is as listed, there was a prior entry referencing "A book called Anthony and

---

263 Chambers, *WS* 2, 322.

Cleopatra" on May 20, 1608, the same day *Pericles* was entered. Bullough lists ten sources, including North's translation of *Plutarch's Lives* and plays by Mary Sidney Herbert and Samuel Daniel.

14. *The Tragedy of Coriolanus* (SR: 1623, November 8; no Meres reference) Bullough lists six sources, including North's translation of *Plutarch's Lives*.

15. *The Winter's Tale* (SR: 1623, November 8; no Meres reference) This is the "shipwreck in Bohemia" play, based largely on Greene's *Pandosto*. Simon Forman reported a performance in May 1611, and there is a record of another performance at court in November of that year. Bullough records ten sources, Greene being prominent. There are no apparent alternate authors.

16. *Cymbeline King of Britaine* (SR: 1623, November 8; no Meres reference) Simon Forman recorded seeing a performance in April 1611. Bullough lists eight sources, the main one being Holinshed's *Chronicles*. Beaumont, Massinger, Chapman, and Peele have all been mentioned as alternative contributors.

17. *The Tempest* (SR: 1623, November 8; no Meres reference; record of performance at Court in November, 1611) Bullough lists twelve sources, including three concerning discovery literature written in 1610 (but not published until years later). These much-disputed precursor texts are supposed to be a silver bullet to the Oxford candidacy, but that rejoinder ignores the fact that Looney never believed Oxford wrote this play. Other sources include Montaigne (as discussed), Jacob Ayrer's *Beautiful Sidea* (no later than 1605, when he died), and Ovid (because the renunciation speech is copied from *The Metamorphoses*). Beaumont, Chapman, and Heywood have all been suggested as alternative authors, at least in part.

18. *The Life of King Henry the Eighth* (SR: 1623, November 8; no Meres reference; record of performance June 29, 1613) The recorded performance also caused a fire at the Globe Theater. Bullough lists three sources, including Holinshed's

Chronicles, Foxe's *Book of Martyrs*, and a play by Samuel Rowley, *When You See Me, You Know Me* (1605). This play has long been considered a collaboration between Shakespeare and Fletcher. Massinger has also been suggested as a replacement for Shakespeare.

The attributions of the Folio plays are less secure than for the Quarto plays, because unlike most of the quarto plays we have only the Folio attribution to go on—although we do have credible attributions of performances by the Lord Chamberlain's/King's men for several. However, as we know from the performances of Jonson's *Every Man in His Humour* and Dekker's *Satiro-mastix*, the performance of a play by Shakespeare's company does not mean that Shakespeare wrote the play in question. Actually, given what we know of Henslowe's productions, it is hard to understand why anyone would propose that the Lord Chamberlain's/King's men performed only Shakespeare plays, or that Shakespeare wrote all the plays for the company—a point that, in turn, undercuts the attribution of most of the Folio plays to Shakespeare.

Now that we have surveyed the canonical plays, we can see that a number of the plays have twins. Below is an incomplete table in two columns, first the Quarto version of a given play, and then the Folio version.

Quarto	Folio
Romeo and Juliet, Q1	Romeo and Juliet
Chronicles	Henry V
Merry Wives Q1	Merry Wives of Windsor
Hamlet Q1	Hamlet
The Contention	Henry VI, Part 2
True Tragedy	Henry VI, Part 3
Leire	King Lear
A Shrew	Taming of the Shrew
Troublesome Raigne	King John

The first four entries in the first column constitute the Bad Quartos as originally defined. The next two were added later. The last three are plays that are normally supposed to have antedated Shakespeare's version by several years. All of them are shorter, sometimes significantly so, than the Folio versions. Many of them contain padding that includes identified plagiarisms from other authors of the time.

Chambers' comments about *The Contention* and *True Tragedy* could fairly apply to all of them: [264]

> The method of the cuts is interesting. Much of the poetry goes out, the similes, the classical allusions; all the Latin. This is noticeable even in short *lacunae*, which we would normally put down to the reporter. There is a process of vulgarization.

With respect to the plays in the first column, if they are not assigned to Shakespeare, they are assigned to the usual suspects: Marlowe, Greene, Lodge, Peele, Kyd. We have large bodies of texts for most of these authors (as well as for Lyly and Nashe), so we have a good sense of their style. We know that they tended to be verbose, liberal in their use of classical and mythological allusions, and ostentatious in their learning and use of Latin. By contrast, we have very little extrinsic evidence of Shakespeare's style, aside from the Folio.

Given the plays in the two columns, we may reasonably consider the Elizabethan Beats on the one hand, and Shakespeare on the other. To which do we assign the plays in the first column? To which do we assign the plays in the second column? We will return to this question.

---

264 Chambers, *WS* 1, 284.

22 | APOCRYPHA, POEMS, SONNETS

In addition to the plays which appeared in Quarto format and those that appeared only in the First Folio, there is a third category of Shakespearean attributions, usually referred to as the "Shakespeare Apocrypha" (perhaps in deference to the title of Charles Brooke's 1908 compilation[265]). The attribution claims of these plays are varied; the main group comprises the seven plays that were added to the Third and Fourth Folios. Of these seven, only *Pericles* is considered canonical, largely on the basis of the 1608 Quarto. In addition, there are three that were found in a volume of plays in the library of Charles II, and there is also *The Two Noble Kinsman*, published in 1634 and titled as a collaboration of Shakespeare and Fletcher. Several other plays, including *Sir Thomas More*, fall into this category. These have had their advocates over the past three centuries.[266]

1. *Arden of Faversham* (SR: 1592, April 3; Q1 published anonymously in 1592; Q2 in 1599; Q3 in 1633) This play was never included in a Shakespeare collection, but the notion that Shakespeare had a hand in it began in 1770 and has had some advocates since; otherwise it is attributed to Kyd. One delicious point about the play is that the two thugs are named "Black Will" and "Shakebagg," which might be a satiric reference to Shakespeare (and his moneylending)—except for the fact that the play is based on Holinshed's *Chronicle* of the murder in 1551, and those are the names recorded.

---

265 Brooke, Charles Frederick Tucker, *The Shakespeare Apocrypha* (Oxford, Oxford UP: 1908).

266 The main source for the Apocrypha is Charles F. T. Brooke's collection (1908), to which should be added Bate and Rasmussen, *William Shakespeare and Others* (2013), which has excellent essays by Jonathan Bate and Will Sharpe.

2. *Locrine* (SR: 1594, July 20; Q1 published in 1595 with the ascription "Newly set foorth, overseene, and corrected by W. S.", and not again until the Third and Fourth Folios which is where the tie in comes with Shakespeare) An annotation discovered by Collier assigns this play to Charles Tilney, a cousin of Edmund Tilney who was Master of the Revels and who crossed out major parts of the Sir Thomas More manuscript. Charles Tilney was among those executed in the Babington Plot in the fall of 1586. This attribution has been disputed; otherwise Marlowe, Greene, and Peele have all been argued, mainly because there are several passages that plagiarize those authors, as well as Edmund Spenser.

3. *Edward III* (SR: 1595, December 1; Q1 published anonymously in 1596; Q2 in 1599) The first assignment to Shakespeare came in a playlist in 1656, but it was never formally published as by Shakespeare. The theory of Shakespearean participation was first advanced by Capell in the 18th century but didn't gather momentum until the late 19th century. Typical attributions include Lodge, Greene, and Kyd. Because of the "Lilies that fester" line in Act II (among other reasons), it has become common to attribute a large chunk of that act to Shakespeare.[267]

4. *Mucedorus* (SR: no entry; Q1 published anonymously in 1598, followed by at least a dozen other quarto versions before the closing of the theaters in 1642) This play has been assigned to Shakespeare on the strength of a play list entry and because it was one of three plays found in a bound volume owned by Charles II. The original title page indicates it was performed at "the Globe," Shakespeare's theater. The play was clearly popular and has a good critical estimation; usually assigned to Peele, Greene, or Lodge.

5. *Sir John Oldcastle* (SR: 1600, August 11; Q1 published anonymously in 1600; Q2 published the same year as "Written by William Shakespeare"; not included in the First Folio, but included in the Third and Fourth) Henslowe's Diary carries a notation for October 16, 1599, that Anthony Munday,

---

[267] This note was originally tied to news reports but Shakespeare attribution concerning Edward III now has a bibliographic grounding in *William Shakespeare and Others: Collaborative Plays* (2013). For Edward III, see 233–235, and consult the essays of Jonathan Bate and Will Sharpe in that volume.

Michael Drayton, and two others were paid ten pounds to write two plays to be titled "Sir John Oldcastle," so that settles the attribution issue. However, it does not answer how the play ended up in Shakespeare's hands. At minimum, this and other evidence indicates commerce between the Lord Chamberlain's and Admiral's Men.

6. *Thomas Lord Cromwell* (SR: 1602, August 11; Q1 published 1602, "Written by W. S."; two more quartos followed in the teens; published in the Third and Fourth Folios) No one accepts the Shakespeare ascription today; normally assigned to Greene or Heywood.

7. *London Prodigal* (SR: No entry; Q1 published 1605 "As it was plaide by the Kings Maiesties seruants. By William Shakespeare"; published in the Third and Fourth Folios) As with most of the apocryphal plays, this one is rarely assigned to Shakespeare today; Drayton has been suggested as the author.

8. *The Puritan* (SR: 1607, August 6; Q1 published 1607, "Written by W. S."; published in the Third and Fourth Folios) Not argued as a Shakespeare play today; Middleton, Marston, and Jonson have all been proposed.

9. *A Yorkshire Tragedy* (SR: 1608, May 2; identified as "written by Wylliam Shakespeare" in the actual SR entry; Q1 in 1608, also attributed to Shakespeare; Q2 in 1619; included in the Third and Fourth Folios) Not argued as a Shakespeare play today; Middleton and Wilkins have been proposed.

10. *The Merry Devil of Edmonton* (SR: 1607, October 22; Q1 published in 1608 specifies "his Maiesties Seruants, at the Globe," i.e., Shakespeare's company at Shakespeare's theater) Never assigned to Shakespeare until an SR notation of 1653. Along with *Mucedorus*, this is one of three plays bound in a volume in the library of Charles II. The play has a fair critical estimation and there are numerous quarto versions. Sometimes assigned to Drayton.

11. *Fair Em* (SR: No entry; Q1 published without date; Q2 published 1631) This is the third and last play from the bound volume in Charles II's library. There is no known

connection to either Shakespeare or any of his immediate contemporaries. Chambers thinks it might date to the early 1580s in some form.

12. *The Two Noble Kinsmen* (SR: 1634, April 8; both the SR entry and the Q1 of 1634 specify authorship by John Fletcher and William Shakespeare; some contextual evidence backdates the play to 1613) This is the only play in the apocrypha that has a strong tradition of ascription to Shakespeare, at least in part. Other attributions include Beaumont and Massinger.

13. *The Birth of Merlin* (SR: No entry; Q1 published in 1662, "by William Shakespear and Wiliam Rowley") Not argued as a Shakespeare play; Rowley's contribution accepted; others suggested include Middleton.

14. *Sir Thomas More* (SR: No entry) This is the same MS that was discovered in 1841 and published by Dyce in 1844, so the issue is whether Shakespeare contributed about a tenth of the text of the play.

15. *Second Maiden's Tragedy* (SR: 1653, September 9) Never published, the original manuscript originally listed Thomas Goffe as the author, then George Chapman, and finally "by William Shakespear." This is not considered a Shakespeare play today. Middleton and Massinger have been suggested. Chambers dates the play to about 1611.

16. *Edmund Ironside* (SR: No entry) This is another anonymous play that exists only in manuscript form. It is assigned by some to Shakespeare—notably Eric Sams, who dates the play to 1587.

17. *Cardenio* (SR: No entry) This is a play known to have been performed by the King's Men in 1613. It is sometimes referred to as *Double Falsehood*. Shakespearean advocacy goes back to Theobald in the 18th century, who claimed to have had a copy. In recent years Gary Taylor has reconstructed what he believes to have been the original Shakespearean text.

18. *Thomas of Woodstock* (SR: No entry) Sometimes called

> *Richard II, Part One*, this is another manuscript play which has sometimes been attributed to Shakespeare. Marlowe has also been mentioned as a possible author.

19. *The Spanish Tragedy* (SR: 1592, October 6; Q1 published without date) This play is attributed to Kyd on the strength of Heywood's reference in 1613. It has very recently been proposed that Shakespeare made additions.

This study is devoted primarily to the authorship controversy as it pertains to the idea that one person wrote the contents of the First Folio more or less as presented. For the sake of completeness, however, we should say a bit about the other works attributed to William Shakespeare. While such other works usually comprise two long poems and 154 sonnets, our brief survey will also consider another body of work that it is relevant to the issue of attribution.

The first literary work published with the name "Shakespeare" was the 1,200 line poem *Venus and Adonis*, which was published sometime in 1593. The SR entry (April 18, 1593) identifies the printer, Richard Field, who was from Stratford. The actual quarto—which went through over a dozen printings, rivaling and even surpassing *Mucedorus*—does not have Shakespeare's name on the title page, but on the second page there is a brief dedication to Henry Wriothesley, the Duke of Southampton. In the dedication, the poem is described as the "first heir of my invention" and there is a reference to a "graver labour" that he has in store. It is signed "William Shakespeare."

The second long poem was *The Rape of Lucrece*, which had an SR entry for May 9, 1594. The poem was printed the same year, again by Richard Field, this time in octavo. There would be several reprints over the ensuing 50 years. The obsequiousness of the dedication—again signed "William Shakespeare"—is notable: "What I have done is yours, what I have to do is yours, being part in all I have, devoted yours."

The next poetical publication to bear Shakespeare's name is *The Passionate Pilgrim*. There is no SR entry for this octavo pamphlet, but the earliest surviving copy is dated 1599, so it is generally assumed that it was published at that time.[268] *The Passionate Pilgrim* contains 20 short poems, several of them in sonnet form. About half a dozen

---

[268] On this point I would demur, since there is no governing SR entry and there is another copy of *Pilgrim* with the cover page missing. A previous publication, in, say, 1598, would be the easiest explanation for the reference by Meres to Shakespeare's "sugared sonnets" in his book, whose SR date was in September, 1598.

can be traced either to plays or to Shakespeare's sonnets that would be published later. However, the main point to make for present purposes is that while the book claims "By W. Shakespeare" on the title page, about two-thirds of the poems were not by Shakespeare. Indeed, literary scholarship has done a lot of work in assigning these remaining poems to other poets.

The final major publication[269] that can credibly be assigned to Shakespeare is *The Sonnets*, which was published in 1609. There are two SR entries. The first entry, which Chambers considers relevant, is dated January 3, 1600, and reads: "A booke called *Amours* by J. D. with certain other sonnetes by W. S." The second entry is for May 20, 1609, and reads: "a book called Shakespeares sonnettes." *The Sonnets* was published in quarto in that year, the title page describing "*Shakespeares Sonnets*" and declaring "*Never Before Imprinted.*" The quarto also includes "*A Lover's Complaint*," which is a poem of about 300 lines. The main source of interest among critics is the rather obscure dedication, which follows the title page. It reads:

> TO.THE.ONLIE.BEGETTER.OF.
> THESE.INSUING.SONNETS.
> Mr.W.H. ALL.HAPPINESSE.
> AND.THAT.ETERNITIE.
> PROMISED.
> BY.
> OUR.EVER-LIVING.POET.
> WISHETH.
> THE.WELL-WISHING.
> ADVENTURER.IN.
> SETTING.
> FORTH.
> T.T.

There has been endless speculation about the meaning of this dedication.[270] There has also been endless speculation about the integrity of the sonnets themselves. While some critics argue that Shakespeare

---

269 I am omitting from discussion the 67 line poem, *The Phoenix and the Turtle*, which appeared as an appendix in a volume of poetry by Robert Chester in 1601. The poem consists of two parts: 52 lines introducing a 15-line threnos signed "William Shakespeare." It is very odd and hard to interpret, and has also been the source of endless speculation; however, it has no contemporary or occasional flavor and has no relation to the other poetry in the volume. Gililov considers it a key to the Rutland candidacy. Consult Chambers, *WS*, I:549-550.

270 "T.T." is just the name of the printer, Thomas Thorpe.

wrote all of the sonnets, others contend that there are inauthentic ones included.[271] The one point upon which everyone seems to agree, however, is that Shakespeare had nothing to do with the publication of the sonnets; they were not indicated as "by William Shakespeare," and there was no dedication or introduction by Shakespeare.

Chambers' reference to the 1600 SR entry may have been prophetic. In a recent monograph,[272] Brian Vickers concludes on the basis of internal evidence that *A Lover's Complaint* was written by John Davies of Hereford (who, we recall, was the professional copyist who called Shakespeare "Our English Terence"). If Vickers is correct, then that would explain the reference to "J. D." in the earlier SR entry. But it would also suggest that *The Sonnets* may have been a miscellaneous aggregation of sonnets that Shakespeare had obtained, or written, or received as payment in lieu of debts. If the 1600 SR entry is correct (which should actually be 1599, if we are calculating correctly[273]), then it would follow that someone had a mass of sonnets in late 1599 that they wished to publish but which were held out for almost ten years.

Of course, whether or not Shakespeare wrote the poems attributed to him is of little value in terms of assigning the rest of the Shakespearean canon; we have to be wary of a Milkmaid and Bucket sequence here. But we do know that Shakespeare's authorship of *Venus* and *Lucrece* was questionable when they were published, and we know that *The*

---

[271] Robertson doubted as many as 50, the range of other analysts ranged from 8 to 120. Brooks, in *Dyer's Hand*, 139–171, devotes considerable space to discussing the sonnets and various proposed authors. Brooks' first assumption is that the sonnets were likely written by those who had written dedications to Henry Wriothesley, the Earl of Southampton (the same dedicatee as *Venus* and *Lucrece*). These included not only Shakespeare, but also Thomas Nashe, Samuel Daniel, and Barnabe Barnes. Brooks goes on to include Thomas Lodge, Robert Greene, George Peele, John Lyly, and Michael Drayton as possible authors.

Brooks' assumption of a link with Southampton, because of the "fair youth" and the encouragement to marry, looks back to *Venus and Adonis*, and by extension to *Lucrece*. But this raises two problems, the first of which is the oft-indicated homoerotic tone of the sonnets. In opposition to this, C.S. Lewis once wrote, "The incessant demand that the Man should marry and found a family would seem to be inconsistent [....] with a real homosexual passion. It is not even very obviously consistent with normal friendship. It is indeed hard to think of any real situation in which it would be natural. What man in the whole world, except a father or a potential father-in-law, cares whether any other man gets married?" Lewis, C.S., *English Literature in the Sixteenth Century*, 503.

We can therefore summarize the problem of the Sonnets this way: (1) at least at the outset, they have a homoerotic tone, (2) they seem to be encouraging marriage, (3) they have a marked change in tone, which is however (4) comparable to many of the poets of the time, but (5) who among them would have advertised a homosexual relationship with an Earl, much less have taken it upon themselves to tell him to get married? For this reason, the interpretation of Joseph Sobran, who in *Alias Shakespeare* argues that in the Sonnets Southampton was the target of the bisexual Oxford, who was known to have attempted to get Southampton to wed one of his daughters, has considerable force. However, none of this explains how the Sonnets were written, or when (but apparently before 1600) and how they ended up in Shakespeare's hands, much less in the hands of the mysterious "W.H."

[272] Vickers, John, *Shakespeare, 'A Lover's Complaint' and John Davies of Hereford* (Cambridge, University Press, 2007).

[273] The New Year in England for several centuries up to 1752 began on March 25, the date of the Feast of the Annunciation, casually referred to as "Lady Day." This would seem to imply that while Elizabeth I's death occurred on March 24, 1603, it actually occurred on the last day of 1602, according to the current reckoning.

Passionate Pilgrim remains the only group of poems that bore the ascription "by William Shakespeare" on the title page.

In reviewing the Shakespearean apocrypha alongside the body of poetry traditionally assigned to William Shakespeare, we soon encounter a curious problem. With reference to the apocrypha, there are number of works that are not normally assigned to Shakespeare, even though his name or initials appear on many of the title pages. With reference to the poems, there are works that are normally assigned to Shakespeare, despite the absence of title page ascriptions—and even as scholars continue to contest the authorship of individual sonnets. The net effect of this situation is to throw into question the reliability of title page ascriptions in general—not only for the apocryphal plays, but for the poems, the quartos, and even the First Folio.

23 | SHAKESPEARE BACK TO FRONT

Shakespeare's Life ~ Circumstances and Challenges ~ Known Activities ~ Probability of Fitting the Known with the Assumed (Playwriting) ~ "On Poet-Ape"

Buttressed by the foregoing survey of Shakespearean criticism, document discovery, and the attributed literature, we are now in a position to recapitulate what we actually know about the life and career of William Shakespeare. This will be a critical appraisal.

Little is known about Shakespeare's background. His parents appear to have been from families long native to Warwickshire and of no particular distinction.

Even less is certain about Shakespeare's education. It is generally assumed that he attended grammar school in Stratford during his youth, but if he had been a precocious student one would expect that, like so many of his literary contemporaries, he would have been singled out for higher education. While Marlowe, Nashe, and Daniel also came from poor (or at least undistinguished) families, they were still allowed to attend university more or less on scholarship. But since we know that Shakespeare attended neither Oxford nor Cambridge, it is likely that he was a middling student at best.

Shakespeare's failure to achieve any higher education may be the source of the legend that he quit school at 14 in order to help support his family. To the extent that this legend is taken seriously, it is of course difficult to reconcile with the expansive erudition on display in the plays. The supposition that such a vast store of knowledge could have been assimilated on the fly by a gifted autodidact may be plausible under some circumstances, but how exactly is this accomplished when one is working to support one's family from the age of 14? Perhaps Shakespeare's remarkable rise should be considered in the spirit of sundry "Horatio Alger" stories that find enterprising youths or young men mastering disciplines while working from a young age, all by dint of guile and Herculean effort. David Sarnoff, Hans Winckelmann, and Franz Schubert all come to mind. But none of them achieved these goals with a wife and children in tow.

This leads to the issue of Shakespeare's marriage. We know that Shakespeare was married at 18 and was the father of three children before his 21st birthday. One would expect—indeed, his own times would demand—that a father in that kind of situation would be turning his energies to providing for his wife and children, not devoting his time to reading obscure literary and historical works, nor spending his time mastering dead or foreign languages for some unclear purpose, let alone going on tours to Italy and other countries.

One can point to cases where authors have abandoned their families in order to follow their muse (Sherwood Anderson is perhaps the most notorious). But Shakespeare doesn't fit the mold. He returned to his family in Stratford at what appears to have been the earliest opportunity and lived out his life in their midst. He made explicit reference to his wife and children and their future progeny in his Will. In fact, his Will was concerned with little else.

When African-Americans were freed from slavery, there followed a decades-long argument as to how the emancipated should improve their lives. One side, which later came to be associated with W.E.B. Dubois, advocated acquiring higher education as the first step in advancement. The other side, associated primarily with Booker T. Washington, advocated hard work, the accumulation of capital, and economic stability. In his autobiography, Washington excoriated those who emphasized the learning of Latin and Greek in place of remunerative work, and he provided an unforgettable image of

> ...a young man, who had attended some high school, sitting down in a one-room cabin, with grease on his clothing, filth all around him, and weeds in the yard and garden, engaged in studying a French grammar. [274]

Add a wife and three children, and this would have been William Shakespeare.

---

274 Washington, Booker T., *Up From Slavery*, gutenberg.org

The earliest record we have of Shakespeare, after the birth of his twins, and at the end of the "lost years," is the Clayton loan of seven pounds in 1592 (assuming we accept that this document applies to Shakespeare). Combining this with the characterization of *Groatsworth* that fall, we can reasonably surmise that by 1592 Shakespeare was already involved in the theater, involved in making money, and involved in lending it.

The rest is hypothesis, but not all hypotheses are equal. For example, it has been conjectured that Shakespeare was a schoolmaster (named "Shakeshaft") in Warwickshire but for some reason gave up his work for the traveling life of an actor. It has been argued that he was a legal clerk, who gave up that job to get involved in theatrics.[275] These and similar hypotheses have to be squared with the facts that are implied: that a young married man with several dependents would sacrifice security and domesticity for the roving, uncertain, and poorly paid job of actor or playwright. I am reminded of the famous Bob Newhart standup routine in which an Abraham Lincoln created by an advertising firm needed to be constantly reminded of the details of his made-up biography: that he was a rail splitter, and then an attorney; not the other way around. The fact that Shakespeare had sufficient capital to be making loans by 1592 suggests that he had been involved in the stage business for some time. It further suggests that his family in Stratford was not in the dire straits presumed to explain his lack of education. At any rate, Shakespeare would not have been able to lend seven pounds simply on the strength of writing.

This brings us to Shakespeare in London. We can assume that he was active there for most of the 1590s and perhaps well into the 1600s, although there is no agreement as to when he gave up his life in London and returned home to Stratford for good. During this interval, we know that he received payments for performances in the Lord Chancellor's Men, that he was a shareholder in that company (as well as the King's Men company that followed), and we know that he was, at least occasionally, an actor. We also know that in 1596 he was involved in a confrontation with William Wayte that led to a "surety of the peace" (something like a restraining order) being issued against

---

[275] This point of view is most associated with Eric Sams, whose two books on the subject argue for an early start for Shakespeare. Another author who points towards the "early start" of Shakespeare's work is Honigmann, who seems to arrive at his position based on his conclusion that *King John* must have preceded *Troublesome Raigne*.

Shakespeare and other parties. The context of this event suggests that Shakespeare was involved in business opportunities other than playwriting and acting.[276]

The "surety of the peace" episode brings up Shakespeare's association with George Wilkins (fl. 1607), a minor writer often cited as a co-author of *Pericles*. Wilkins' literary career came to a mysterious end in 1608, but his career as a defendant was just beginning: from 1610 to 1618 he was the subject of no less than 18 complaints for various crimes including a couple of ugly assaults on women (in one case he kicked a pregnant woman in the belly; in another, he beat and stomped on a woman so badly that she had to be carried away).[277] It is likely that Shakespeare and Wilkins were friends, as they both testified in a suit concerning a dowry involving a Huguenot couple that Shakespeare had lived with in London for several years. Evidence further suggests that Wilkins was a pimp, and his inn a brothel, reinforcing the impression we have had since Robert Greene that the theater in those days had one foot firmly planted in the underworld. How much of this may have rubbed off on Shakespeare, while he was warbling his native woodnotes wild, is a matter of speculation.

Shakespeare must have also been the lead personality of his company, and as such he was at least informally presented as the writer of its plays. There's no other way to explain the enumeration of plays by Francis Meres. Here the anti-Stratfordians are bound to make an admission, since not only does Meres attribute several plays to Shakespeare, but the title pages, beginning in 1598, also show Shakespeare's name. There are two possible explanations: either Shakespeare really was writing these plays, or he was considered to be the man responsible for their production—as impresario, producer, director, stage manager, script doctor, and occasional actor. Such a characterization of Shakespeare's duties would make him indeed a *Johannes factotum*: a jack of all trades, just as Greene described him.

Here I have to record my belief that Shakespeare's functions were oriented more toward management—he may have been the first professional producer and director—than playwriting. I have several

---

276 Barber, *Shakespeare Examined*, 410–412. Briefly, Wayte took out a restraining order against Shakespeare, Richard Langley, and two women. The women are unknown, but Langley, in addition to being involved in theater building, was also a moneylender. Wayte, meanwhile, was the stepson of Richard Gardiner, another moneylender. This evidence tends to put Shakespeare in the middle of the loansharking business in Elizabethan London, which is suggested by other evidence. Meanwhile, the two women suggest other rackets associated with the theater, including gambling and prostitution.

277 *Oxford Pericles*, edited by Gary Taylor, 6, based on the research of Roger Prior published in 1972.

reasons. The first is that the managerial and productive functions—which Shakespeare almost certainly fulfilled—would have taken up all of his time. The second is that there are a number of plays thus accredited to Shakespeare, or put on by his company, that no one claims as his, since the selection in the First Folio remains the gold standard for his authorship. A third reason is that, if my interpretation of Dekker's *Satiro-mastix* is correct, that play too was understood as a "Shakespeare play" prior to its publication. To all of this I would add that Shakespeare could not have made his fortune merely by writing, nor was his acting ever described as being on the level of Edward Alleyn. It thus follows that he must have been in the revenue stream by some other means. Setting aside any other business ventures, directing the company seems the most likely source of regular income. And beyond such matters of logistical and practical account, the plays themselves simply do not mesh well with any concept of single authorship. A "Shakespeare play" in those times would have been understood as a play put on by William Shakespeare and his company.

Another purely practical reason can be proposed for why Shakespeare did not write the plays. Shakespeare had money. The numerous playwrights surrounding him in London did not. Nothing would have been easier than for Shakespeare to acquire, buy, broker, or commission the writing or revision of plays. Keep in mind also the deaths or departures of his contemporaries: Greene died in 1592, Marlowe was killed in 1593, Kyd was dead by 1594, Lodge abandoned the stage in 1595, Peele died in late 1596, Nashe abandoned London in 1597 (and died by 1600). We could also mention Lyly's retirement by the mid-90s, the several years Dekker spent in debtor's prison, or a number of other factors that would have prevented Shakespeare's contemporaries from publicly objecting if a play in which they had a hand was published under Shakespeare's name.

There are a limited number of reasons why someone should choose to write at all. The reasons one might choose to write a play, let alone follow a break-neck schedule to produce two plays a year over a span of decades, are more limited still. The notion of writing to promote a specific political or social agenda is one appealing rationale, as is the notion of writing in order to advance a new literary genre. But such explanations are called into question once one examines the plays in detail. Rather than a thematically coherent or markedly original body of work, we find a gnarly concatenation of derivative plots and characters, long stretches of pedestrian dialogue, and labored speeches (often virtually borrowed wholesale from sources like Holinshed and North) that serve little purpose. To note such characteristics of the plays is not to scant their numerous beauties, about which volumes have been written, but to press the question: why would Shakespeare even bother to write the plays? He was not writing for a muse, nor was he writing because he had an easy pen. But even if we set aside the clumsiness of his signature, his apparent inability to write virtually anything outside of the plays sets him apart from his contemporaries. If Shakespeare could not have been writing for an artistic vision or due to graphomania, he certainly wasn't writing for money: the going rate for a play throughout his career was perhaps six pounds, or even less—and upon receiving this compensation, a playwright lost all rights to the players, the company, and the publisher. There's no reason why Shakespeare, by the late 1590s, would invest months of his time scribbling two versions of *Henry V* while investing hundreds of times that amount on real estate investments and church tithes in his native town of Stratford.

Similar difficulties emerge when, following the approach stressed by James and Rubinstein, we attempt to fit the chronology of the plays to Shakespeare's life. The standard chronology supposes that Shakespeare wrote mainly histories to start, then ventured into comedies in the mid- to late 1590s; then, at some point around 1600, he went in a radically new direction that culminated in the great tragedies of *Lear*, *Hamlet*, and *Macbeth*. Following this phase of singular brilliance, Shakespeare goes on to write what are referred to as his "problem plays."[278] It is very difficult to square that chronology with the biographical fact that during those years Shakespeare was enjoying his greatest financial success.

This is what we know about the writing of dramas in Elizabethan times: collaboration was the norm. This was true even in the case of *Gorboduc*, the first blank verse tragedy. We also know that declarative authorship was *dangerous*. Nashe and Jonson were imprisoned for their part in the writing of the *Isle of Dogs*, and Marston, Chapman,

---

278 The "Problem plays" coinage is credited to Frederick S. Boas in the 1890s. It refers to the later Shakespeare plays that were identified as being ambiguous as comedy or tragedy, i.e., *All's Well that Ends Well*, *Measure for Measure*, and *Troilus and Cressida* (Boas also put *Hamlet* on his list, somewhat illogically). I would argue that the percieved "ambiguity" has much to do with the treatment of women in these later plays, where the passion and simplicity of Juliet, or the screwball comedy of *Much Ado* or *As You Like It*, has been traded for more complex, if not demeaning, characterization (compare *Pericles*, John Ford's *Tis Pity*, Dekker and Middleton, *Roaring Girl*, etc.). Boas got his name from a common reference to Ibsen, but see *Hedda Gabler* and *A Doll's House*. The cited books by Germaine Greer are relevant. Part of the reason for identifying "Generation J" is the notion of changing perceptions, perceptions common for Jacobean theater but not for Elizabethan times and similarly uncommon for the earlier, but not the later, plays attributed to Shakespeare.

and Jonson were imprisoned for *Eastward Ho!* Even Samuel Daniel fell under suspicion for his *Philotas*. We also know that there were dozens of talented playwrights in London during the time that Shakespeare was active.

There is nothing in William Shakespeare's background or activities that suggests an incentive to write plays. This is a man who in 1597 paid 60 pounds toward a new house in Stratford, who purchased 120 acres five years later for 340 pounds, who two years after purchased a tithe in the church's property (and, incidentally, the right to be buried in the church's chancel, along with the famous bust) for 440 pounds. The idea that he would have worried himself with writing three plays in 1599 (not including a rewrite of one of them—*Henry V*), for the going rate of six pounds a piece makes little sense.

Of course, none of this will prevent advocates from insisting that Shakespeare was, despite all contrary evidence, a writing machine. Even if he could barely sign his own name, they prefer to believe that he wrote until he literally dropped, penning some autumnal sonnet in his garden in Stratford.

We began with Ben Jonson's folio, which contained a number of plays, masques, and poems. One of these, "On Poet-Ape" seems to speak directly to the issues under discussion:[279]

> Poor Poet Ape, that would be thought our chief,
> whose works are e'en the frippery of wit,
> From Brokage is become so bold a thief,
> As we, the robbed, leave rage and pity it.
> At first he made low shifts, would pick and glean,
> Buy the reversion of old plays, now grown
> To a little wealth and credit on the scene,
> He takes up all, makes each man's wit his own,
> And told of this, he slights it. Tut, such crimes
> The sluggish, gaping auditor devours;
> he marks not who twas first, and aftertimes
> May judge it to be his, as well as ours.
> Fool! As if half-eyes will not know a fleece
> From locks of wool, or shreds from the whole piece.

There is ongoing argument as to whether this poem refers to

---

[279] Jonson, *"On Poet-Ape," Epigrams, Complete Works*, 789.

Shakespeare.[280] With the verdict forestalled, it is hard not to conclude that Jonson provides an accurate account of how the plays were put together. Once you have a sense of how Elizabethan and Jacobean theaters operated, the answer to the authorship question is actually rather simple: everyone, but no one.

Old plays, like the *Comedy of Errors*, *Midsummer Night's Dream*, *The Merchant of Venice*, and *Love's Labour's Lost* were purchased from failed companies and worked into something new. More recent plays like *King John*, the *Henry VI* plays, *King Lear*, and *Hamlet* were cut down into racy performance versions—to be dubbed "bad quartos" by later generations, while the originals were squirreled away with the other manuscripts that Shakespeare, with good instincts, had either purchased or accepted as payment on outstanding loans.

This may be the most likely description of Shakespeare's career. It need not derogate that career. Shakespeare was clearly the preeminent stage manager of his time, as evidenced by his fortune as well as the positive memory so many of his contemporaries held of him. The fact that he did not write the words of the plays attributed to him does nothing to dislodge his position as the Father of Modern Theater.

---

280 The key is that the poem conveys three facts: 1) that someone has pretensions to literary dominance, 2) that someone is a plagiarist, and 3) that someone is cobbling together texts from multiple authors. Because of the third point, most unitarians of any affinity dispute the applicability to Shakespeare, since it undercuts not only Shakespeare but any other sole author. On the other hand, the charge of plagiarism can be leveled against numerous Elizabethan authors, including, at least in part, Shakespeare himself. However, he "would be our king" dovetails nicely with the suggestion that Shakespeare at times played kingly roles (compare also the epigram of John Davies of Hereford). One proposed explanation is that Jonson is targeting both Dekker and Marston, because they were Shakespeare's opponents in the War of the Theaters. Yet the poem does not indicate multiple targets, and the proposal seems otherwise unconvincing.

24 | LEGENDS OF THE NOBLE HAND

Edward Ravenscroft ~ The Pinner of Wakefield ~ Other Oblique References ~ The Test That All the Candidates Fail ~ Lack of Direct Evidence ~ The Likely or Possible Activities of the Earl of Oxford

One of the small clues that students turn over in the quest for evidence in the authorship controversy is the plate at the front of a book, published in 1612, that shows a hand reaching out from behind a curtain, quill in hand, writing the words, "MENTE VIDEBORI," which is assumed to be an incomplete Latin phrase for "In the mind thou shalt be seen."[281] The image has been taken by many anti-Stratfordians to buttress the case for their claimants, but we will seize on the image solely to pursue the notion of a mysterious noble hand writing the plays and poems of Shakespeare. First, we will look at some of the evidence that in fact confirms that hidden authorship was a widely held belief in Elizabethan times; then we will move on to consider the actual evidence supporting the alternative candidates, nearly all of whom are from the nobility.

We recall that Edward Ravenscroft as far back as 1687 had indicated the notion of hidden authorship for at least one Shakespeare play. But the idea was commonly expressed elsewhere. One example concerns a notated copy of an anonymous play called *The Pinner of Wakefield*.[282] The writing on the cover page of this play has been identified as the hand of George Buc (1560–1622), who was the successor to Edmund Tilney as the Master of the Revels, an officer who

---

281 Michell, *Who Wrote Shakespeare*, 184.

282 A "pinner" is something like an animal control officer.

oversaw public dramatic performances.[283] On this copy of the play Buc had written:[284]

> Written by .... a minister who ac[ted]
> Th pinners pt in it himself. Teste W. Shakespea[re]
> Ed. Iuby saith that this play was made by Ro. Gree[ne]

Evidently, Buc did not know who had written this play, asked around and got some answers, perhaps two different answers. At any rate, the inscription is one of the main reasons why the play is now assigned to Robert Greene.

It is important to keep in mind that there were a lot of anonymous publications in this era. In his survey of the Elizabethan stage, Chambers discusses more than 80 plays that were printed anonymously, and the number of anonymously or pseudononymously published sonnet cycles, poems, and other miscellaneous writings must have been enormous. On occasion one will also find cryptic references to hidden authors. For example, George Puttenham, in his *The Art of English Poesie* (1589), made the following remarks:[285]

> Among the nobility or gentry as may be very well seen in many laudable sciences and especially by making poesy, it is so come to pass that they have no courage to write and if they have are loath to be known for their skill. So as I know very many notable gentlemen in the Court that have written commendably, and suppressed it again, or else suffered it to be published without their own names to it: as if it were a discredit for a gentleman to seem learned.

A little farther on, Puttenham is more specific:

> Noblemen and Gentlemen of Her Majesty's own servants, who have written excellently well as it would appear if their doings could be found out and made public with the rest, of which number is first that noble gentleman Edward Earl of Oxford.

When Puttenham's book was published the writings of Sir Philip Sidney had circulated unpublished for years, so it is possible that he had such writings in mind. But Puttenham is also asserting that Oxford

---

283 As we have seen in the case of Edmund Tilney and the manuscript to *Sir Thomas More*; this was also a post that decreed censorship and other interference in the texts of plays.

284 Title page of a facsimile copy of the play (*The Pinner of Wakefield*); the part in brackets was added by the editor.

285 Sobran, *Alias Shakespeare*, 134.

had concealed writings—an allegation that cannot be easily dismissed.

There are other references to hidden authorship and assumed pseudonymous authorship as well. We are familiar, for example, with Greene's accusations from *Groatsworth*, in which someone is accused of using someone else's writings; but this is actually a complaint that Greene made on at least two other occasions.

It is clear that in the Elizabethan era there were suspicions as well as complaints about hidden authorship, and specifically, hidden noble authorship. While such suspicion cannot validate the attribution of the literature of the age, nor even the Shakespeare plays and poems, we should be alert to this well-documented contemporary belief—even if the belief is not true.

The fact that most alternative candidates were members of the nobility has often led to the claim that the people promoting alternatives were snobs. Today, they would be considered "elitist" or "classist" in their orientation, or they might be stuck with the more recently branded "denialist" epithet. The problem with such name calling is that it tends to circumvent further inquiry as to why so many candidates have noble background. This in turn gets us back to the notion of "special knowledge," so in the following summary we will elaborate on that as well.

- The main reason so many Shakespeare alternatives are nobles is because the plays demonstrate extensive miscellaneous knowledge, as well as knowledge of foreign and dead languages. This in turn implies the time and resources to acquire such knowledge, since that is after all the main purpose of a university education. All of the alternative candidates were so educated.

- Whoever wrote Shakespeare seemed to have an extensive knowledge of the law: many of the noble candidates had such knowledge.

- Whoever wrote Shakespeare appears to have traveled widely on the European continent, including France and Italy. Again, this applies to nearly all the noble candidates.

- Whoever wrote Shakespeare was a political conservative, who portrayed the nobility in a favorable light, while caricaturing the lives of the peasantry. More: whoever wrote

Shakespeare seemed thoroughly conversant not only in how the nobility acted, but also seemed obsessed with the minor details of rank and succession.[286]

All of these are valid observations about the plays. The normal Shakespearean response is that Shakespeare somehow managed to acquire the necessary knowledge. But hopefully at this point it will have been noticed that these ostensibly noble characteristics apply to many of Shakespeare's playwriting contemporaries as well. For example, Marlowe, Greene, Peele, Lodge, Nashe, Lyly, Daniel, and many others attended university; Marlowe, Greene, Nashe, Daniel, Munday and several others visited the continent and even made it to Italy; Lodge, Marston, Ford, Middleton and others seemed to have either attended law school or were well versed in the law, and so on. In addition, many of them seemed to have other types of special knowledge that would appear in the plays: Lodge's experiences on his two voyages would make him a master mariner among his peers; Daniel's first book was on the subject of crests; Chapman was a learned classical scholar; Drayton's possessed encyclopedic knowledge, as displayed in his *Poly-Olbion*; and so on. Thus the knowledge base scattered among Shakespeare's literary contemporaries was widely and casually dispersed.

The noble or class orientation of the plays is also less remarkable when we recall that nearly all of Shakespeare's contemporaries were either under the patronage of nobility or seeking such patronage. This was in fact the normal path to job security among the educated non-nobility at the time. We can see indications of this in the florid dedications that accompany many works, the defense of certain nobility by various writers (e.g., the defenses of Oxford by Greene and Nashe), as well as by the fact that several of these authors actually worked in the homes of the nobility as tutors.[287]

While the need for a nobleman (or noblewoman) to serve as a replacement for Shakespeare is not really justified, the tradition has nevertheless been to propose mostly noble candidates as alternatives to Shakespeare. We will review these claims briefly.

---

286 Thus Joseph Sobran once quipped that following the speeches in *Richard III* was "like trying to follow a 500-year-old pennant race." Sobran's quip goes back to a column written in March, 1997, but which I have been unable to trace further.

287 Tutors to the nobility include Daniel, Davies of Hereford, and Nashe.

Francis Bacon (1561–1625) Bacon was the original alternative candidate, and his selection appears to have been based on a series of simple clan associations: he was a lawyer, he was extraordinarily learned, and he would have been well-situated to write the plays and poems if he had wanted to. There is some secondary evidence that supports his candidacy; some satires from about 1600, including one by John Marston, appear to point to the belief that Bacon wrote *Venus and Adonis* and *Lucrece* at the time, and there is the Northumberland manuscript, discovered in the 19th century, which shows the linkage of Bacon and Shakespeare several times on a sheet of parchment, and which is hard to explain to this day. On the other hand, there is no evidence that Bacon ever wrote any plays, there is no reference to him as a playwright, and no one has ever provided a mechanism to explain how and why Bacon would have used Shakespeare as a front. The Bacon candidacy continues today in muted form, but there is no question that it was seriously damaged by the long-discredited code and cipher hunting initiated by Donnelly.

William Stanley, 5th Earl of Derby (1564–1642) Derby's candidacy came next in 1891. The case is actually rather strong, provided we envision him as the provider of precursor texts for some individual plays. Derby is the one candidate for whom we have contemporary evidence that he actually wrote plays; he came from a family that sponsored an acting troupe, and he fit the other criteria for education and worldliness. In addition, he appears to have been the only candidate who actually visited the French court in Navarre, which plays a large role in *Love's Labour's Lost*, and his association with the occultist John Dee is a plausible explanation for the character Prospero in *The Tempest*. However, there is really no meaningful way to tie Stanley into the entirety of the Shakespeare canon, so his candidacy has always been somewhat minor, and usually associated with various group theories. A piquant touch is that he was married to one of the daughters of Edward de Vere, the Earl of Oxford.

Christopher Marlowe (1564–1593) Marlowe's candidacy was first proposed in 1895. Although he is the only non-noble among the major claimants, we should discuss the case here. While his death in late May 1593 would seem to make his name excludable from any serious list of alternative candidates, the first thing we have to concede is that we really have no idea what literary remains he left behind. Looking at the plays that are indisputably his, and then comparing them to the Shakespearean corpus, it is not hard to find his influence in the early history plays, the *Henry VI* series, *Richard III*, *The Merchant of Venice* and *Taming of the Shrew*. It is much harder to find his influence in the later plays. If Marlowe had an influence in the earlier plays, either directly, or indirectly through his literary remains, then that would suffice to show his continuing influence in death. As to his death, I think the historical record supports the traditional view. But it is not inconceivable that the life crisis he was experiencing in the spring of 1593 resolved itself with some skulduggery and that Marlowe was spirited off to continue his intellectual career in a more congenial climate. If I were making that kind of argument, I would place him in Germany, because that would be a way of explaining the various German versions of Shakespeare plays associated with Jacob Ayrer.

ROGER MANNERS, 5TH EARL OF RUTLAND (1576–1612) Rutland emerged as a candidate in the early years of the 20th century. The case is not very strong, aside from the usual assumptions about nobility in terms of leisure and learning, and his actual visit to Denmark. To be sure, he was a fascinating individual who had a tragic life (as did his wife). But given his youth there is little to square with the proposed chronology of the plays, or even a backdated chronology. It is also worth pointing out that the one particular piece of evidence that supported his candidacy—that he attended the University of Padua with Rosenkrantz and Guilderstern—is apparently false.[288]

In the 21st century there have been four new candidates. While none of them have the tradition behind them that the others do, they have their positive points. We will discuss them, and then we will conclude with Oxford.

SIR HENRY NEVILLE (1564–1615) The candidacy of Sir Henry was first proposed by Brenda James and William Rubinstein in 2005, in their book, *The Truth Will Out*.[289] The James-Rubinstein theory has a few points in its favor. There are original documents in favor of the claimant, and some suggestive documentation on the writing of *Henry VIII*. It is also one of the few alternative theories to integrate the

---

[288] Fields, *Players*, 267.

[289] James, Brenda; Rubinstein, William D., *The Truth Will Out: Unmasking the Real Shakespeare*, Harper, NY: 2005

cryptic Northumberland Manuscript; unnoticed by virtually everyone else, Neville's name actually appears on the document.[290] There is much circumstantial evidence supporting the thesis as well; for example, Neville actually knew Henry Wriothesly, the Earl of Southampton, who was the dedicatee of *Venus* and *Lucrece*. James and Rubinstein also give much attention to the biography implied by the chronology of the plays; thus, according to the standard enumeration, something happened to Shakespeare around 1600 that caused the preparation of the great tragedies: *Hamlet, Lear, Othello,* and *Macbeth.* Neville was actually in prison at this time, for his role in supporting the Earl of Essex' rebellion, and was also imprisoned with Southampton. However, despite the large amount of research, including many primary sources, the theory largely points to some influence on Neville's part in the writing of *Henry VIII*, but little more. There is also the fact that Neville was not even in London during the time that Shakespeare flourished. The idea that Neville wrote the plays and then sent them by post to the London stage to be worked into shape for performance has little force to recommend it.

MARY (SIDNEY) HERBERT, DUCHESS OF PEMBROKE (1561–1621) Mary Sidney (using her maiden name) is one of the more intriguing candidates. We have already discussed her evident intelligence and skill, as well the Wilton circle of poets and dramatists that surrounded her. The first full exposition on her behalf was argued by Robin P. Williams in 2006, in *Sweet Swan of Avon*, although she does not claim unitary authorship on her behalf. There are three points in Sidney's favor. First, her feminine and aristocratic voice could conceivably inform the speeches of some of Shakespeare's greatest heroines, for example, Rosalind in *As You Like It* and Cleopatra. Second, her patronage and association with Samuel Daniel puts her right in the middle of a certain aspect of Shakespearean creativity. Third, she was the mother of the two dedicatees of the First Folio. At minimum, she is an interesting alternative candidate for part of the Shakespearean canon, but her role would be hard to define.

SIR THOMAS NORTH (1535–1604) The case for Sir Thomas was made by Dennis McCarthy in 2011. There are many things to praise in McCarthy's treatment, especially inasmuch as he focuses on neglected

---

290 Gibson's argument in *The Shakespeare Claimants* (224–236) is that the binder cover was simply a scratch pad for a couple of scribes. However that does not explain away the suggestive juxtaposition of names and titles, which remains a mystery, and is hard to accept as mere coincidence.

sources of Elizabethan thought and interprets what I believe to be the proper relationship of the Quarto versions of the plays to the Folio versions (i.e., that the Quartos are generally rewrites of the originals, which appeared for the first time in the Folio[291]). On the other hand, the case for North rests almost entirely on the fact that North's translation of *Plutarch's Lives* (1579, 1595, 1603) was paraphrased, copied, or plagiarized to a significant degree in plays like *Coriolanus* and *Anthony and Cleopatra*. This information has long been known, but McCarthy makes a strong underlining of it. However, instead of leading one to think that, therefore, North must have written all the plays of Shakespeare, this information actually causes one to rethink the plays themselves. Consider that if the plays in the Folio are to be regarded as some kind of unitary artistic or philosophical vision, it is difficult to square that claim with blatant copying (either from North, or Holinshed, or any other author that we find quoted in the canon). On the contrary, it suggests that the plays were oftentimes written hurriedly in order to meet an obligation.

McCarthy attempts to support his argument by showing that there are *Hamlet*-like touches in North's *Diall of Princes* (1557) and *The Moral Philosophy of Doni* (1570), but he gives very little acknowledgment to the fact that the *Diall of Princes* is a translation Guevara's *Reloj de principes*, which in turn is a kind of novelization of the *Meditations* of Marcus Aurelius, or that the *Philosophy of Doni* is a reworking of the *Fables of Bidpai*, otherwise known as the *Panchatantra*. McCarthy certainly deserves credit for acknowledging the importance of Hellenistic philosophy and Indian animal tales in Elizabethan times, but in his effort to praise North, he neglects to explore these issues in any detail and he fails to recognize that in all of his writings North was first and foremost a translator (there is no evidence either of dramatic writings, or even an association with the theater). Other arguments are weak: it is claimed that *Groatsworth* is about North, but it would make little sense for a man who was over 50 years old (and who was to be knighted for his translations) to choose to go live in London and write plays for a few pounds apiece, and there is no evidence supporting the claim.

Sir Thomas Sackville, 1st Earl of Dorset (1536–1608)

The case for Sir Thomas was first made by Sabrina Feldman in *The Apocryphal William Shakespeare* in 2011. One point in favor of this

---

291 McCarthy, Dennis, *North to Shakespeare* (2011).

interpretation is that Sackville was a known playwright; in his youth he co-wrote *Gorborduc* (1561) with Thomas Norton, and the seminal role of that play in the evolution of Elizabethan blank verse drama has long been acknowledged.

Feldman is very modest in her claims, suggesting only that Sackville could have been the author of the plays, or was, at any rate, the hidden noble poet whose existence was alleged at that time. The route she takes follows the proliferation of quartos, and in particular, the apocryphal plays assigned to Shakespeare. This is a very attractive line of inquiry because it sets up a logical fallacy of the traditional unitarians: if we know that Shakespeare wrote the plays because his name is on the title page, then we cannot exclude the other plays with his name on the cover. If we do exclude those plays because of stylistic weakness, then we are using the same arguments that the analysts have used for centuries to re-assign canonical plays to other authors. This is precisely the sort of issue that came to a head in the 1980s as a result of the attributions of Gary Taylor and Donald Foster.

Feldman comes to the same conclusion as McCarthy, which is that the quartos represent the stage version of the plays that Shakespeare edited, and that the Folio versions represent the more or less untouched original versions, while the apocryphal plays were plays that either Shakespeare wrote himself or worked up to completed form in the usual manner. The layout of Feldman's treatment is unique since it consists mostly of 81 separate vignettes engaging primary source documentation from the era, with generally cautious and sober analysis. But the case for Sir Thomas Sackville as Shakespeare must remain in limbo.

Finally, we return to the case of **Edward de Vere, The 17th Earl of Oxford**, whose candidacy we have already discussed in some detail. The best that can be said for de Vere is that he knew everyone, was well educated, well traveled, a fair poet, a patron of many of the best writers of his time, and that he sponsored an acting troupe. He could have written the plays and poems attributed to Shakespeare, but there is absolutely no direct evidence that he did.

It is precisely at this point that the orthodox Shakespeareans rise and claim that the entire issue of alternative authorship is a waste of time, and that it must follow that William Shakespeare wrote the plays and poems after all. This objection, however, tends to ignore the main point: absent the title pages, and the First Folio, we don't have any direct documentary evidence that Shakespeare wrote the plays, either. But the plays *were* written; someone, or some people, must have written them. So it is legitimate to ask who wrote them. What is required are plausible explanations for the genesis of the plays and poems, whether by one author, or by many.

As noted at the beginning of this chapter, one of the main reasons that noble authors are proposed is based on the idea that anonymity was desired due to the "stigma of print." Yet there are a number of reasons why an author, whether noble or not, would have wanted to avoid identification with the plays.

In the first place, if the normal practice for playwriting was collaborative, then there would be little point in claiming credit for a contribution to a play. At best, claiming credit would suggest sole authorship, at worst, claiming credit would associate the author with parts of a play which he might not care to be associated. Nashe's insistence that he had little to do with the *Isle of Dogs* is an example. Second, and directly related, is that claiming credit was potentially dangerous. Jonson was imprisoned twice, simply for his involvement in *Isle of Dogs* and *Eastward Ho!*, and even Samuel Daniel, when he finally put forth a play found himself in trouble for *Philotas*. A third related reason is what we might call the "Alan Smithee Effect." There is no such person, but "Alan Smithee" is a name that has been used since the 1960s to denote a person who did not want his name associated with a given film project. Suppose a writer collaborated on a given play and did not like the finished product—would he or she not be grateful that someone else was putting their name on the title page, and not sullying their own name, reputation, or beliefs? I think this is a likely scenario, and a better explanation than the legend of the Noble Hand.

Yet another factor involved with anonymity was simply a lack of concern for credit, as Nashe alluded to in his memoir of Robert Greene:[292]

> A good fellow he was and would have drunk with thee for more *angels* than the Lord thou libelledst on *gave thee in Christ's College*; and in one year he pissed as much against the walls, as thou and thy two brothers spent in three. In a night and a day would he have yarkt up

---

[292] Quoted in Alden Brooks, *Dyer's Hand*, 41, from *Strange News* (Nashe, *Complete Works*, Grosart edition, II: 220–221), and somewhat modernized. Nashe was in the process of attacking Gabriel Harvey in this excerpt; an "angel" is a coin. Moreover, the "lord thou libellest" is a reference to the Earl of Oxford. The text comes just before the description of the legendary luncheon with Will Monox, etc. discussed earlier.

a Pamphlet as well as in seven year, and glad was that printer that might be so blest to pay him dear for the very dregs of his wit.

He made no account of winning credit for his works, as thou dost, that dost no good works, but thinks to be famoused by a strong faith in thy own worthiness. His only care was to have a spell in his purse to conjure up a good cup of wine at all times.

A final reason for authors to lack concern for credit was purely practical. A collaborative play, bought and paid for on commission, belonged to the players, and then the company, before being sold to the printers: it did not belong to the author or authors. We should also keep in mind that in that era, fame was considered something of a chimera. John Marston's dedication to his *Scourge of Villainy* in 1598 may serve as our epitaph for Shakespeare's contemporaries:[293]

> Let others pray
> For ever their fair poems flourish may;
> But as for me, hungry Oblivion,
> Devour me quick, accept my orison,
> My earnest prayers, which do importune thee,
> With gloomy shade of thy still empery
> To veil both me and my rude poesy.

---

[293] *The Works of John Marston*, ed. A. H. Bullen (200 copies privately printed, London: 1887; here, Kindle edition).

25 | BEETHOVEN'S STAIRCASE

Beethoven's Ninth ~ The "Death of the Author" ~ Vickers' Protestations ~ The Intentional Fallacy ~ The Genetic Fallacy ~ Reader Response ~ Hermeneutics (Dilthey) ~ Loss of Secure Subject, 20th Century Intellectual Trends ~ Love's Types of Authorship (Precursory, Executive, Declarative, Revisory)

There is a legend that Beethoven got the idea for the beginning of the Scherzo in his Ninth Symphony while descending a staircase. Yet any edition of the symphony that one might consult lists only Beethoven as the composer. The staircase receives no credit at all—even though, if the legend is true, the staircase was instrumental in the derivation of that theme.

I want to use the image of Beethoven's staircase to address the larger issue of authorship, and more specifically the argument concerning "the death of the author" that emerged in the 1960s. In turn, I will propose some guidelines for assessing influence and collaboration. Above all, I mean to suggest a model to dampen the volatility of the authorship controversy.

The first part of the problem concerns the willingness to detach a work of art (or a document, or a text) from any kind of causal context. This is the general result of the strategy advanced by William Wimsatt and Monroe Beardsley in their famous article on the "Intentional Fallacy" in aesthetic criticism.[294] While it is certainly true that relentlessly

---

[294] William K. Wimsatt, Jr. and Monroe Beardsley, two American academics, published two articles in the *Sewanee Review*, "The Intentional Fallacy" (LIV, Summer, 1946) and "The Affective Fallacy" (LVII, Winter, 1949), which were strong statements of what became known as the "New Criticism," a school which meant to focus merely on the text in question in order to derive meaning. It is clear from reading the actual articles that they were motivated by a desire to avoid the heavy contextualization of previous readings (e.g., that Coleridge had actually read about "Kubla Khan" before he wrote his poem; whether Donne was familiar with cosmological theories when he wrote his, and so on). The two articles, along with several others, mainly by Wimsatt, were published as *The Verbal Icon* in 1954.

contextualizing a text ultimately leads to impressionism and relativism, and ultimately to the disappearance of the text itself,[295] it is also true that focusing on the context or the causative context of a text creates a theoretically endless learning curve before one can even begin to engage the text itself. This situation provides a partial account of why the authorship controversy, which is so short on direct objective evidence, should be given short shrift in literature courses. At some point, after all, students must get down to the business of actually reading the plays and poems.

As Wimsatt and Beardsley further note, the Intentional Fallacy is an offshoot of the Genetic Fallacy (judging an object by its origins) and the Affective Fallacy (judging an object by its results), and in neither case do these fallacies have any intrinsic relation to the object itself. Tension thus arises when the study of history is involved. Since historical research is overwhelmingly concerned with causes, the imposition of these fallacies, designed to facilitate the engagement with a text, have the result of de-historicizing literary objects to the extent that causal understanding is cast aside. Yet causal explanations of how a text came to be are not only of primary interest to historians but also to the general public. Put simply, How and Why are not going away. To be sure, this is one of the ways in which Stratfordians and anti-Stratfordians are doing the same thing: they are both attempting to link the creation of the plays to the biography of one person or another. That is one of the reasons I prefer to conceptualize them as unitarians and unitarian revisionists. It may be that Charlton Ogburn and Mark Anderson go too far in attempting to reconstruct the life of the person who wrote the Shakespeare plays, but so do people like A.L. Rowse, James Shapiro, and Stephen Greenblatt.

Now if we take a text—in this case, a play or a poem—completely out of context, we succeed in preventing that text from being submerged into the surrounding historical (or biographical) details in which it was created. But we have also caused the creator of the text to vanish. I believe this is what it means to speak of the "death of the author." The phrase itself comes from a brief essay by the French author Roland Barthes. Written in the same opaque language of most French structuralists and post-structuralists, the essay has the typical grand gestures, thus: "The removal of the Author [...] is not merely an historical

---

[295] Wimsatt and Beardsley, *The Verbal Icon*, 21. In the follow-up article they asserted that due to such techniques "the poem itself, as an object of specifically critical judgment, tends to disappear." Of course, by removing the context from the poem, I would argue they have also caused the author to disappear.

fact or an act of writing; it utterly transforms the modern text …" and "Once the Author is removed, the claim to decipher a text becomes quite futile" and "the birth of the reader must be at the cost of the death of the Author."[296] The concept has also been extensively elaborated by Foucault.

One reason all of this is relevant is that Brian Vickers, who has written and edited extensively on Shakespeare, seems to have taken the matter very seriously. Consequently, Vickers has written extensively in an effort to prove that authors actually exist (and that they write texts). In *Appropriating Shakespeare*, Vickers sought to trace the problem to Saussure, whose linguistic theories are supposedly the root of the "death of the author" business.[297] The detail and complexity of Vickers' exposition, deeply tied to modern secondary studies, commands respect, and, since I have used Saussure myself for my own purposes, some admiration. However, I don't think the problem is that complicated.

In the first place, Barthes' article can be read as nothing more than an extravagant restatement of what Wimsatt and Beardsley were saying with regard to the intentional fallacy—perhaps with a kind of subordinate restatement of "reader response" theory[298] added to the mix. But these writings are concerned with how to read and interpret texts: they are not dictates on how to construe historical reality.[299] For all his analytical labors, I think Vickers is digging in the wrong soil—which is not to say that there are not larger philosophical issues at stake.

The variability of meaning in a literary text, whether it is assumed to derive from formal analysis or, if one prefers, the "performance" of the text (as opposed to the notion that the reader supplies meaning to the text), is acceptable. After all, literary analysis is primarily concerned

---

296 Barthes, "The Death of the Author" in *Image, Music, Text*, 142–148; 145, 147, 148.

297 Vickers, *Appropriating*, especially Chapter 2 "Creators and Interpreters" and Chapter 1 "The Diminution of Language: Saussure to Derrida." We might summarize the matter this way: Wimsatt and Beardsley's approach causes the author to disappear, but Vickers' complaint is that recent critical approaches have caused the notion of a single shaping intelligence behind a text to disappear, namely, the authors of the plays, generally assumed to be Shakespeare.

298 Although there were some previous writings in this area, the idea that readers define the meaning of a text by their experience of a text was most famously articulated by Stanley Fish in his *Surprised by Sin* (1967), which argued that Milton's *Paradise Lost* was meant to elicit a change of mind or metanoia in the reader. As he subsequently argued in an appendix ("Discovery as Form in *Paradise Lost*"), the meaning of the poem lies in the experience of the reader of it, compared to which, on some level, the form of the poem itself is, in some sense, "incidental and even irrelevant," 341.

299 Hirsch, E.D., Jr., *Validity in Interpretation*, is a useful corrective to the vulgarization of concepts pertinent to literary criticism only, discussing Wimsatt, Saussure, Dilthey, and Gadamer. (Fish is not discussed, probably because both books were published in 1967.)

with a text as an aesthetic object.[300] In the study of history, however, the ambition is to achieve objectivity. Of necessity, this implies that there is a specific—and ideally discoverable—meaning and intent inherent in any text or document. To be sure, there are many who would argue that such objectivity is impossible, since all readers or students bring themselves into the equation.[301] While a recondite treatment of this objection is beyond the scope of the present study, it is useful to briefly explore some of the philosophical issues at play.

In the late 19th century, the German historian Wilhelm Dilthey sought to create a solid footing for historical study. According to Dilthey, the mental structures associated with Kant, but shaped by our lived experience, would make it possible for a student to correctly discern the meaning and intent of a text. However, Dilthey's somewhat imprecise approach to historical truth, which depends on process and experience[302] only works if a text is assumed to have a fixed meaning (as with the Bible) or if it is assumed that the result of the thinking process (i.e., phenomenology) will have a specific end point (as with Hegel's "Idea"). The problem is that 20th century trends in philosophy, particularly the analysis of thinking as a process (phenomenology) or thinking as a kind of being (Heidegger) brings us to a point where we have to acknowledge not only the insecurity of the subject, or student, or reader, but also the insecurity of the *creator* of the object, or text, or document. As a later critic of Dilthey, Hans Georg Gadamer, expressed it, the reader will have a horizon (determined by experience) while the creator of the object will also have had a horizon (also determined by experience), and because these horizons are always in flux, a definitive determination of meaning and intent is not possible. The end result is a hermeneutic circle that is interactive (or, if you prefer, intersubjective

---

300 I see the distinction between Wimsatt and Beardsley and Fish as being the difference between a formal analysis on the one hand, and a subjectively informed analysis on the other; thus Fish's approach carries with it notions of "process" to which predicates like phenomenological, hermeneutical, performance (in the Judith Butler sense), and ontology (in the Heideggerian sense) would pertain.

301 Peter Novick's *That Noble Dream* is a good introduction to the problem of the impossibility of historical objectivity in American historiography; Novick used the work of the historian Mircea Eliade to open the door for the play of structures that we bring to bear on experience, but this is common in most social sciences, linguistics, and philosophy since Kant and Hegel—not because they are to be blamed, but because of the subjectivity involved in any analysis of human experience.

302 It is not an accident that Dilthey wrote a biography of Schleiermacher, whose biblical studies introduced the study of hermeneutics (see chapter 7). One of the core concepts with Dilthey is *Erlebnis*, that is, experience. I think that what he meant by invoking this term was simply to point out that our patterns or categories of perception and understanding, instead of being rigidly defined, would change as a result of our lived experience. Of course, this insight can be dismissed as little more than a common sense appreciation of wisdom, or attendance at the school of hard knocks; or it can be appreciated as a useful distinction that separates the human sciences from hard sciences, allowing us to achieve insights on the basis of intuition, or empathy, or through our own lived experiences, with regard to the actions of other humans and their artifacts that would otherwise remain elusive. While it is certainly an operative principle in my own analyses, the non-empirical nature of such an attitude can easily be dismissed due to its vagueness.

and intertextual), and which, no matter how wide the context, never achieves finality.[303]

Recall that we began with John Aubrey wandering among the stones at Avebury. We observed that his discovery was contingent on a variety of objective factors (time of day, angle of approach, and so on) as well as subjective factors (the knowledge he possessed, the things that were on his mind, and so on). Now recall our discussion of Biblical hermeneutics, where we conceptualized a circle in which the reader was required to go from part to whole, and from whole to part, in an ever-widening context. If we put these things together, we have a situation in which Aubrey's discovery requires a hermeneutic approach of relating the single stones to the entire circle, while the Biblical student would be involved in a dynamic process with his or her text that would depend on the text under examination, the student's frame of mind, as well as such acquired knowledge and experience that the student brings to the text.

We could have more fun with our gathered images. Imagine the inhabitants of Avebury living in a Black Iron Prison and completely oblivious to the third millennium BCE hologram surrounding them—until the John Aubrey/Horselover Fat hero, disordered by pink laser beams, discovers the awful truth. Or we could imagine Aubrey, challenged by a ten-foot-tall stone text, locked in a form of phenomenological insight, such that the stone served as a lure and a challenge to his emerging consciousness. The tableau might suggest that the stones at Avebury had been placed for the same reason as the famous sentinel stones in Arthur C. Clarke's *2001*.

If it seems that I've drifted astray, that's the point. These kinds of speculations are characteristic of much modern discourse in philosophy and literary criticism. The farther we wade into the mire of hermeneutics, or linguistic theory, or even analytical philosophy, the stronger the tendency toward solipsism and non-communication.[304] And so we will stop it where it is: the "death of the author" simply means that human subjects, either as creators or as readers, are variable, and mutable,

---

303 Abstracted by my readings of the the relevant philosophers, including Dilthey and Gadamer, and secondary studies by Ermarth, Hodges, Bambach, and Howard. E. D. Hirsch, *Validity in Interpretation*, has a good appendix criticizing Gadamer, but Hirsch's argument is really about degrees of uncertainty; he does not endorse the notion of absolute validity in interpretation.

304 Howard, *Three Faces of Hermeneutics* is a good summary in this direction. The variability and incompleteness of perception and judgment really shouldn't be an issue, except when one attempts to go from epistemological to ethical issues: that is where most of the outrage pertaining to "relativism" resides, and that is the basis for most criticism of modern (or "postmodern") theory (opacity, subjectivity, and difficulty could be other grounds).

and unstable. What this can only mean beyond that is that humility, modesty, and uncertainty have a place in our judgment.

Instead of getting further bogged down in debates as to what constitutes an "author," let's step back and look at the issue from a historical point of view. We have a body of plays and poems. These plays and poems presuppose a general body of knowledge and erudition, which can be charted on a case by case basis. Assuming Shakespeare gets the title credit (which he does), we may proceed to the next question: how did this knowledge get into Shakespeare's head, so that it could go out through his hand?

The usual explanation is that Shakespeare was either a precocious student or a great listener. The first explanation is unsupportable because he left behind no books, manuscripts, letters, or written remains of any kind. He came from an illiterate environment, and to this environment he returned for several years before his death. The second explanation, that he gained his knowledge secondhand, is not so easily dismissed. Yet it requires that we imagine a Shakespeare who was far more sociable and curious than extant data suggest. If Shakespeare really was the sort of person who went to local drinking establishments to get the lowdown on legal terminology, Italian geography, hawking, or what have you, then one would expect more contemporary references to him as a real person. This is not what we find. Almost all the references to him are based strictly on the title page attributions of the plays and poems. That means that if the title page ascriptions are inaccurate, then the references to Shakespeare are inaccurate as well.

In his 2002 study *Attributing Authorship*, the late British scholar Harold Love distinguishes between four types of authorship: precursory, executive, declarative, and revisionary.

Precursory authorship represents any kind of contribution that leads to the creation of a text. Beethoven's staircase would fit in here, but so would a prior text (say, Holinshed's *Chronicle*), or an interpretation of a text. In his discussion of precursory authorship, Love usefully brings up film, and suggests that an actor (his example is Clint Eastwood) can have a profound effect on how a text is written or even how it is finally constituted. This, in essence, is why we talk about actors "creating" roles.

In a sense, the notion of precursor texts would be accepted by all sides, since everyone knows that the Shakespeare plays are dependent (often heavily dependent) on prior texts. Basic plots and characters are often thus derived, and there are numerous examples of paraphrasing and even outright plagiarism. This is why Shakespeareans emphasize Shakespeare's special gift for plot changes or secondary characterizations. It's also why anti-Stratfordians frequently argue that their candidate not only wrote a particular play, but the text it was based on as well.

On the subject of precursory authorship we should also note that when we are discussing the plays of Shakespeare, we are not actually describing the plays of Shakespeare; we are discussing only the *words* of the plays of Shakespeare. A Shakespeare production would have involved many other elements besides the simple text—blocking, acting, choreography, costume design, special effects, music, and so on. Referring back to Wagner, we can say that Wagner wrote his own libretti, but these are pale simulacra of the actual performances of Wagnerian opera. The same can be said about the emphasis, or even over-emphasis, on the words of the Shakespeare canon; whoever wrote the words, no one questions that the productions at the time were under the supervision of William Shakespeare.

This observation about Shakespeare's controlling role in production leads to Love's next category, *executive authorship*. By this he means the individual who makes the final decisions about what to include, omit, highlight or soft-pedal in a text. Again, regardless of "who wrote the plays" there is no question that Shakespeare was the executive author (except in such cases where he squirreled away an unadulterated manuscript or prior playscript among the theater's papers).

Nor is there any question that Shakespeare meets Love's criteria for *declarative authorship*. Either Shakespeare's name, or no name, is on the title pages of the texts.

Finally we come to *revisionary authorship*. This should be self-explanatory, and the possibility of revision must loom large whenever we discuss a Shakespeare text. Excepting *Venus and Adonis* and *Lucrece*, there is no assurance that Shakespeare had anything to do with the quartos of the plays or the Sonnets, and he died years before the Folio was assembled.

If we put Harold Love's categories of authorship on a timeline from left to right, we get:

precursory > executive > declarative > revisionary

Since no one seriously questions Shakespeare's executive and declarative authorship, the controversy mainly concerns precursory and revisionary authorship. But since revisionary authorship must be more or less assumed (as we have no guarantee of the integrity of any manuscript collected and published years after Shakespeare's death), let's place the emphasis on precursory authorship for now.

Suppose, as the story has it, that someone brought Shakespeare a play entitled *Titus Andronicus*. Shakespeare made some adjustments, and put it on the stage. Hence, it was a Shakespeare play. At some point, someone sent it on to be printed. Because Shakespeare had made the final alterations to the play, and had staged it, the play was published under his name. This is in fact the kind of understanding most people would have about *Titus*, so long as it was also understood that Shakespeare wrote all the good parts.

But let's suppose the same scenario with *Romeo and Juliet*, or *Othello*. Most people would object to the idea that anyone other than Shakespeare wrote the actual words to these plays. Yet we already know that the plots and characters of both tragedies were borrowed from Italian literature, so in effect we already know there were precursory authors to these plays. We also know (in the case of *Romeo*, in any case) that there are markedly different versions of the play, and it is unlikely that Shakespeare would have written two different versions. At this point, we are proposing different levels of precursory authorship—distant, like a staircase, but also near, like a manuscript or prior script.

My impression is that while nearly everyone will accept some distant precursor, the notion of a near precursor, as in the form of a manuscript, would be much less acceptable. And yet I am inclined to think that the latter is closer to the truth.

26 | The Folio Unbound

Speculations on Henry V ~ Suggestion of Quartos Being Shakespeare's Revisions ~ The Case for Hamlet ~ The Tempest ~ Individual Play Analysis Advocated for Purposes of Chronology and Context

As we are winding up our presentation I hope the reader will at least agree that there is considerable gray area surrounding the creation of the plays and poems under discussion. The real problem with the authorship controversy, to my mind, is the over-willingness of both sides to accept pat explanations that settle the matter once and for all. As I stated at the outset, it is not my desire or intention to refute anyone's candidacy—even Shakespeare's. I do, however, think there is ample room for speculation, which, in turn, might eventually lead to the discovery of new documents, new connections, and more satisfactory explanations for the creation of these literary documents. In that spirit, I will take this opportunity to deliberately present my own opinions.

The first issue to explore is the idea of "bad quartos" in the sense of unauthorized memorial reconstructions of original texts. A good test case is afforded by *Henry V*. We have two versions of this play: *The Chronicle History of Henry the Fifth* (the quarto published in 1600), and then *Henry V* as presented in the First Folio in 1623. So which was written first? Donnelly felt that the *Chronicle* came first and then was expanded to the Folio version. Chambers believed that *Henry V* came first and that the *Chronicle* was a one-time shortening. Others argue that the *Chronicle* is a reconstruction. The Folio text is usually preferred because it is longer, and makes more logical sense in many points. However, I would argue that the *Chronicle* is actually a better performance piece for three reasons: first, it omits the chorus parts which were already somewhat old-fashioned by the time the play was supposed to have been written in 1599; second, it omits the tiresomeness of the scene in Act V, partly in French, between Henry and Katherine; and third, because it truncates the speech of the Archbishop of Canterbury in Act I, Scene 1. (This speech sets out the justification for the war in legal terms. In the Folio, the speech is long, ornate, and uses Latin. In the quarto, the speech is shorter, simpler, and in English only.) Therefore I conclude that the Folio version was the original text, which was then deliberately cut down to make the play more accessible.

However, if the Folio text was written in 1599 and then shortened in 1599 in order to be published in 1600, then question arises as to who did the shortening and why. We assume that Shakespeare was by this time a practiced man of the theater. Why would he write a learned and pedantic speech for the Archbishop of Canterbury originally, and then cut it down and assign it to a bishop later the same year? Why would he write the well-known choruses ("Oh, for a muse of fire!" etc.) only to omit them the next year?

Let's take another example, the "Band of Brothers" speech in Act IV. The exhortation in the Folio is about 50 lines, in the quarto about 20 lines shorter. Here it is as it is set forth in the Folio:

> This story shall the good man teach his son;
> And Crispin Crispian shall ne'er go by,
> From this day to the ending of the world,
> But we in it shall be remember'd;
> We few, we happy few, we band of brothers;
> For he today that sheds his blood with me
> Shall be my brother; be he ne'er so vile,
> This day shall gentle his condition:
> And gentlemen in England now a-bed
> Shall think themselves accursed they were not here,
> And hold their manhoods cheap whiles any speaks
> That fought with us upon Saint Crispin's day.

And here is the quarto version of the same passage:

> This story shall the good man tell his son;
> And from this day unto the general doom,
> But we in it shall be remember'd;

> We few, we happy few, we band of brothers;
> For he today that sheds his blood by mine,
> Shall be my brother; be he ne'er so base,
> This day shall gentle his condition:
> Then shall he strip his sleeves and show his scars,
> And say, these wounds I had on Crispin's day;
> And gentlemen in England now a-bed
> Shall think themselves accursed,
> And hold their manhood cheap
> Whiles any speaks
> That fought with us
> Upon Saint Crispin's day.

Note that the speech has been shortened so that it no longer strictly scans in pentameter. The added line "strip his sleeves" comes from a segment cut out earlier in the speech. Note also the substitution of the word "base" (as in low-born) for "vile." "Vile" technically meant "servile," that is, again, low-born, but it also carried connotations of "being disgusting."[305] The substitution was likely made to appeal to a broader audience.

To sustain the conclusion that Shakespeare wrote both plays, we must imagine that he was at once an experienced man of the theater and a playwright who did not mind duplicating effort.[306] We would also have to maintain that he was a playwright who did not know what he was doing. If that seems harsh, consider the speech of the Archbishop of Canterbury in the Folio version, which reads like a memorandum drafted by a legal wonk who is excited by arcane details. It makes little sense that a man trying to write for a popular audience would indulge in such turgid disquisition.

I conclude that the 1623 Folio version of *Henry V* is the original version, which Shakespeare then revised downward in 1599 in order to put it on the stage. The *Chronicle* is, in effect, an adapted play, written by William Shakespeare. But who wrote the original version? That question cannot be answered with finality. However, because of the use of the chorus, it seems reasonable to suppose that it was originally written in the early 1590s or the 1580s, and by someone with a trove of legal and historical knowledge at his fingertips.

---

305 In the same sense that "villein" (low born) gave way to "villain," see the usage in the Wat Tyler rebellion and compare Nietzsche's *Genealogy of Morals*. "Vile" on the other hand has its more ordinary meaning in *King Lear*, "Out, vile jelly!" (III: 7), which is a reference to the notorious eyeball extrusions, not to Marmite.

306 Keep in mind Shakespeare is supposed to have written two other plays in 1599.

The same reasoning can be applied to *2 Henry VI*, and *3 Henry VI*. Again, for many years it was felt that these were upward revisions of the anonymous *The Contention* and *True Tragedy*. The more modern concept is that they are memorial reconstructions. On the other hand, it could be that the longer versions that we know from the Folio were the actual original versions, with the others being mere stewards of their excellence. Then we would have a case where Shakespeare shortened these plays, and, incidentally, made the gaffe about the succession from Edward. Such an interpretation would also help explain Greene's outburst in *Groatsworth*.

Now let us take up the case of *Hamlet*. We have five versions: the version referenced by Nashe and Lodge (the so-called "*Ur-Hamlet*"), the German version of uncertain date, the 1603 quarto, the 1604 quarto, and finally the Folio version of 1623. Excluding the *Ur* version, we are talking about essentially two versions, the 1603 quarto and the German version (which is very similar), and then the 1604 version and the 1623 version which are essentially the same play (although the 1604 version is about 10% longer).

Shakespeare scholar Paul Werstein has argued that the 1623 version comes before the 1603 and 1604 versions. That would make it the basic version of the play.[307] If Werstein is correct, then that would suggest that the 1603 version—along with the German version—was a deliberate simplification of the play for stage performance, while the 1604 version was expanded from the 1623 version by a few hundred lines to make it more relevant to the time when it was published.

There are other grounds that would support Werstein's conclusion. The 1604 quarto and the 1623 Folio correctly describe the flat topography of Elsinore. They also provide the correct names for Rosencrantz and Guilderstern (two real people). The use of the name "Polonius" also approximates the name of hereditary servitors to the Danish throne, the Ploennies family.[308]

It's also useful to contrast the famous soliloquy in the 1603 version with the 1604/1623 versions:

> To be, or not to be—that is the question:
> Whether 'tis nobler in the mind to suffer

---

307 Rosenbaum, *Shakespeare Wars*, 200–202. Werstine's book seems to support the priority both of the 1623 version of *Hamlet* and the later (fuller) quartos of *Romeo and Juliet*, but does not appear to support the idea of derivative versions made for performance purposes.

308 Michell, *Who Wrote Shakespeare?*, 220–222.

The slings and arrows of outrageous fortune
Or to take arms against a sea of troubles
And by opposing end them. To die, to sleep—
No more--and by a sleep to say we end
The heartache, and the thousand natural shocks
That flesh is heir to. 'Tis a consummation
Devoutly to be wished. To die, to sleep—
To sleep—perchance to dream: ay, there's the rub,
For in that sleep of death what dreams may come
When we have shuffled off this mortal coil,
Must give us pause: there's the respect
That makes calamity of so long life;
For who would bear the whips and scorns of time,
The oppressor's wrong, the proud man's contumely,
The pangs of disprized love, the law's delay,
The insolence of office and the spurns
That patient merit of the unworthy takes,
When he himself might his Quietus make
With a bare bodkin? Who would these fardels bear
To grunt and sweat under a weary life,
But that the dread of something after death,
The undiscovered country, from whose bourn
No traveler returns, puzzles the will
And makes us rather bear those ills we have
Than fly to those that we know not of.

Versus:

To be, or not to be, I there's the point,
To Die, to sleepe, is that all? I all:
No, to sleepe, to dreame, I mary there it goes,
For in that dreame of death, when wee awake,
And borne before an euerlasting Iudge,
From whence no passenger euer retur'nd,
The vndiscouered country, at whose sight
The happy smile, and the accursed damn'd.

The difference is no mere simplification. The first excerpt sounds almost like a paraphrase of Seneca's 82nd Epistle in the Lodge translation, as cited earlier. The second, however, has been awkwardly Christianized, with intrusive religious references to "an everlasting Judge" and "the accursed damned" making nonsense of the remainder ("sleep of death," "undiscovered country," and so on). I would argue not only that the 1623 Folio version precedes the 1603 quarto, but that it was written by a different person (or by different people) with completely different ideas about the subject under discussion.

This raises the question of where to place the 1623 version, especially since we know that the *Ur-Hamlet* was being performed just a few years before, and was perhaps referenced as far back as 1586.[309] The simplest path would be to assume that the 1623 version is identical to the *Ur-Hamlet*, written sometime before 1589, probably in the mid- to late 80s.

Let us now go back to Nashe's remarks in *Menaphon*, taking his cue to bleed Seneca line by line:

> But lest I might seem, with these night-crows, *Nimis curiosus in aliena republica* [to meddle in affairs not my own], I will turn back to my first text of studies of delight, and talk a little in friendship with a few of our trivial translators. It is a common practice now-a-days amongst a sort of shifting companions, that run through every art and thrive by none, to leave the trade of *noverint* whereto they were born and busy themselves with the endeavours of art, that could scarcely Latinize their neck-verse if they should have need;

The first point is that Nashe wants to talk about translators, who have had no fixed employment, but whose mastery of foreign languages would barely allow them benefit of clergy (hence the reference to "neck-verse"[310]) and who have abandoned the trade of *noverint*, that is, either a scrivener or a law clerk ("born" implies heredity, and we know that Kyd's father was a scrivener).[311] On the other hand, the term *noverint* is also frequently held synonymous with lawyering, so anyone trained in the law could be covered.

> ...yet English Seneca read by candlelight yields many good sentences, as Blood is a beggar, and so forth, and if you entreat him fair in a frosty morning, he will afford you whole *Hamlets*, I should say handfuls, of tragical speeches.

---

309 This interpretation depends on a "to be to he" reference in Nashe's preface to Philip Sidney's *Astrophel*, and has been argued to show the age of *Hamlet*; since Sidney died in 1586 there have been arguments to pre-date *Hamlet* to that point. However, the linkage of the quote is not certain, and Nashe's preface was not published until 1591, so we cannot be certain when he wrote it.

310 The term "neck verse" is commonly understood to be a reference to a passage from the Bible (usually, Psalm 51): "Have mercy upon me, O God, according to thy lovingkindness ..." which, read by an accused in a capital case, would confer benefit of clergy. It was, in effect, a literacy test, and underscored the rarity and importance of literacy at that time.

311 "Noverint" from "Noverint universi per praesentes," i.e., to all that shall know these presents, a common opening for legal documents of the period (compare "to all that shall see these presents, greetings"—a common salutation in armed services promotions to this day).

This, the most famous line, has already been quoted. One point that seems to go unnoticed by commentators is that Nashe is making a pun on the word, "hamlet." He invokes "*Hamlets*" to mean entire villages of tragical speeches, but he is also making a reference to a play of the same name. This is perhaps an important thing to note, in that while he may be identifying the play by name and by its central character, he is not necessarily discussing either the play or its author. He may simply be saying that *Hamlet*, as a derivative of Seneca, is full of tragical speeches.

Also here we have a distinction between reading "English Seneca" at night, which I interpret as "Englished Seneca" followed by plays full of tragical speeches in the morning. This is an image of someone reading a pretty good draft translation of Seneca at night (although "Blood is a beggar" remains elusive) and then the next morning finding a pamphlet hawked in St. Paul's churchyard (the traditional market for book stalls) full of Senecan speeches; or it may mean that someone started with translations and ended up with a play. But even here we have not settled on a specific candidate.

> But O grief! *Tempus edax rerum* [Time devours all things], what's that will last always? The sea exhaled by drops will in continuance be dry, and Seneca, let blood line by line and page by page, at length must needs die to our stage,

Here Nashe seems to be saying that such diluted Senecan writings will not last, and will fail on the stage. This does not appear to be the case with the *Spanish Tragedy*. On the other hand, the reference to Seneca "line by line and page by page" is usually taken as a reference to his tragedies, whereas I would take it as a nod to his philosophical writings. Nashe also seems to be referencing the manner of Seneca's death by cutting his veins.

> ...which makes his famished followers to imitate the kid in Aesop, who, enamoured with the fox's newfangles, forsook all hopes of life to leap into a new occupation,

This is the second most famous line and more than any other is the reason Kyd has been identified as the author of the *Ur-Hamlet*. But consider the original fable. The goat and the fox go into a well in order to drink water; the fox gets the goat to stand up, so that the fox can crawl out, and then he leaves the goat in the well. In other words, the goat is in a hole and cannot escape.[312] That would seem an apt metaphor for an indentured writer—the sort of thing Greene described in *Groatsworth*.[313]

> ...and these men, renouncing all possibilities of credit or estimation, to intermeddle with Italian translations, wherein how poorly they have plodded (as those that are neither Provencal men, nor are able to distinguish of articles), let all indifferent gentlemen that have travailed in that tongue discern by their twopenny pamphlets.

So now we're back to the "trivial translators" who have sacrificed careers to make poor translations from Italian, which they sell as cheap pamphlets. This might apply to any number of authors.

> And no marvel though their home-born mediocrity be such in this matter, for what can be hoped of those that thrust Elysium into hell, and have not learned the just measure of the horizon with an hexameter? Sufficeth them to bodge up a blank verse with ifs and ands, and otherwhile, for recreation after their candle-stuff, having starched their beards most curiously, to make a peripatetical path into the inner parts of the City, and spend two or three hours in turning over French dowdy, where they attract more infection in one minute than they can do eloquence all days of their life by conversing with any authors of like argument.

This last passage is of course the most scurrilous. It implies sarcasm in the first instance, insofar as these translators have not mastered hexameter (a dig at Harvey) and write poor blank verse instead—and after their lucubrations spend their time with French prostitutes.

To sum up, the famous paragraph attacks trivial translators of continental languages, who gave up careers in law or scrivening to go about selling cheap translations that are poor in quality, who may be indentured or in debt, whose Latin is poor, who are sexually promiscuous, who are Senecan epigones, and who, among other things, wrote *Hamlet*. All of this could apply to Kyd, but also to others. But it sure doesn't sound like Shakespeare.

---

312 "Fox and Goat" in *Fables of Aesop*, 80. This is from a 1694 version, but given the extreme age of the stories, not particularly relevant.

313 There is extensive exegesis on the point that there is no kid (but rather goat) in Aesop, which leads back to a stanza in Spenser's *Faerie Queen*. See Duthie, *The 'Bad' Quarto of Hamlet* (1941), Jolly, *The First Two Quartos of Hamlet* (2014).

The next question is one of priority for the *Spanish Tragedy* or *Hamlet*. It is generally assumed that *Hamlet* came later, although Harold Bloom believes that the *Ur-Hamlet* (by Shakespeare) came first and that the *Spanish Tragedy* followed.[314] In either case we have a version of *Hamlet* in the mid-1580s.

Placing *Hamlet* in the 1580s makes sense on stylistic grounds. There are several examples of euphuism, as well as the characteristic ostentatious learning and moral didacticism of the genre. Another reason to place the play in the 1580s is that the speech to the actors in Act III is also a reference back to arguments about plays and playacting in the 1580s.

So then who wrote *Hamlet*? The two writers most associated with the euphuistic style were John Lyly and Thomas Lodge, but Lyly's style is nothing like that in *Hamlet*. Lodge on the other hand has a didactic speech in his *Rosalind* that is very similar to the speech of Polonius,[315] and his prose is full of the kind of rhetorical devices found in the play. The long sequence of balanced clauses in the famous Soliloquy are common in Lodge's writing, particularly in his *Wit's Misery*. In addition, Lodge's attitude toward the theater (as expressed in his *Defense of the Theaters*) is somewhat consonant with the advice given in Act III. On this evidence, we can hypothesize that Lodge wrote *Hamlet* in the 1580s as a response to Kyd's *Spanish Tragedy*. We should be able to definitively exclude Kyd as the author of *Hamlet* (or the *Ur-Hamlet*) on two grounds: first, there would be no reason to write another version of the *Spanish Tragedy* so soon after writing the original, and second, the writing styles are completely different.

But what exactly is to be gained by assuming (for the moment) that Lodge wrote *Hamlet*, or something approximating the *Hamlet* we know? What, in other words, is the functional purpose of this attribution? Unless we are attempting to purify the canon for devotional reasons, it would seem that the proper purpose of positing attribution is simply to increase our understanding, if only for heuristic purposes. Through this lens, we might see the play as a rebuttal to both Gosson and Philip Sidney. Or with regard to the players, we might construe the famous "to be or not to be" soliloquy as being less about the cosmic value of life over death

---

314 Bloom, *Shakespeare*, 396-398, 408.

315 Partly quoted above in chapter 3. This kind of didacticism is common in his other works, e.g., *Wit's Miserie*.

and more directly about the roving players who arrive at the castle ("who would these fardels bear?")—which would make the name of the book Hamlet is carrying irrelevant.[316] Given Lodge's education, we might also reflect on the overall purpose of the play. We may discern that the "tragical speeches" that Nashe referenced are not dramatic, but *didactic*. Looking closer, we find the verse turning over resonant themes in Hellenistic philosophy, and in particular, Seneca's writings.

Then again, there is much portrayal of mental illness or melancholia in the play, and there is also a ghost. But even here there is some ambiguity, as evidenced by Hamlet's initial skepticism; in effect, the contrast between external apparition and inner voice is raised. Such questions remind us that *Hamlet*—whenever it was penned, and whoever wrote it—was written about halfway between Reginald Scot's debunking *Discoverie of Witchcraft* (1574) and Robert Burton's *Anatomy of Melancholy* (1621).[317] The play is clearly concerned with psychological and philosophical issues of deep meaning to the author. Yet there are no prior plays by Shakespeare with this orientation, and only a few after (*King Lear* and *Macbeth* come to mind). On the other hand, there are a small number of other authors of the time who explored these types of themes, either in poetry or prose. Among such writers we may count Nashe, Lodge, Daniel, Chapman, and Davies of Hereford. Of the five, only Nashe and Lodge wrote specifically on psychological or psychopathological themes. And of these two, Nashe's style does not jibe. So again we are left with Lodge.

There are various ways to buttress the Lodge attribution. We know that he was well educated, that he was involved in the stage and that he wrote plays, and we know that he left the law to pursue a literary career (in fact, several careers) before becoming a physician in the late 1590s.[318] We know that Lodge's inheritance from his mother was lost because he discontinued his legal studies, and his father did not even

---

316 Note that the "fardels" reference is omitted from the 1603 quarto.

317 Another reference that is perhaps relevant is 1586, the year Timothy Bright's *Treatise of Melancholie* was published.

318 Lodge received BA 1577 but did not receive his MA in 1581 because he was arrested, either for debt or for his Catholicism, and spent that summer in prison (Tenney, Edward Andrews, *Thomas Lodge*, 80). It is known that he maintained an address at the law school at Lincoln's Inn for several years. We have already discussed Collier's insight—or forgery—that Lodge was an actor; we know, however, that William Prynne (1600-1660) characterized him as one in his *Histrio-Mastix* (1633): "these players Lodge & Haywood [sic!]" Paradise, N. Burton, *Thomas Lodge*, 73.

mention him in his Will.³¹⁹ We may consider his status as a recusant Catholic and whether this may have had something to do with the handling of ghosts and purgatory in *Hamlet*.³²⁰ In addition, we know that Lodge was plagiarized several times. He even complained about it, though we do not know the specific cases he had in mind.³²¹ Lodge was also accused of plagiarism himself, inasmuch as several of his poems were simply translations from French and Italian originals—yet this reminds us that his skills in classical languages must have been formidable. In the 1600s he published translations of both Josephus and all of Seneca's moral and philosophical writings. These must have taken many years to complete.³²²

Did Nashe ever refer to Lodge at any other time? This is a point of some dispute, but there is a passage from *Pierce Penniless*, from 1592, which bears an uncanny resemblance to Lodge. It was written while Lodge was on his second voyage:³²³

> A young heir or cockney, that is his mother's darling, if he have played the wastegood at the Inns of Court or about London, and that neither his student's pension, nor his unthrift's credit, will serve to maintain his college of whores any longer, falls in a quarrelling humour with his fortune because she made him not King of the Indies, and swears and stares after ten in the hundred that ne'er a such peasant as his father or brother shall keep him under; he will to the sea, and tear the gold out of the Spaniards' throats, but he will have it, byrlady. And when he comes there, poor soul, he lies in brine in ballast, and is lamentable sick of the scurvies; his dainty fare is turned to a hungry feast of dogs & cats, or haberdine and poor-john at the most, and, which is lamentablest of all, that without mustard.

---

319 Paradise, *Thomas Lodge*, contains all of the family wills. The stipulation of the mother was that Lodge (one of six children and five sons) would remain in the law until he was 25; he failed to do so (201). The father's will is at 208-211. Beginning in 1594, Lodge would litigate his inheritance with his brother (11).

320 Tenney, describing the pamphlet *The Devil Conjured* (1596). 147-148. Briefly, the Protestant Church of England decreed all ghosts as agents of the Devil, as opposed to the Catholic Church, which allowed for beneficial or neutral spirits (because of the existence of Purgatory). As a Catholic, Lodge would have argued this position. For insight into how it ties into *Hamlet*, compare Greenblatt's *Hamlet in Purgatory*.

321 Paradise, 37, indicating that this was a common complaint. This is as good a place as any to note that Lodge's poem, *Historie of Glaucus and Scilla* (1589), provided the model, including the unusual meter, for Shakespeare's first publication, *Venus and Adonis* (Harman, Edward George, *Countess of Pembroke's Arcadia*), 191. Harman somewhat overstates Sidney Lee's acknowledgment of this and claims Shakespeare copied Lodge. Harman also claims that Bacon used Lodge as a front, 187. Late in life Joseph Sobran also claimed that Lodge's sonnet cycle *Phillis* was also written by the Earl of Oxford.

322 If we enlist Lodge's translation of Seneca's 82nd epistle as precursor to *Hamlet*, we will certainly have to assume that the translation existed in manuscript for many years. This would be unusual but not that remote a possibility (compare the writings of Sir Philip Sidney, as well as the arguments for the influence of Strachey's manuscript on *The Tempest*, and so forth). It is worth keeping in mind that the letter comprises four pages in a thousand-page long set of translations.

323 Tenney, *Thomas Lodge*, 130-131.

I propose that Lodge wrote *Hamlet* more or less in the 1623 folio form, either before or after Kyd's tragedy, subsequent to a visit either by Lodge himself or by an intimate who had been to Denmark in 1585.[324] The play was meant to be a model Senecan tragedy, with room for the development of the author's interests in philosophy, psychology, and drama. That's why it was so long, and why it failed. The play was then cut down and shortened for stage performance (including a version with chorus that later migrated to Germany). Lodge disowned the play, leaving the country to study medicine. In 1603, the vulgarized adaptation (or a version thereof) was published, and the following year the original, longer version—with some additions—was also published. Because of these modifications, both versions could rightly be characterized as "Shakespeare plays." Finally, when the First Folio was prepared, a clean copy of the more or less original manuscript was used. Shakespeare probably purchased it from Henslowe.[325]

The argument could be rebutted by saying that no one attributed *Hamlet* to Lodge, and that Lodge never complained even though he lived until 1625 and referenced *Hamlet* in *Wit's Misery*. These are fair points. I would only rejoin that one way to interpret the reference in *Wit's Misery* is that it comes in the portion where Lodge describes "hate-virtue," the human propensity to tear things down. In that context, the reference to *Hamlet* could mean simply that the high-flown ambition of the original play had been degraded into a catchphrase, that Lodge's creation had been vulgarized into a popular play that he wanted nothing to do with.[326] I would also note that Lodge was frequently out of England after his conversion. As a Catholic he had good reasons to keep a low profile, and by 1596 he had resolutely turned his back on his earlier literary life.

Beyond this, and again, the rebuttals are fair. I have no desire to pursue the argument. If Thomas Lodge were ever recognized as a precursory author to *Hamlet*—and, I further suspect, *Lear* and

---

324 Fleay had the idea that Greene was in Elsinore in 1584 with Leicester's Men; we know that Greene and Lodge cowrote at least one play.

325 Lodge had chronic debts throughout his life. One debt, for seven pounds to the tailor Topping, ended up in Philip Henslowe's lap, Paradise, 46-48.

326 There is also a possibility that, if Lodge had a hand in *Hamlet*, he was self-promoting here; Nashe's reference to Talbot in *Pierce Pennilesse* is taken by many to support the idea that he contributed to *Henry VI, Part 1*; Dekker made a pun about *Patient Grissel* in his *Wonderful Year* (1603), and Greene's reference to "Tiger's heart" in *Groatsworth* is an arguable self-reference to *Henry VI, Part 3*.

Edward III—then we could at least read these plays in light of his writings. And that, I am convinced, would enhance our understanding of "Shakespeare."[327]

---

327 Other plays can be evaluated for their relationship to other authors, and in terms of broader historical context. For example, it has already been suggested that Daniel may have had a hand in *Romeo*; and given his friendship with Nashe, it is not hard to see Nashe in the character of Mercutio (whoever actually wrote his speeches). Daniel seems a likely source to consult for *Richard II*, as well as for *Anthony and Cleopatra*. Being aware of the Henslowe plays of *Cesar's Fall*, *The Spanish Moor*, and *Troilus and Cressida*, it also does not require a lot of imagination to see the hands of Dekker, Drayton, Chapman, Middleton and company in any number of the post-1600 plays, including *Julius Caesar*, *Othello*, and *Troilus*.

With regard to *The Tempest*, I have already noted the tendency of Stratfordians to date the play to after 1610 (on the thesis that the playwright must have consulted the Strachey manuscript). In reaction to this, Oxfordians have recently argued that the play bears a relationship to an unknown play entitled *The Spanish Maze*. Yet both arguments ignore the fact that *The Tempest* bears a strong resemblance to *The Beautiful Sidea* of Jacob Ayrer, whose death in 1605 must mean that *The Tempest*—or something very much like it—must have been written before then. Given that Ayrer's plays (and other old German plays) include several with a strong resemblance to Shakespeare plays, as Cohn describes, it is reasonable to conclude that *Sidea*, like the others, was a German reworking of an original English play. So what play might that have been?

With regard to *The Tempest* there are numerous tantalizing elements, not just the Montaigne quote noted earlier. There is also a reference to men with their heads in their chests, in Act III, scene III, whose appearance yields the following comment:

> *Who would believe that there were mountaineers*
> *Dew-lapp'd like bulls, whose throats had hanging at 'em*
> *Wallets of flesh? or that there were such men*
> *Whose heads stood in their breasts? which now we find*

The second part of this quote was recognized as far back as 1839, by Joseph Hunter, as being a possible reference back to Sir Walter Raleigh's book, *The Discovery of Guiana*, in 1596. But the trope also turns up in *Othello*, as well as in Lodge's *Wit's Miserie* from 1595. Ultimately the motif may be traced to *The Travels of Sir John Mandeville*, a hugely popular travelogue first circulated in the 1350s. Bearing in mind that there is an unknown play from the 1580s entitled *Mandeville*, it would be easy to suggest a linkage among them. In addition, the first part of the quotation concerning dew-lapped mountaineers seems to be a reference to the known effects of iodine deficiency in southern Germany and the Alps, which further suggests deeper personal knowledge by the playwright of the region.

Another aspect of *The Tempest* worth exploring is its potential for being perceived as politically incendiary. This concerns the notion that Prospero, as an actor and magician, steps forward at the end of the play not only to receive the plaudits of the crowd, but also metaphorically to regain his crown. Other subversive elements include the Montaigne speech already noted, the part where the noble Ferdinand is reduced to the menial labor of hauling logs, and, I would argue, the witch Sycorax herself. Usually her name is construed as *sus+korax* from the Greek, that is, *pig* and *raven*, with the pig element recalling Circe turning the crew of Odysseus into pigs. I think a more likely etymology would be a Greco-Roman calque of *syco*- (fig in Greek, but a well known vulgar term for female pudenda) and *rex*- (Latin for King), thus "Queen Quim" might be the most polite translation. Some, but not all, of these elements are still present in Ayrer's play. Yet a final element concerns the presence of dogs in two places in the play (the apparitions in Act IV, and the "Bow Wow" song in Act II). This calls to mind a well known incendiary play from 1597: *The Isle of Dogs*.

The Isle of Dogs is an actual location in northeast London, a low lying area at a tight bend in the Thames; but it has also been noted as being identical in meaning to the Canary Islands, a Portuguese holding. During the summer of 1597, the Earl of Essex (who would lead a rebellion against Elizabeth few years later) led an expedition to the region to seize a Spanish treasure fleet, and it was during this time that *The Isle of Dogs* had its abortive performances. When we combine these facts with the subversive elements of the play—a King denied his throne but requesting the audience's applause to regain it, an evil queen with a misshapen son, nobles reduced to hauling logs, discussions of a different social order—we can imagine that a performance of such a play would lead to political demonstrations as well as furious suppression, whether such political interpretation was intended or not. In short, I would suggest that *The Tempest*, while comprising many other elements, is primarily a palimpsest for *The Isle of Dogs*.

27 | "Shakespeare—Who?"

Traditional Attribution to Shakespeare Is Unassailable ~ But That Doesn't Make it Unquestionable ~ Unitarians versus Analysts, Irreconcilable Approaches ~ Gombrowicz's Ferdydurke ~ Psychological Reactions to Unknowing: Hate-Virtue, Milkmaid and Bucket ~ Chain of Reasoning versus Skein of Reasoning ~ Forgery and Fraud ~ Gluttony-Virtue or Vedic Expansions ~ Black Iron Prison or Epistemic Closure ~ Accusations of Denial ~ Traditional Categories: Internal Evidence (Moot) ~ External Evidence (Title Pages) ~ Contextual Evidence (Anyone but Shakespeare) ~ Expand the Pantheon

In the preceding chapters, we have tried to put the Shakespeare authorship controversy into a progressively wider context. We have seen that it arose in the context of the corrupt and divergent nature of the texts left behind by Shakespeare, and we have seen how this contextual backdrop informed the attribution studies of the 18th century and beyond. We have seen also that the controversy was fed by the discovery and publication in the 1840s of the *Sir Thomas More* manuscript and Philip Henslowe's Diary, both of which provided documentary proof for the collaborative authorship of Elizabethan and Jacobean plays.

Over the course of almost four hundred years, no document has ever been unearthed to directly support the claim that William Shakespeare wrote the plays and poems that are attributed to him. There are only the title page attributions. Even if we accept the attribution of the two excerpts in *Sir Thomas More* to Shakespeare, there is no logical point connecting that attribution to the rest of the Shakespeare canon. At the same time, it is only fair to add that no document has ever emerged directly ascribing the plays, or any single one of them, to anyone else.

There seems little doubt that the authorship controversy arose organically from the body of Shakespeare criticism. While is true that global reassignments of the canon were not pushed forward until the 1850s, doubts about attributions are as old as Shakespearean criticism itself. More interesting is the way in which the controversy has tended to split into two competing groups. On one side we find "unitarians" who are convinced that the First Folio is a calculated artistic (or political, or philosophical) statement that traces to a single genius. On the other side are the "analysts" who, depending on where one draws the line, are convinced that some or much or all of the canon derives from other heads and other hands.

In the broadest sense, the argument between unitarians and analysts may never be reconciled—and this may be the case whether the subject is Homer, the Bible, or Shakespeare. The problem is that it represents not so much a discourse, but two states of mind. The impulses to take apart and put back together will always be in conflict. The situation is nicely captured in Witold Gombrowicz's novel *Ferdydurke*, in which Filidor, a professor of Synthesology at the University of Leyden, enters into a duel with Anti-Filidor, a professor of Higher Analysis at Columbia University:

> Anti-Filidor walked over to our table and silently looked daggers at the Professor, who rose to his feet. The Analyst pressed coolly from below, the Synthesist responded from above, with a gaze charged with defiant dignity. When the duel of looks gave no definite result, the two spiritual enemies began a duel of words. The Doctor and master of Analysis declared:
> "Noodles!"
> The Synthetologue responded:
> "One noodle!"
> The anti-Filidor responded:
> "Noodles, noodles, namely a mixture of flour, eggs, and water!"
> Filidor retorted instantly:
> "Noodle, namely the higher being of the Noodle, the highest Noodle himself!"[328]

To put it another way, the real divide is not between those who think Shakespeare wrote the plays, and everyone else; it is between those

---

328 Gombrowicz, *Ferdydurke*, 88–89.

who think Shakespeare or Oxford or Bacon (or whoever) wrote the plays, and those who think the plays are in the last analysis a more or less fortuitous compilation gathered together and published in 1623. (The relative few who argue that the plays were written by many, but were overseen by the prodigious mind of one person, may be considered for their attempt to have the best of both approaches.)

We thus begin with a kind of Elizabethan Rorschach test that reveals various psychological attitudes. This is the inevitable result of the background reality that cannot be over-emphasized: aside from title page ascriptions and the like, we have no direct evidence that *anyone* wrote the plays.

"Hate Virtue" seems to be one prominent attitude. But while the accusation is often made, there really doesn't appear to be much in the way of hatred underlying the various attempts to wrest the plays away from Shakespeare. From the earliest days to the present era, dissenters seem to have been motivated by honest, if perhaps sometimes naïve, doubts.

Perhaps more interesting are the various psychological habits and sleights employed by the parties. The "Milkmaid and Bucket" sequence is one, whereby a chain of deductions is created with a view toward supporting a particular conclusion. Yet in all likelihood this approach masks a presupposed conclusion, obtained intuitively then guided along by motivated reasoning or confirmation bias. It remains a common problem in this field, but it is a common problem in many fields. A prior intuition will often seem stronger than any rational explanation, and it is here that the minutiae of clang associations shade over into what we might normally call paranoia.

Another psychological approach works from the top down. We might call this "virtue gluttony" or "Vedic expansion." This is where a generally assumed premise of authorship—or a generally assumed premise of anything—based on little tangible evidence, is then expanded into an ever larger edifice of explanation. This is also a common mental failing, not exclusive to Shakespeare studies. Again we find the spider webs of reasoning, even in the complete absence of evidence. At the prickly outer edges, the expansionist mindset may give way to grandiose megalomania and devotionally charged wish fulfillment.

In both of the above cases we are talking about psychological issues that arise from *not knowing*. The cure, in both cases, is clear and direct evidence. But in the present case the dearth of direct evidence leads not only to rational distortions, but also into other more obscure realms such as cipher decoding, grave excavations, telepathic stunts, spirit conversations, etc. While it can be tempting to dismiss such obsessive pursuits as manifestations of some underlying psychopathology, this misses the point. It would be better to say that they are normal reactions of human beings confronted with the inability to find answers. When the cloud of unknowing has become a brick wall, one reaches for a chisel. For most of us, the temptation to chisel away is mercifully held in check in our day-to-day lives. Yet the human disposition to seek—and invent—answers, to fill in the gaps of our own ignorance, is deeply rooted. If we are thus wired to never take "no evidence" as an answer, we should also expect instances of forgery and fraud to occasionally be introduced as ersatz gap-fillers. Indeed, we have seen this in the case of Shakespeare through the activities of Ireland and Collier.

There is another kind of mental reaction that deserves attention. Recalling the rigidity of "epistemic closure" that finds expression in Philip K. Dick's "Black Iron Prison," we may consider such hostile complementary strategies that are exemplified by vilification and, more recently, by accusations of "denial." One way to react to uncertainty is to simply declare certainty by fiat and then demean anyone who thinks differently. While the denigration of contrary opinion has become commonplace in many scholarly controversies, it is both unproductive and cruel. When one party proclaims the unassailable truth of his or her own position in the authorship controversy, a core problem (beyond mere rudeness) may stem from the implicit invocation of the "context of discovery and justification" to achieve a purpose for which it was never intended. Regardless, demeaning the character of one's opponent represents not only a failure of communication at its most basic level, but also a failure to acknowledge the fundamentals of trust, civility, and charity that should rule in public discourse. Such polarities may at times leave an amusing detritus (as in the Harvey-Nashe quarrel), but more often the hostile reaction simply inflames prejudice and does nothing to advance knowledge or understanding.

So how exactly do we proceed with a subject, when we do not know what we most wish to know? The first step, which we borrow from hermeneutics, is to seek an ever-widening context. If a problem remains stubbornly obscure at its point, then widen the circle and learn what you can. Eventually a plausible pattern may come into view, one that is at least grounded in evidence. Surely, John Aubrey never would have gained his insight at Avebury just by standing still.

The second step is to mimic the understanding of a problem as it happened over time. The benefit of a "historical" or "chronological" approach is that one can see how the assumptions upon which a particular explanatory model was built evolved over time, and did or did not change as more evidence accumulated. This is the true relevance of the discovery/justification context, and its applicability to the paradigm shift that Thomas Kuhn described.

Beyond these techniques, we simply must reconcile ourselves to the insecurity of our knowledge and the incompleteness of our understanding. Modesty is not relativism, and neither entails the destruction of civilization as we know it.

With this much in tow, we turn once again to the question that is usually paramount. Who wrote the plays? Let's begin by stating the matter using the categories of traditional literary criticism.

Internal evidence is a shaky category for Shakespearean attributions. To begin with, all potential candidates must have received more or less the same education. They also read the same books, attended the same plays, and participated in the same conversations about the world around them. Given these circumstances, it is often quite difficult to tell one author from another. More difficult still is the task of taking two or three potential authors and deciding definitively who wrote what.

It may be useful to frame the argument for internal evidence in another way. There is plenty of evidence that the Homeric works, in their dialectical scope, cover centuries in time and hundreds of miles in geography. We know this because of changes in grammar and word usage and, of course, by studying their narrative content. And yet to this day, there is no agreement as to whether these works were compiled or written by a sole author. There is no reason to expect otherwise with the Shakespeare plays, which were focused in a single city over the course of a mere couple of decades. To be sure, there are many cases in which the form of expression, or even specific words, may point to a specific author, or away from another. But arguments over characteristic expression and special knowledge are hundreds of years old, with no resolution in sight. Add to this the decisive evidence that points to Elizabethan drama as a collaborative enterprise, which presents great obstacles to settling any matter on internal evidence. Schoenbaum observed more than once that, while William Faulkner collaborated on the screenplay for the 1955 film *Land of the Pharaohs*, it would be very difficult to identify which parts he wrote.[329] The difficulty is vastly more daunting when applied to the entirety of Elizabethan and early Jacobean drama.

External evidence is also not a reliable measure. To be sure, we have Shakespeare's name on various title pages, but we also find his name on texts that are almost never attributed to him. And there are other texts, now ascribed to him, which were originally published anonymously. Bearing in mind Erasmus' dictum that "[n]othing is easier than to place any name you want on the front of a book," it follows that external evidence at this level is also unreliable. The simplest explanation for the plays attributed to Shakespeare, as well as the Shakespeare apocrypha, is that these were the plays that were at one time or another in the possession of his theater company—the Lord Chamberlain's Men, or after 1603, the King's Men.

There is another way of looking at the external evidence. Condell, Heminge, and Jonson clearly thought that the plays in the First Folio constituted a body of work in which Shakespeare had at least a leading part. For most of the plays, it is likely that they would have relied upon clean copies that had been set aside for safekeeping; and we know that for the remainder printed quartos were probably used. The burning of the Globe in 1613 may have had an impact on these decisions. The problem is that there is no sure way of differentiating the versions presented in the First Folio from the manifold quarto versions, nor can we be sure which versions came first.

However, the differences between the quarto and Folio versions create another problem for attribution. Remember that the quarto versions tend to be shorter and more direct, while the Folio versions tend to be longer, more ornate, abstract, and dramatically inert. The quarto versions may also contain deliberate plagiarisms from other plays ("A Shrew"), historical inaccuracies ("The Contention") and geographical and factual inaccuracies ("Hamlet"). Again, let us keep in mind what we know about plays in Elizabethan times: they were written collaboratively, they were frequently revised and touched up, and many of the people involved in writing plays were prolix and ostentatious in their other (undisputed, and voluminous) writings. We also know that writing plays was not a particularly lucrative activity (writers complained

---

[329] Schoenbaum, *Internal Evidence and Elizabethan Dramatic Authorship*, 168.

about their status compared to the actors and moneylenders). If we maintain that Shakespeare was responsible for the quartos, then he must have written the quartos after the folio versions for performance purposes. But that would mean that in writing the Folio versions, Shakespeare did not know what he was doing.

We could imagine another scenario in which a number of creative and alienated young men—the "Elizabethan Beats"—sought to avoid the penury of life as a parish priest or a private tutor by writing. Frustrated by the prevailing ideology and infrastructure that allowed few avenues for success, these men would have read the Tudor equivalent of Nietzsche (Machiavelli) or existentialism (Hellenistic philosophy). They would assimilate ideas and aesthetics that would find expression in plays, which they would write and sell for the money it took to fuel their worldly addictions. We might further imagine such bright young men reacting with horror as their plays were dumbed down for the Elizabethan equivalent of network television. This would mean that Shakespeare knew exactly what he was doing.

My interpretation, already set forth, and implied or expressed by several others,[330] is that the "bad quartos" were simply performance versions put together by Shakespeare (and a scribe, since I am convinced that Shakespeare could not write) on the basis of previous manuscripts Shakespeare had received.[331] This seems like a reasonable conclusion, since there appears to be a consensus, going back to Alexander Pope, that the "bad quartos," considered as performance pieces, are in some ways superior to the longer versions.

But even if we set that conclusion aside, we still have to deal with multiple versions, and we still have to deal with the possibility of revisions, even extensive revisions, between Shakespeare's putative "foul papers"[332] and the final publication either in quarto or the First Folio. Thus it is only fair that we should hold the matter of authorship in

---

[330] Including Sabrina Feldman and Dennis McCarthy.

[331] I am not sure why that there are now at least three students of this subject arguing that the quarto plays were illegitimate offshoots of the Folio originals; it would not have been typical among Shakespeareans, because it involves pushing the chronology of the plays further back, while the typical anti-Strat position is to argue that the bad quartos represented first drafts that were later improved. Certainly a major influence has been the work of Laurie Maguire, whose book on the bad quartos ("suspect texts") argued that few of them were memorial reconstructions (Maguire investigated 41 suspect texts, not merely Shakespeare's).

[332] "Foul papers" was a concept popularized by Walter Greg and others in the mid-20th century, and is meant to refer to a more or less final version of a play in the author's own hand before being handed down for performance. All other versions, whether "fair copies," "prompt books," "bad quartos," or even "variant quartos," are meant to be seen as lesser or degraded emanations of the idealized One Noodle "Foul Papers." The concept is meant to address the theoretical need for a foundational or authoritative version of a play, but it remains hypothetical; there is no complete "foul paper" version of any Elizabethan play, much less a Shakespeare play, and as a result the concept has been criticized in recent decades. See Werstine, Ioppolo, McMillin, and Hinman.

suspense. It seems a suitable penalty for Shakespeare's lack of concern for his works or his posterity. The yawning absence of any literary remains ups the ante. Since Shakespeare left nary a scrap to guide us, the idea of collaboration or revision is hard to resist or deny.

All of this leads us to consider the final category of contextual evidence.[333] Once again, Shakespeare falls short. There is nothing in Shakespeare's background, education, life experience, or the wider context of playwriting or play production in the London of his time to support the idea that he simply isolated himself between acting performances and created these plays and poems extemporaneously. On the contrary, all of the contextual evidence points to a profile of Shakespeare as a hard-working businessman—a play producer, actor, and script doctor who was above all concerned with making money, raising his social status, and bestowing his wealth and status on his family.

One irony about contextual evidence is that we have no contemporary evidence of Shakespeare as a playwright or play doctor—except for the possible identification him as the "Poet Ape" in Jonson's epigram. Yet that is the identification that most avoid.

It is the absence of contextual evidence supporting Shakespeare (along with the wider context provided by Henslowe's Diary) that invites consideration of other candidates. This is so even if the candidates proposed often reflect the bent of the individual researcher. Those who are dissatisfied with Shakespeare, but who believe the works add up to some whole, are most likely to propose a candidate of noble background. This is not because of snobbery or classism, but because any unitary approach to the plays will recognize that the author must have been someone of great and variegated learning, and, therefore, someone with the time to acquire such erudition and the time to channel it into plays.

Yet these (usually noble) alternative candidates have other problems. The first one is the plays themselves. Virtually all of them can be traced to earlier or complementary works. Hardly any of the plots, or the characters, were created for the plays. This means that attempts to read biographical details into the plays are fatally flawed. Edward de Vere, the 17th Earl of Oxford, had three daughters, and so did Lear. But Lear

---

333 Wimsatt and Beardsley, *Verbal Icon*, 10–11, generally construe contextual evidence as pertaining to matters that are directly relevant to the author, and this is a formulation most often used (compare Brooks' criticism of Chambers, *Dyer's Hand*, xiv–xv, whereas I construe context in terms of an ever widening circle of evidence based research).

came first, and that does not make him the author of Oxford. The "bed trick" is a common trope in literature and folklore going back to the Bible, but if Oxford was victimized in this way—and that's a big *if*—that would have no bearing on the reappearance of the motif in *Measure for Measure* and *All's Well that Ends Well*. The impulse to create contextual evidence by decoding links between presumed biographical facts and similar tropes in the plays is predicated on a completely unacceptable level of mind reading. However tempting, it is a parlor game that has little place in serious literary or historical analysis.[334]

There is no question that de Vere—more than any of the other alternative candidates—was admirably situated to be engaged on some level with the plays. He knew most of the people, and he was himself deeply involved in literature, patronage, and the putting on of plays. But what harms Shakespeare harms de Vere as well. Oxfordians are thus left to contend with the absence of any direct evidence that de Vere wrote any play, as well as the absence of any literary remains that touch on anything other than tin mines and money. If we question Shakespeare because of the absence of direct literary evidence, the case for the Earl of Oxford is impaired by the same deficiency.

While the presumed necessity of noble background is a mainstay in critical studies concerned with Shakespearean authorship, we can safely consider the proposition false. The elite values that inform the suspected history plays are actually common to all history plays—not just the ones attributed to Shakespeare. Just as important, it can be assumed that anyone writing for patronage, or in the hope of securing patronage, would write in a manner suited to reflect the values of the potential patron. It is absurd to suggest that any of the numerous authors who wrote for Oxford would have been unfamiliar with his views on class or rank. The writers in his orbit were learned men who would have cultivated a nuanced understanding of the aristocratic worldview, and they would have been adept in expressing that worldview, whether they themselves accepted it or not. A similar argument about educational attainment can likewise be dispatched. There were many educated people in London at the time; rank had little to do with it.

---

[334] The issue is not whether biography can or will manifest itself in art; the problem is rather with inferring biographical facts from the plays (e.g., the "bed trick"), or projecting vague biographical facts into the plays (e.g., Oxford got into a sword fight, ergo Montagues and Capulets in *Romeo and Juliet*; or Hamnet Shakespeare died aged ten, which is sad, so therefore Shakespeare wrote *Hamlet*, which is also sad, etc.), and using such to prove attribution of a play, let alone the entire body of plays. One could just as easily argue, based on a minute examination of court depositions, that George Wilkins wrote all of Shakespeare.

At this point we might ask once more: What really is the point of attribution? For the experts, such as Brian Vickers or Harold Love, it is clearly very important. But the importance of any identification is vacuous if it does not ramify into further study, or to the identification of a specific authorial intent. If such issues are rarely engaged in the study of the Shakespeare plays, it is probably because the plays are generally quite derivative.

Since it is generally useless to seek biography in the plays and poems—and this is really what Wimsatt and Beardsley were arguing—what would be the possible consequences of identifying de Vere, or Bacon, or Shakespeare as the author of the plays? One can forecast two possible results. First, it would lead to a close reading of one of Shakespeare's contemporaries. Second, it would lead to an attempt to place the plays in a wider chronology in terms of history and the history of ideas. In neither of these cases is attribution particularly important, except in one sense: by attributing the plays to Shakespeare we are bound to have them all written at arbitrary dates between 1590 and 1610.

To further interrogate the value of attribution, it is useful to recall Harold Love's distinction between precursory and executive authorship. A line between the two needs to be drawn, but where? And how important is it where that line is drawn? We know, for example, that *As You Like It* and *Winter's Tale* are deeply indebted to precursor texts by Lodge and Greene: is it really worth the time and effort to determine precisely where Lodge and Greene stepped out, and Shakespeare stepped in? It seems to me that time would be better spent actually reading Lodge and Greene.

I would suggest that we go back to the wider context. We know that hundreds of plays were produced in the thirty years between 1580 and 1610 (I have seen totals as high as 1,500), and we know that the vast majority of these plays are lost, with many of the remainder having been published anonymously. We also know—from a variety of sources—that the London of this time was the home of dozens of highly educated, talented, and impoverished writers. We know that many of them gravitated to the stage in order to make money. We know that they generally—though not always—collaborated in the writing of plays. Pressed into semi-servitude because of their debts, they came up with plots, wrote outlines, and churned out copy. When they needed a little extra punch, they would call upon one of their number to provide a pretty speech, or a little jargon in French or Welsh. Locked in a room, fired with tremendous ambition, they wrote or translated tracts written in a high style and festooned with not terribly original philosophical or theological observations. Their efforts would later be edited down, cut to size by hands more practiced in the rudiments of actual theatrical production. Whether we call them the Elizabethan Beats or the Braceros of Bankside, I think these were the true creators of the body of Elizabethan theater.

The next question would concern who wrote what. I have already recorded my appreciation of Lodge, Nashe, and Daniel, but I would not want the trouble of attempting to argue on the basis of unreliable internal evidence. As an antidote to the endless Vedic expansions of unitarians, such that Shakespeare or Oxford is identified as the author of all the good bits in English Renaissance literature, I would argue for an expansion, not of the canon, but of the *pantheon*. Shakespeare, and even Oxford, have received far too much attention and adulation, and far too much unwarranted biographical reconstruction. It is time to focus at least a little bit of this attention on the works and individual lives of their remarkable and gifted peers.

In this respect I should declare my agreement with Jonathan Bate that the Folio should remain as is. This seems wise as a matter of tradition, or simple practicality (though we might make an exception for *Pericles* and *Two Noble Kinsmen*). Regardless of what the Folio actually represents, it remains the only large scale collection of Elizabethan drama that we have. Our understanding of Elizabethan literature would be better served if the authorship controversy were to move from adoration to more of a *mu* state, to allow for more flexible analysis. The largest problem with understanding the plays is the straitjacket provided by the very narrow chronology. It would be better to allow the chronology to relax, not so much to detract from Shakespeare, but simply in recognition that an earlier chronology makes better sense for several of the plays.

Instead of focusing on authorship and what must have been on Shakespeare's mind (or whoever's mind) when the plays were composed, we would better advised to discern what we can about the plays (and their various versions) on an individual basis. Then, if we must, we may turn back to the question of attribution. A few of the plays seem to rise above mere entertainment to engage in philosophical, political, or aesthetic discourse. In what way? What was the author trying to achieve? Who, among the writers of the time, showed a particular interest in these questions? Of course there have already been many answers to these questions. I think if we focus on the issues rather than the brass ring of authorship, we will get better answers.

William Shakespeare may not have seen the best minds of his generation destroyed by madness. But he knew them. He helped support them. In his own way, he gave them immortality. Gifted with intelligence, and skilled in the workings of words and ideas, two generations converged on London to live and die by their wits. It is fashionable to disparage many of Shakespeare's contemporaries as "second raters" or as "hacks" (as though there isn't quite a bit of hack work in the plays themselves), but such judgments seem gratuitous; worse, they seem to stem from a position of security that ignores the stark choices facing generations of young men whose skills were unsuitable for a livelihood outside of an overfull academic or ecclesiastical environment. If, as Samuel Johnson once said, "no one but a blockhead ever wrote a book for money," the same could be said for a play: and if one writes for one's daily bread that does not diminish the talent, spirit, and aspiration that will nevertheless find a way to peek out from columns of expository drama.

To quote a king, but probably not Shakespeare:[335]

> I have been studying how I may compare
> This prison where I live unto the world:
> And for because the world is populous
> And here is not a creature but myself,
> I cannot do it; yet I'll hammer it out.
>
> My brain I'll prove the female to my soul,
> My soul the father; and these two beget
> A generation of still-breeding thoughts,
> And these same thoughts people this little world,
> In humours like the people of this world,
> For no thought is contented.
>
> The better sort,
> As thoughts of things divine, are intermix'd
> With scruples and do set the word itself
> Against the word:
> As thus, 'Come, little ones,' and then again,

---

335 *Richard II*, V:v.

'It is as hard to come as for a camel
To thread the postern of a small needle's eye.'
Thoughts tending to ambition, they do plot
Unlikely wonders; how these vain weak nails
May tear a passage through the flinty ribs
Of this hard world, my ragged prison walls,
And, for they cannot, die in their own pride.

Thoughts tending to content flatter themselves
That they are not the first of fortune's slaves,
Nor shall not be the last; like silly beggars
Who sitting in the stocks refuge their shame,
That many have and others must sit there;
And in this thought they find a kind of ease,
Bearing their own misfortunes on the back
Of such as have before endured the like.
Thus play I in one person many people,
And none contented: sometimes am I king;
Then treasons make me wish myself a beggar,
And so I am: then crushing penury
Persuades me I was better when a king;
Then am I king'd again: and by and by
Think that I am unking'd by Bolingbroke,
And straight am nothing: but whate'er I be,
Nor I nor any man that but man is
With nothing shall be pleased, till he be eased
With being nothing.

The long-standing deification, not of Shakespeare, nor Oxford, nor Bacon, but of the First Folio itself, has cast its hungry creators into the shadows; and though they might have been content with oblivion, it is past time to bring them forth and acknowledge that the lives they lived and the things they made were something more than nothing.

Acknowledgments

I wasn't kidding when I said in the preface that I have been thinking about the Shakespeare authorship problem for close to fifty years. Of course, there are a couple of ways to take this. For those who agree with my interpretation, such long and hard study may be taken as an authority move. For those who disagree, it can be pointed to as proof of the fact that one can think for a long time about a subject and yet learn nothing. But actually the background to this book is both shallower and simpler, and in both cases the "onlie begetter" of *William Fortyhands* is my publisher and editor, Richard "Chip" Smith.

What happened was that about seven years ago Chip approached me with the idea of publishing some texts I had written in the late 1990s on the subject of the Holocaust and its revision. I was reluctant for obvious reasons, but I agreed. As I set about working up these old essays for publication, Chip further suggested that I should also write a summary of recent developments in the field. So I flogged my memory for concepts and categories I could use to make my points. *The Gas Chamber of Sherlock Holmes* was published by Nine-Banded Books in spring, 2011.

Despite the forbidding aura of its subject, *Sherlock* is largely concerned with "how do we know what we know" type questions, or epistemological questions. After it was published Chip and I kept in touch, and our correspondence ensured that I would keep turning those questions over in my mind. In the late summer of 2012, Chip asked me to write about some books that seemed especially relevant. My review-essay, subsequently published online as "The Limits of Understanding," while putatively about some books by Errol Morris, W. Joseph Campbell, and Michael Shermer, also allowed me to throw in another group of concepts that I had been carrying about in my brain-fardel.

About six months later Chip wrote me a note asking me what I was working on. I wrote him back with a couple of themes that were on my mind, and that I intended to write about someday. He liked the Shakespeare idea, so I started on that. At that point, Chip and the redoubtable novelist, translator, and cat person Ann Sterzinger were sharpening their pencils to deconstruct my text, and to oblige their curiosity I sent them a draft near the end of 2013.

The next year and a half were blurred by a number of physical breakdowns, affecting me and family members, so a serious return to actually finishing the MS was delayed. Never say never, but if it were not for the constant encouragement and prodding of Chip this text might never have been completed. Finally in the summer of 2015, Chip and Ann went to work, and while it took six months to get back to me, the final draft was much improved.

It follows from the above that the main acknowledgment I have to make is to Chip, whose influence has been large. But I reference the background for another good reason: because I ended up working into the design all of the concepts I had been turning over in the prior book and article. This was deliberate, partly because I am convinced that knowledge and understanding grow organically but also because by introducing those ideas I could ensure that whatever it was I had to say on the subject, it would not have been said before in precisely the same way. At least, that is the aspiration; there is nothing new under the sun.

In addition to Chip and Ann, I need to thank the novelist James Nulick and the essayist Anita Dalton for their encouragement and careful reading. I also need to shout out to our cover designer Kevin Slaughter, who did such a splendid cover for *Sherlock* and who was assisted this time by the mischieviously gifted cartoonist Josh Latta. I want to thank my teachers, some of whom have been exposed to my alternative ideas, but who have always encouraged me. I want to thank my children, who have always supported me. And last, I wish to thank my mother, with whom I have spent innumerable hours for many decades discussing just this subject. Death of the author or no, all have had a hand, no mere main finger, in this book.

Samuel Crowell
March 14, 2016

SOURCES CONSULTED

Many of the texts consulted for this book were obtained from the Internet, either from Google Books or Archive.org. However, since the manner of accessing these books changes from time to time, it seemed best to simply list them by their title pages in Section III below in order to provide a more secure point of contact for the interested reader. Several other online resources were used, and some of them are mentioned in the first group below. The second group comprises complete editions of Shakespeare, which have been sorted by the names of the relevant editors, while the third group comprises books and articles in the normal way. Many books that exist only in a proprietary electronic format (e.g., Kindle) are also listed in that section.

I. Internet Sources

Archive.org – An online source for many books published before 1923

Books.google.com – An online source for many books published before 1923

Dictionary of National Biography, First Edition, 63 vols., 1885–1900, at en.wikisource.org

Gutenberg.org – An online source for many books published before 1923, fully searchable but not in facsimile format

Oxford-Shakespeare.com – An Oxfordian site with many of the writings of Robert Greene and Thomas Nashe in modern spelling in PDF, maintained by Nina Green

Questia.com – An online source (paywall) for a variety of scholarly materials

Stoics.com – A website devoted to exploring the connection between

Stoic philosophy and Shakespeare and his times; includes many Classical and Renaissance authors in HTML format, based usually on recent translations (e.g., Loeb Library); maintained by Ben R. Schneider, Jr.

II. Collected Works of Shakespeare

This section is meant to highlight compilations of Shakespeare only; his contemporaries are listed by editor in Section III. I should also mention the *Arden Shakespeare*, second and third series, published by A&C Black, London, whose annotated versions for all of the individual plays were consulted throughout (although the only one to be referenced in text was the Jowett edition of *Sir Thomas More*).

Bate, Jonathan; Rasmussen, Eric, eds., *William Shakespeare Complete Works* (RSC Shakespeare) (NY, Modern Library:2007)

Bate, Jonathan; Rasmussen, Eric, eds., *William Shakespeare & Others: Collaborative Plays* (RSC Shakespeare) (NY, Palgrave MacMillan:2013)

Chalmers, *The Plays of William Shakespeare* (8 vols.) (London: 1826)

Furness, Horace Howard, *A New Variorum Edition of Shakespeare* (Philadelphia, Lippincott: 1877)

Greenblatt, Stephen; others, eds. *The Norton Shakespeare*, 2nd Edition (2 vols.) WW Norton, NY:nd)

Harrison, G. B., *Shakespeare: The Complete Works* (Harcourt, Brace & World, NY:1968)

Moston, Doug, ed., *The First Folio of Shakespeare – 1623* (NY, Applause: 1995)

Shakespeare, William, *The Complete Works of Shakespeare*, Latus ePublishing, np, nd (Kindle)

Wells, Stanley; Taylor, Gary, eds. *The Oxford Shakespeare: The Complete Works*, 2nd Edition (Oxford, Oxford UP: 2005)

III. Books and Articles

Acheson, Arthur, *Shakespeare and the Rival Poet* (London, John Lane: 1903)

Adams, Robert M., ed., *Ben Jonson's Plays and Masques* (NY, Norton: 1979)

Anderson, Mark, *'Shakespeare' By Another Name: The Life of Edward de Vere, Earl of Oxford* (NY, Gotham: 2005)

Anon., [E. C. Esquier], *Emaricdulfe* (London, Matthew Law: 1595)

Anon., *The Life and Adventures of Common Sense: An Historical Allegory* (London, Montagu Lawrence: 1769)

Anon., *The Pilgrimage to Parnassus*, with the two parts of *The Return from Parnassus* (Oxford, Oxford UP: 1886)

Aubrey, John, *'Brief Lives,' chiefly of Contemporaries, set down by John Aubrey between the Years 1669 & 1696* (Andrew Clark, ed., 2 vols.) (Oxford, Oxford UP: 1898)

Aufrecht, Monica, *On Reichenbach's Contexts* (University of Notre Dame, 2009)

Bacon, Delia, *The Philosophy of the Plays of Shakspere Unfolded* (London, Groombridge: 1857)

Bambach, Charles R., *Heidegger, Dilthey, and the Crisis of Historicism* (Ithaca, NY, Cornell UP: 1995)

Bantas, Hercules, *Understanding Dilthey: Hermeneutics, The Reluctant GeE. K.*, np, nd (Kindle)

Barber, Ros, *Shakespeare: The Evidence* (np, Leanpub.com: 2015)

Barthes, Roland, *Image, Music, Text* (NY, Hill and Wang: 1977)

Bassett, Samuel E., "Homeric Criticism," *Sewanee Review*, v. 30 n. 4 (Oct, 1922) (Johns Hopkins UP)

Bate, Jonathan, "The Case for the Folio" (np, 2007)

Bate, Jonathan, *Soul of the Age: A Biography of the Mind of William Shakespeare* (NY, Random House: 2009)

Baxter, James Phinney, *The Greatest of Literary Problems: The Authorship of the Shakespeare Works* (Boston, Houghton Mifflin: 1915)

Beauclerk, Charles, *Shakespeare's Lost Kingdom: The True History of Shakespeare and Elizabeth*, Grove/Atlantic (NY:2010) (Kindle)

Bednarz, James P., *Shakespeare and the Poets' War* (NY, Columbia UP: 2001)

Bentley, Gerald Eades, *The Jacobean and Caroline Stage* (7 vols.) (1941–1968)

Bevington, David, others, eds. *English Renaissance Drama* (WW Norton, NY: 2002)

Bierce, Ambrose, *The Collected Works*, vol. 6 (NY, Neale:1911)

Black, Joseph L., *The Martin Marprelate Tracts: A Modernized and Annotated Edition* (Cambridge, Cambridge UP: 2008)

Blackwell, G., *An Enquiry into the Life and Writings of Homer* (London: 1735)

Bloom, Harold, *Shakespeare: The Invention of the Human* (NY,

Riverhead Books: 1998)

Boas, Frederick S., *Marlowe and His Circle: A Biographical Survey* (Oxford, Oxford UP: 1929)

Boas, Frederick S., *Shakespeare and the Universities* (NY, Appleton: 1903)

Boas, Frederick S., *Shakspere and his Predecessors* (NY, Charles Scribner: 1900)

Boas, Frederick S., ed., *The Works of Thomas Kyd* (Oxford, Oxford UP: 1901)

Bompas, George C., *The Problem of the Shakespeare Plays* (London, Sampson Low, Marston: 1902)

Bond, R. Warwick, ed., *The Complete Works of John Lyly* (3 vols.) (Oxford, Oxford UP: 1902)

Bote, Hermann, *Till Eulenspiegel*, German Edition, np, nd (Kindle)

Brazil, Robert Sean, *Edward de Vere and the Shakespeare Printers* (Seattle, WA: 2010)

Brett, Cyril, ed., *Minor Poems of Michael Drayton* (Oxford, Oxford UP:1907)

Bright, T., *A Treatise of Melancholie* (London, Vautrollier: 1586)

Brink, Jean R., *Michael Drayton Revisited* (Boston, Twayne Publisher: 1990)

Britton, John, *Memoir of John Aubrey* (London, J. B. Nichols: 1845)

Brooke, Charles Frederick Tucker, *The Shakespeare Apocrypha* (Oxford, Oxford UP: 1908)

Brooks, Alden, *Will Shakspere and the Dyer's Hand* (NY, Scribners: 1943)

Brooks, Alden, *Will Shakspere: Factotum and Agent* (NY, AMS: 1974)

Bullen, A. H., ed., *The Complete Works of John Marston* (3 vols.) (np, 1887) (Kindle)

Bullough, Geoffrey, *Narrative and Dramatic Sources of Shakespeare* (8 vols.) (NY, Columbia UP: 1957–1975)

Burgess, Anthony, *A Dead Man in Deptford* (NY, Carroll & Graf: 1995)

Burgess, Anthony, *Shakespeare* (Chicago, Ivan R. Dee: 1970)

Burroughs, William, *Naked Lunch* (NY, Grove: 1990)

Bush, Douglas, *English Literature in the Early Seventeenth Century, 1600–1660*, 2nd Edition (London, Oxford UP: 1973)

Cardanus Comforte (London: 1573)

Chambers, E. K., *Shakespearean Gleanings* (Oxford, Oxford UP: 1944)

Chambers, E. K., *The Elizabethan Stage* (4 vols.) (Oxford, Oxford UP: 1923)

Chambers, E. K., *The Medieval Stage* (NY, Dover: 1996)
Chambers, E. K., *William Shakespeare: A Study of Facts and Problems* (2 vols.) (Oxford, Oxford UP: 1930)
Charters, Ann, ed., *The Portable Beat Reader* (NY, Penguin: 1992)
Chiljan, Katherine, *Shakespeare Suppressed: The Uncensored Truth About Shakespeare and His Works* (SF, Faire Eds.:2011)
Cohn, Albert, *Shakespeare in Germany in the Sixteenth and Seventeenth Centuries* (London, Asher & Co.:1865)
Collier, John Payne, *Memoirs of Edward Alleyn* (London, Shakespeare Society: 1841)
Daniel, Samuel, *The Poetical Works of Mr. Samuel Daniel* (London, Gosling:1718)
de Peyster, J. Watts, *Was THE Shakespeare, after all, a Myth?* (np, nd)
Dekker, Thomas, *Satiro-Mastix* (Hans Scherer, ed.) (Louvain, Uystpruyst: 1907)
Dick, Philip K., *VALIS and Later Novels* (NY, Library of America: 2009)
Dilthey, Wilhelm, *Hermeneutics and the Study of History* (Selected Works, vol. IV, Makreel and Rodi, eds.) (Princeton, Princeton UP: 1996)
Disraeli, Benjamin, *Venetia* (London, Frederick Warne: 1869)
Dobson, Michael; Wells, Stanley, eds., *The Oxford Companion to Shakespeare* (Oxford UP, Oxford: 2001)
Donaldson, Ian, *Ben Jonson: A Life* (Oxford, Oxford UP: 2011)
Donne, John; Walton, Izaak; Jessopp, Augustus; Alford, Henry, *John Donne Complete Works Ultimate Collection* [Annotated] (Everlasting Flames Publishing, nd) (Kindle)
Donnelly, Ignatius, *The Great Cryptogram: Francis Bacon's Cipher in the So-Called Shakespeare Plays* (Chicago, R.S. Peale: 1888)
Drummond, William, *Notes of Ben Jonson's Conversations* (London, Shakespeare Society: 1842)
Dyce, Alexander, *Strictures on Mr Collier's New Edition of Shakespeare, 1858* (London, John Russell Smith: 1859)
Dyce, Alexander, ed., *The Dramatic and Poetical Works of Robert Greene & George Peele* (London, George Routledge: 1883)
Dyer, Edward, *Poems* (np, poemhunter.com:2004)
Edmonson, Paul; Wells, Stanley, eds., *Shakespeare Beyond Doubt* (Cambridge University Press:2013) (Kindle)
Edwards, William H., *Shaksper not Shakespeare* (Cincinnati, Robert Clarke: 1900)

Eliot, T. S., *Essays Ancient and Modern* (Houghton Mifflin Harcourt, NY:nd) (Kindle)

Eliot, T. S., *Essays on Elizabethan Drama* (Houghton Mifflin Harcourt, NY:nd) (Kindle)

Eliot, T. S., *Selected Essays* (Houghton Mifflin Harcourt, NY:nd) (Kindle)

Elliott, Ward; Valenza Robert J., "Oxford by the Numbers," *Tennessee Law Review* 72 (2014): 323–453

Elliott, Ward; Valenza Robert J., "Shakespeare's Vocabulary: Did it Dwarf All Others?" in *Stylistics and Shakespeare's Language: Transdisciplinary Approaches* (New York, Continuum: 2011)

Ellis, David, *The Truth About William Shakespeare: Fact, Fiction and Modern Biographies, Edinburgh University Press* (Edinburgh:2012) (Kindle)

Elze, Karl, *Essays on Shakespeare* (London, MacMillan: 1874)

Erdman, David V; Fogel, Ephim G, eds., *Evidence for Authorship: Essays on Problems of Attribution* (Ithaca, Cornell UP: 1966)

Ermarth, Michael, *The Critique of Historical Reasoning* (Chicago, University of Chicago: 1981)

Fairholt, F. W., *The Dramatic Works of John Lilly* (2 vols.) (London, John Russell Smith:1858)

Feldman, Sabrina, *The Aprocryphal William Shakespeare* (Indianapolis, IN, Dog Ear: 2011)

Fields, Bertram, *Players: The Mysterious Identity of William Shakespeare* (NY, Regan: 2006)

Fish, Stanley, *Surprised By Sin: The Reader in Paradise Lost* (Berkeley, UC Press: 1967)

Fleay, Frederick, *A Biographical Chronicle of the English Drama 1559–1642* (2 vols.) (London, Reeves and Turner: 1891)

Fleay, Frederick, *A Chronicle History of the Life and Work of William Shakespeare* (London, Nimmo: 1886)

Fleay, Frederick, *A Chronicle History of the London Stage, 1559–1642* (NY, Stechert: 1909)

Fleay, Frederick, *Introduction to Shakespearian Study* (London, Collins: 1877)

Fleay, Frederick, *Shakespeare Manual* (London, MacMillan: 1876)

Fleay, Frederick, *The Life and Death of King John, Troublesome Reign of King John* (London, William Collins: 1878)

Foster, Donald W., *Author Unknown: On the Trail of Anonymous* (NY,

Henry Holt: 2000)

Foster, Donald W., *Elegy by WS: A Study in Attribution* (Cranbury, NJ, Associated UP: 1989)

Frazer, Robert, *The Silent Shakespeare* (Philadelphia, William J. Campbell: 1915)

Freeman, Arthur and Janet Ing Freeman, *John Payne Collier: Scholarship & Forgery in the Nineteenth Century* (2 vols.) (New Haven, CT, Yale UP: 2004)

Friedman, William F. and Elizabeth S., *The Shakespearean Ciphers Examined* (Cambridge, Cambridge UP: 1958)

Gadamer, Hans Georg, *Truth and Method* (NY, Crossroad: 1985)

Gassner, John, ed., *Medieval Tudor Drama* (NY, Applause: 1987)

Gibson, H. N., *The Shakespeare Claimants* (NY, Barnes & Noble: 1963)

Gifford, William, ed., *The Works of Ben Jonson* (NY, D. Appleton: 1879)

Gililov, I., *Igra ob Uil'iame Shekspire: ili Taina Velikogo Feniksa* (Moscow: 1997)

Gililov, I., *The Shakespeare Game: The Mystery of the Great Phoenix* (NY, Algora: 2003)

Gilvary, Kevin, ed., *Dating Shakespeare's Plays: A Critical Review of the Evidence* (Tunbridge Wells, UK, Parapress: 2010)

Gladstone, W. E., *Studies on Homer and the Homeric Age* (Oxford, Oxford UP: 1858)

Gombrowicz, Witold, *Ferdydurke* (New Haven, Yale UP: 2000)

Gosse, Edmund W., ed., *The Complete Works of Thomas Lodge* (4 vols.) (Hunterian Club: 1883)

Greg, Walter W., *Henslowe's Diary* (2 vols.) (London, AH Bullen: 1904)

Grosart, Alexander B., ed., *The Complete Works of John Davies of Hereford* (2 vols.) (Private: 1878)

Grosart, Alexander B. ed., *The Complete Works in Verse and Prose of Samuel Daniel* (4 vols.) (Private: 1885)

Grosart, Alexander B., ed., *The Complete Works of Thomas Nashe* (6 vols.) (Private: 1883–84)

Grosart, Alexander B., ed., *The Life and Complete Works in Prose and Poetry of Robert Greene* (15 vols.) (Private: 1881–1886)

Grosart, Alexander B., ed., *The Non-Dramatic Works of Thomas Dekker* (5 vols.) (Private: 1884)

Grosart, Alexander B., ed., *The Works of Gabriel Harvey* (3 vols.) (Private: 1884)

Gosson, Stephen, *The School of Abuse* (London, Shakespeare Society:

1841)

Greenblatt, Stephen, *Hamlet in Purgatory* (Princeton, Princeton UP: 2001)

Greenblatt, Stephen, *Will in the World: How Shakespeare Became Shakespeare* (NY, Norton: 2004)

Greenwood, G. G., *Is There a Shakespeare Problem?* (London, Bodley Head: 1916)

Greenwood, G. G., *Shakspere's Handwriting* (London, Bodley Head: 1920)

Greenwood, G. G., *The Shakespeare Problem Restated* (London, Bodley Head: 1908)

Greer, Germaine, *Shakespeare* (NY, Sterling: 1986)

Greer, Germaine, *Shakespeare's Wife* (NY, Harper Collins: 2007)

Greg, Walter W., *Henslowe's Diary* (in two parts, text and commentary) (London, Bullen: 1904)

Grosart, Alexander B, *The Complete Works of John Davies of Hereford* (two volumes) (privately printed, np: 1878)

Gurr, Andrew, *Shakespeare's Opposites: The Admiral's Company, 1594–1625* (Cambridge, Cambridge UP: 2009)

Halliwell-Phillipps, *Outlines of the Life of Shakespeare* (London, Longmans, Green: 1883)

Harman, Edward George, *The Countess of Pembroke's Arcadia* (London, C. Palmer: 1924)

Harris, Frank, *The Man Shakespeare and His Tragic Life-Story* (NY, Mitchell Kennerley: 1909)

Hart, Joseph C., *The Romance of Yachting* (NY, Harper & Brothers: 1848)

Harvey, Gabriel, *Four Letters and Certain Sonnets* (London, John Wolfe: 1592)

Hirsch, E. D., Jr., *Validity in Interpretation* (New Haven, Yale UP: 1979)

Hodges, H. A., *The Philosophy of Wilhelm Dilthey* (London, Routledge & Kegan Paul: 1952)

Hoffman, Calvin, *The Murder of the Man Who Was 'Shakespeare'* (NY, Julian Messner: 1955)

Honan, Park, *Christopher Marlowe: Poet and Spy* (Oxford, Oxford UP: 2005)

Honigmann, EAJ, *Shakespeare's Impact on His Contemporaries* (Totowa, NJ, B&N: 1982)

Hooker, Elizabeth Robbins, "The Relation of Shakespeare to Montaigne,"

PMLA v. 17 n. 3 (1902) (Modern Language Association)

Hooper, Richard, ed., *The Complete Works of Michael Drayton* (3 vols.) (London, John Russell Smith: 1876)

Hope, Warren; Holston, Kim, *The Shakespeare Controversy: An Analysis of the Authorship Theories*, 2nd ed. (Jefferson, NC, McFarland: 2009)

Hopkinson, A. F., ed., *A Warning for Fair Women* (London, Sims: 1893)

Hotson, J. Leslie, *The Death of Christopher Marlowe* (London, Nonesuch Press:1925)

Howard, Roy J., *Three Faces of Hermeneutics: Introduction to Current Theories of Understanding* (Berkeley, UC Press: 1982)

Hughes, Charles, *Willobie His Avisa* (London, Sherratt and Hughes: 1904)

Hunter, Joseph, *A Disquisition on the Scene, Origin, Date etc. etc. of Shakespeare's Tempest* (London, Whittingham: 1839)

Hyman, Stanley Edgar, *The Armed Vision: A Study in the Methods of Modern Literary Criticism* (NY, Vintage: 1955)

Ilsemann, Hartmut, *William Shakespeare Dramen und Apokryphen* (Bd. 1) (Aachen, Shaker: 2014)

Ingleby, C. M., *A Complete View of the Shakspere Controversy* (London, Nattali: 1861)

Ingleby, C. M., *The Shakespere Allusion-Book* (2 vols) (NY, Duffield & Company: 1909)

Ingleby, C. M., *Shakespeare Hermeneutics* (London, John Allen: 1875)

Ingleby, C. M., *Was Thomas Lodge an Actor?* (London, Richard Barrett: 1868)

Ioppolo, Grace, *Revising Shakespeare* (Cambridge, Harvard UP: 1991)

Jack, Albert E., "Thomas Kyd and the Ur-Hamlet," *PMLA* v 20, n 4 (1905)

James, Brenda; Rubinstein, William D., *The Truth Will Out: Unveiling the Real Shakespeare* (NY, Harper: 2006)

Johnson, Samuel, *Delphi Complete Works of Samuel Johnson, Illustrated Series Four*, Delphi Classics, (Kindle)

Jonson, Ben, *Complete Works of Ben Jonson Illustrated*, Delphi Classics, (Kindle)

Kirschbaum, Leo, *Shakespeare and the Stationers* (Columbus, OH, Ohio State UP: 1955)

Kuhn, Thomas S., *The Structure of Scientific Revolutions*: 50th Anniversary Edition, University of Chicago Press, (Kindle)

Lang, A. A., *Hellenistic Philosophy: Stoics, Epicureans, Sceptics* (Berkeley,

UC Press: 1986)

Langbaine, *An Account of the English Dramatick Poets* (Oxford, George West: 1691)

Lawrence, Edwin Gordon, *Sidelights on Shakespeare* (Boston, Stratford Company: 1918)

Leahy, William, ed., *Shakespeare and his Authors: Critical Perspectives on the Authorship Question* (London, Continuum: 2010)

Lee, Sidney, *A Life of William Shakespeare* (NY, MacMillan: 1901)

LeFranc, Abel, *Sous le masque "William Shakespeare" – William Stanley VI Comte de Derby* (2 vols) (Paris, Payot: 1919)

Lewis, C. S., *English Literature in the Sixteenth Century* (NY, Oxford UP: 1954)

Lewis, C. S., *Selected Literary Essays* (NY, HarperCollins) (Kindle)

Lewis, C. S., *Studies in Medieval and Renaissance Literature* (NY, HarperCollins) (Kindle)

Lodge, Thomas, trans., *Lucius Annaius Seneca Works, Translated into English by Thom. Lodge* (London, 1620)

Lodge, Thomas, *Rosalynde, or, Euphues Golden Legacy*; Edward C. Baldwin, ed. (Boston, Ginn: 1910)

Looney, J. Thomas, *"Shakespeare" Identified in Edward de Vere the Seventeenth Earl of Oxford* (NY: Frederick A. Stokes: 1920)

Looney, J. Thomas, *The Poems of Edward de Vere* (London, Cecil Palmer: 1921)

Lord, Albert B, *The Singer of Tales* (NY, Atheneum: 1978)

Love, Harold, *Attributing Authorship: An Introduction* (Cambridge, Cambridge UP: 2002)

Luce, Alice H., *The Countess of Pembroke's Antonie* (Weimar, Felber: 1897)

Macaulay, Thomas, *Lord Macaulay's Essays and Lays of Ancient Rome* (London, George Routledge: 1892)

Maguire, Laurie E., *Shakespearean Suspect Texts: The 'Bad Quartos' and Their Contexts* (Cambridge, Cambridge UP: 1996)

Marlowe, Christopher, *Complete Plays and Poems*, ED Pendry, ed., JC Maxwell, advisor (London, Everyman: 1976)

Marston, John, *The Works of John Marston* (3 vols.) Transcript (Kindle)

Matus, Irvin Leigh, *Shakespeare in Fact* (NY, Dover: 2012)

McCarthy, Dennis, *North of Shakespeare* (np: 2011)

McClarran, Steve, *I Come to Bury Shakespeare: A Deconstruction of the Fable of the Stratfordian Shakespeare* (np: 2012)

McClinton, Brian, *The Shakespeare Conspiracies* (Aubane, Ireland, AHS: 2007)
McCrae, Scott, *The Case for Shakespeare: The End of the Authorship Question* (Westport, CT, Praeger: 2005)
McGinn, Colin, *Discovering the Meaning Behind the Plays: Shakespeare's Philosophy* (Harper Collins e-books, nd)
McKerrow, Ronald B., *The Works of Thomas Nashe* (3 vols.) (London, Bullen: 1904)
McMillan, Scott; MacLean, Sally-Beth, *The Queen's Men and Their Plays* (Cambridge, Cambridge UP: 1998)
Michell, John, *Eccentric Lives and Peculiar Notions* (Canada, Adventures Unlimited: 1999)
Michell, John, *Who Wrote Shakespeare?* (London, Thames & Hudson: 1996)
Milton, John, *The Poetical Works of John Milton* (Kindle)
Montaigne, Michel de, *Essays Complete with Table of Contents*, Popular Classical Books (Kindle)
Morgan, Bill, *The Typewriter Is Holy: The Complete, Uncensored History of the Beat Generation*, Free Press (Kindle)
Munday, Anthony, *A Brief Chronicle of the Successe of Times, from the Creation of the World to this Instant* (London, Jaggard: 1611)
Munday, Anthony, *A Second and Third Blast of Retraite from Plaies and Theaters* (London: 1580)
Munday, Anthony, *The English Romayne Lyfe* (London, Bodley Head: 1925)
Munro, J. J., ed., *Brooke's 'Romeus and Juliet' Being the Original of Shakespeare's 'Romeo and Juliet'* (NY, Duffield: 1908)
Nagy, Gregory, *Homeric Questions* (Austin, U Texas: 1996)
Nashe, Thomas, *The Unfortunate Traveller and Other Works*, J. B. Steane, ed. (London, Penguin: 1972)
Nicholl, Charles, *The Reckoning: The Murder of Christopher Marlowe* (Chicago, UC Press: 1992)
North, Thomas, *The Earliest English Version of the Fables of Bidpai, "The Moral Philosophie of Doni,"* Joseph Jacobs, ed. (London, Nutt: 1888)
Oates, Whitney J., ed., *The Stoic and Epicurean Philosophers* (NY, Modern Library: 1940)
Ogburn, Charlton, *The Mysterious William Shakespeare: The Myth and the Reality*, 2nd ed. (McLean, VA, EPM Publications: 1992)
Ogburn, Dorothy and Charlton, *This Star of England* (NY: Coward McCann: 1952)

Oliver, James A., *The Pamphleteer* (London, IA: 2010)

Osborne, Grant R., *The Hermeneutical Spiral: A Comprehensive Introduction to Biblical Interpretation* (Downes Grove, IL, IVP: 2006)

Paradise, N. Burton, *Thomas Lodge: The History of an Elizabethan* (New Haven, Yale UP: 1931)

Patrick, David, ed., *Chambers Cyclopedia of English Literature* (volume 1) (London, Chambers: 1901)

Patterson, Annabel, *Reading Holinshed's Chronicle* (Chicago, UC Press: 1994)

Patterson, ed., *Ben Jonson's Conversations with William Drummond of Hawthornden* (London, Blackie and Son: 1923)

Pierce, William, *An Historical Introduction to the Marprelate Tracts* (NY, E. P. Dutton: 1909)

Pinksen, Daryl, *Marlowe's Ghost: The Blacklisting of the Man Who Was Shakespeare* (NY, Universe: 2008)

Pointon, Anthony, *The Man Who Was Never Shakespeare*, Parapress (Kindle)

Pollard, Alfred W., *Shakespeare's Fight with the Pirates and the Problems of the Transmission of His Text* (Cambridge, Cambridge UP: 1920)

Pollard, Tanya, ed., *Shakespeare's Theater: A Sourcebook* (Malden, MA, Blackwell: 2004)

Price, Diana, *Shakespeare's Unorthodox Biography: New Evidence of an Authorship Problem* (Westport, CT, Greenwood Press: 2001)

Price, Diana, *Shakespeare's Unorthodox Biography: New Evidence of an Authorship Problem*, 2nd ed. (Westport, CT, Greenwood Press: 2012)

Purdy, Gilbert Wesley, *Edward de Vere Was Shakespeare: at Long Last, the Proof, The Collected Poems of Edward De Vere*, GWP Editions (Kindle)

Reynolds, CD; Wilson, NG, *Scribes and Scholars: A Guide to the Transmission of Greek and Latin Literature*, 2nd ed. (Oxford, Oxford UP: 1974)

Rhys-Davids, Caroline AF, ed. and trans., *Stories of the Buddha: Being Selections from the Jataka* (NY, Dover: 1989)

Riggs, David, *The World of Christopher Marlowe* (London, Henry Holt: 2004)

Robertson, J. M., *Montaigne and Shakespeare and Other Essays on Cognate Questions* (London, Adam and Charles Black: 1909)

Robertson, J. M., *The Baconian Heresy: A Confutation* (London, Herbert Jenkins: 1913)

Robertson, J. M., *The Shakespeare Canon* (London, George Routledge: 1922)
Robertson, J. M., *The State of Shakespeare Study* (London, George Routledge & Sons: 1931)
Rollet, John M., *William Stanley as Shakespeare: Evidence of Authorship by the Sixth Earl of Derby* (Jefferson NC, McFarland: 2015)
Rosenbaum, Ron, *The Shakespeare Wars: Clashing Scholars, Public Fiascoes, Palace Coups* (NY, Random House: 2005)
Rowse, AL, *Shakespeare the Man* (NY, St Martin's: 1988)
Royle, Nicholas, *After Derrida* (London, Manchester UP: 1995)
Rubinstein, William D., *Who Wrote Shakespeare's Plays?* (The Hill, Stroud, Amberley Publishing:2012) (Kindle)
Salgado, Gamini, *The Elizabethan Underworld* (Phoenix Mill, UK, Sutton Publishing: 2005)
Sams, Eric, *The Real Shakespeare: Retrieving the Early Years, 1564-1594* (New Haven, CT, Yale UP: 1995)
Sarma, Vishnu; Rajan, Chandra, eds., *The Panchatantra* (London, Penguin: 2006)
Sarrazin, Gregor, *Thomas Kyd und sein Kreis* (Berlin, Emil Felber:1892)
Scarsbrook, M. G., ed., *Christopher Marlowe, The Life & Complete Works Of Christopher Marlowe* (Red Herring, London:nd) (Kindle)
Schmucker, Samuel Mosheim, *Historic Doubts Respecting Shakspere; Illustrating Infidel Objections Against the Bible* (Philadelphia: 1853)
Schoenbaum, S., *Internal Evidence and Elizabethan Dramatic Authorship: An Essay on Literary History and Method* (Evanston, IL, Northwestern UP: 1966)
Schoenbaum, S., *Shakespeare's Lives* (Oxford, Oxford UP: 1970)
Schoenbaum, S., *Shakespeare's Lives, New Edition* (Oxford, Oxford UP: 1991)
Schoenbaum, S., *William Shakespeare: A Compact Documentary Life* (Oxford, Oxford UP: 1977)
Scot, Reginald, *The Discoverie of Witchcraft* (reprint of first edition of 1584, Brinsley Nicholson, ed.) (London, Stock: 1886)
Seneca, CDN Costa, trans., *Dialogues and Letters* (NY, Penguin: 1997)
Shaffer, Lawrence, *Literary Criticism* (New Delhi, Ivy Publishing: 2011)
Shahan, John M., Whalen, Richard F., "Apples to Oranges in Bard Stylometrics," *Oxfordian*, v IX, 2006
Shahan, John; Waugh, Alexander, *Shakespeare Beyond Doubt?* (Aeon Publishing Inc., Lumina Press, np:2013) (Kindle)
Shapiro, James, *A Year in the Life of William Shakespeare: 1599* (London,

Faber & Faber: 2005)

Shapiro, James, *Contested Will: Who Wrote Shakespeare?* (NY, Simon & Schuster: 2010)

Sharpe, Robert Boies, *The Real War of the Theaters: Shakespeare's Fellows in Rivalry with the Admiral's Men, 1594–1603* (Boston, MLA: 1935)

Shepherd, Richard Herne, ed., *The Works of George Chapman: Homer's Iliad and Odyssey* (London, Chatto & Windus: 1903)

Sherbo, Arthur, *Shakespeare's Midwives: Some Neglected Shakespeareans* (Newark, University of Delaware: 1992)

Sidney, Philip, *The Major Works Including Astrophil and Stella*, Katherine Duncan-Jones, ed. (Oxford, Oxford UP: 2008)

Sisson, Charles J., ed., *Thomas Lodge and Other Elizabethans* (NY, Octagon Books: 1966)

Small, Roscoe Addison, *The Stage-Quarrel Between Ben Jonson and the So-Called Poetasters* (Breslau, M&H Marcus:1899)

Smith, C. Gregory, ed., *Elizabethan Critical Essays* (2 vols.) (Oxford, Oxford UP: 1950)

Sobran, Joseph, *Alias Shakespeare: Solving the Greatest Literary Mystery of All Time* (NY, Free Press: 1997)

Stritmatter, Roger A.; Kositsky, Lynne, *On the Date, Sources and Design of Shakespeare's The Tempest*, McFarland, (Kindle)

Strittmatter, Roger and Kositsky, Lynne, "The Spanish Maze and the date of the Tempest," *The Oxfordian*, X, 2007

Sykes, H. Dugdale, *Sidelights on Shakespeare* (Stratford-on-Avon, Shakespeare Head Press: 1919)

Symonds, John Addington, *Shakspere's Predecessors in the English Drama* (London, Smitt, Elder: 1884)

Taylor, Gary, *Reinventing Shakespeare* (Oxford, Oxford UP: 1989)

Taylor, Gary; Lavagnino, John, eds., *Thomas Middleton: The Collected Works* (Oxford, Oxford UP: 2007)

Tenney, Edward Andrews, *Thomas Lodge* (Ithaca, NY, Cornell UP: 1935)

The Travels of Sir John Mandeville (London, MacMillan: 1905)

The Works of Lucius Annaius Seneca, translated by Tho. Lodge (London, Stansby:1614)

Tolstoy, Leo, *O Shekspire I o drame, in Sobranie Sochinennii v dvadtsati tomakh*, t. 15 (Moscow, 1964)

Tolstoy, Leo, *Tolstoy on Shakespeare* (NY, Funk & Wagnalls: 1906)

Twain, Mark, *Is Shakespeare Dead?* (NY, Harper & Brothers: 1909)

Vickers, Brian, *Appropriating Shakespeare: Contemporary Critical Quarrels* (New Haven, Yale UP: 1993)

Vickers, Brian, *'Counterfeiting' Shakespeare: Evidence, Authorship, and John Ford's Funerall Elegie* (Cambridge, Cambridge UP: 2002)

Vickers, Brian, *Shakespeare, A Lover's Complaint, and John Davies of Hereford* (Cambridge, Cambridge UP: 2007)

Vickers, Brian, *Shakespeare, Co-Author* (Oxford, Oxford UP: 2002)

Vickers, Brian, *Shakespeare: The Critical Heritage, 1623–1801* (6 vols.) (London, Routledge & Kegan Paul: 1974–1981)

Virkler, Henry A.; Ayayo, Karelynne Geuver, *Hermeneutics: Principles and Processes of Biblical Interpretation* (Grand Rapids, MI, Baker Academic: 1981)

Volkmann, Richard, *Geschichte und Kritik der Wolfschen Prolegomena zu Homer* (Leipzig, Teubner: 1874)

Warnke, Karl; Proescholdt, Ludwig, *Pseudo-Shakspearian Plays: Arden of Faversham* (Halle, Niemeyer: 1888)

Warren, Roger, *A Reconstructed Text of Pericles, Prince of Tyre* (W. Shakespeare and G. Wilkins) (Oxford, Oxford UP: 2003)

Watson, Thomas, *Hekatompathia, or Passionate Century of Love* (reprint, Spenser Society: 1869)

Waugaman M.D., Richard M, *It's Time to ReVere the Works of "ShakeSpeare": A Psychoanalyst Reads the Works of Edward de Vere, Earl of Oxford* (Oxfreudian Press) (Kindle)

Waugaman M.D., Richard M, *Newly Discovered Works by "William ShakeSpeare": a.k.a. Edward de Vere, Earl of Oxford* (Oxfreudian Press) (Kindle)

Waugaman, "The Psychopathology of Stratfordianism", *The Oxfordian*, 2012

Wells, Stanley, *Shakespeare & Co.* (NY, Pantheon: 2006)

Wells, Stanley; Taylor, Gary, William *Shakespeare: A Textual Companion* (NY, Norton: 1987)

Werstine, Paul, *Early Modern Playhouse Manuscripts and the Editing of Shakespeare* (Cambridge, Cambridge UP: 2012)

Whately, Richard, *Historic Doubts Relative to Napoleon Buonaparte*, 3rd edition (Oxford, Baxter, Parker, and J. Hatchard and son, London: 1827)

White, Harold Ogden, *Plagiarism and Imitation During the English Renaissance* (NY, Farrar, Straus, Giroux: 1973)

White, Thomas W., *Our English Homer: Or Shakespeare Historically Considered* (London, Sampson Low, Marston:1892)

Williams, Robin P., *Sweet Swan of Avon: Did a Woman Write Shakespeare?* (Berkeley, Peachpit Press: 2006)

Williams, Simon, *Shakespeare on the German Stage, Volume 1: 1586–1914* (Cambridge, Cambridge UP: 1990)

Wilson, TP, Hunter GK, *The English Drama, 1485–1585* (NY, Oxford UP: 1969)

Wimsatt, W. K. Jr., *The Verbal Icon: Studies in the Meaning of Poetry* (NY, Noonday: 1954)

Wright, Ernest Hunter, *The Authorship of Timon of Athens* (NY, Columbia dissertation: 1910)

Yutang, Lin, ed., *The Wisdom of China and India* (NY, Modern Library: 1942)

Zbierski, Henryk, *Shakespeare and the 'War of the Theaters': A Reinterpretation* (Poznan:1957)

Zeigler, Wilbur Gleason, *It Was Marlowe: A Story of the Secret of Three Centuries* (Chicago, Donohue, Henneberry: 1895)

INDEX

Abbey Road, 116
Aesop, 96, 102, 245, 246n
Alleyn, Edward (1566-1626), 80, 113, 114, 215
All's Well That Ends Well, 171, 199, 216n, 261
Analysts, 88, 91, 127, 139, 142, 162, 183, 209n, 227, 254
Anderson, Mark, 83n, 169n, 181, 182, 186n, 232
Anderson, Sherwood, 212
Anonymous (2011), 172n
Anthony and Cleopatra, 16n, 64, 150, 179, 199-200, 225, 226, 251n
apophenia, 16
Arabian Nights, 102, 172
Arden of Faversham, 100, 180, 203
As You Like It 39, 186, 192, 199, 216n, 225, 262
Aubrey, John, 15-18, 50, 144, 172, 177, 235, 257
Aufrecht, Monica, 176n
Aurelius, Marcus, 104, 226
Avebury, 16, 18, 50, 64, 177, 235, 257

Bacon, Delia, 20, 121, 126-127, 129, 176
Bacon, Francis, 11, 13, 20, 101, 104, 108, 121, 125, 126, 127, 129, 135-137, 140-141, 143, 173, 179n , 185n, 223, 249n, 255, 262, 265
Bad Quartos, 94, 159, 160, 163, 164, 190, 193, 197, 198, 201-202, 218, 239, 246n, 259
Barber, Ros, 164n, 172n, 184n, 214n
Barthes, Roland, 232-233
Bate, Jonathan, 81, 151, 203n, 263
Beat Generation, 35-36, 158
Beatles, The, 116
Beaumont, Francis, (1584-1616) 29, 146, 200, 206
Bible, 22, 88, 89, 90-92, 173, 181, 182n, 234, 244n, 254, 261,
Birth of Merlin, 206
Black Iron Prison, 158, 165, 235, 256
Bloom, Harold, 106, 247
Brooks, Alden, 59n, 144n, 164n, 209n, 228n, 260n

Burbage, Richard, 24, 74
Burroughs, William S., 35, 44n
Byrne, Muriel St. Clare, 161-162, 163, 179

Capell, Edward, 94, 99, 204
Carlyle, Thomas, 111-112, 127
Carr, Lucien, 35
Chambers, E[dmund] K[erchever], 16, 20, 24n, 25n, 40n, 51n, 52n, 95, 109, 118n, 144n, 159, 163, 164, 167, 186, 190n, 197, 202, 206, 208, 209, 220, 239
Chapman, George (1559-1634), 16, 55-56, 57, 58, 68, 69, 70n, 83, 84, 115, 148, 163, 177, 194, 199, 200, 206, 216, 222, 248, 251n
Chatterton, Thomas, 108, 124
Chettle, Henry (1564-1606), 81-82, 84, 115, 116, 119, 154, 160
Clayton Loan, 159, 163, 164n, 213
Collier, John Payne, 109-110, 121, 122, 176, 197, 204, 248n, 256
Combine, The, 36
Comedy of Errors, 83, 122, 197, 198, 218
Condell, Henry, 27-29, 33, 74, 258
Context of Discovery, 175-176, 178n, 187, 256
Context of Justification, 175-176 178n,
convergence of evidence, 104
Coriolanus, 200, 226
Cymbeline, 100, 109, 197, 200
dactylic hexameter, 41, 70-71, 246

Daniel, Samuel (1562-1619), 57, 63, 65-67, 83, 101, 131n, 149, 150, 179, 191, 191, 192, 193, 200, 209n, 211, 217, 222, 225, 228, 248, 251n, 263
Davies, John, of Hereford (1565-1618), 64-65, 67, 76, 81, 209, 218n, 222n, 248
de Vere, Edward (17th Earl of Oxford), 13, 20, 21, 37, 40, 41, 42n, 48, 58, 60, 63, 71, 77n, 82, 83n, 103, 115, 154, 163, 167-173, 181, 185-186, 187, 220, 223, 227, 228, 249n, 260-261, 262
Death of the Author, 101n, 112, 231, 232, 233, 235
Dekker, Thomas, (1572-1632) 77n, 117-118, 119, 146, 148, 151, 160, 186n,

201, 215, 216, 218, 250n, 251n
Denial, Denialism, 183, 184, 187, 221, 256
Devereaux, Robert (Earl of Essex), 60n, 154n, and see Essex Rebellion
Dick, Philip K., 157–158, 256
Dilthey, Wilhelm, 233n, 234, 235n
Disintegration Speech, 20, 163
Disraeli, Benjamin, 111, 123
Donne, John, 15
Donnelly, Ignatius, 129–137, 144, 223, 239
Drayton, Michael, (1563–1631) 52, 57–58, 68, 83, 109, 115, 148, 149–150, 205, 209n, 222, 251n
Droeshout, Martin, 27, 29, 151
Drummond, William (Hawthornden) (1585–1649), 31, 32n
Dubois, W. E. B., 212
Dyer, Edward, 59, 60, 68

Edmund Ironside, 206
Edward III, 162, 180, 204, 251
Elizabethan Beats, 34, 35–37, 41, 43, 149, 202, 259, 263
Emmerich, Roland, 172n
Epicureanism, 104
Epicurus, 104
Epistemic Closure, 256
Erasmus, Desiderius, 89, 163, 258
Essex Rebellion, 154, 225, 251n

Fair Em, 205–206
Feldman, Sabrina, 61n, 226–227, 259n
Ferdydurke, 254
First Folio, 19, 29–34, 35, 50, 53, 63, 90, 91, 92, 84, 103, 125, 130, 136, 145, 147, 159, 163, 164, 170, 180, 189–207 passim, 210, 215, 225, 228, 239, 250, 254, 258, 259, 265
Fleay, Frederick, 20, 21, 139–140, 162, 163, 250n,
Fletcher, John (1579–1625), 146, 201, 203, 206
Folger, Henry Clay, 173
folio (defined), 26
Ford, John (1586–1639), 147, 178, 216n
Foster, Donald, 178, 179, 227
Foul Papers, 259
Fourth Folio, 31, 50, 203–205
Funeral Elegy, 178

Garrick, David, 73
Generation J, 145, 147, 216n
German *Hamlet*, 96
Ginsburg, Allen, 35, 158
Gombrowicz, Witold, 254
Green, Nina, 40n, 42n, 43n, 44n, 77n, 81n, 95n, 154n, 164n, 182
Greenblatt, Stephen, 183, 232, 249n
Greene, Robert (1558–1592), 25, 32, 36, 39, 40–41, 42, 45, 48, 73, 76–82, 84, 85, 95, 97, 100, 115, 116, 122, 125, 131n, 154, 164, 170, 182, 185, 186n, 190, 193, 194, 197, 198, 200, 202, 204, 205, 209n, 214, 215, 220, 221, 222, 228, 242, 246, 250n, 262
Greenwood, George, 20, 140
Greer, Germaine, 216n
Greg, Walter, 259n
Groatsworth of Wit, A 41, 73, 76–82, 85, 86, 95, 97, 101, 115, 116, 126, 159, 164, 171n, 190, 213, 221, 226, 242, 246, 250n
Gunpowder Plot, 154

Halliwell-Phillipps, James, 163, 164, 167
Hamlet 16n, 24n, 41, 65, 93, 95–96, 97, 103, 114, 122, 148, 152, 159, 193–194, 201, 216, 218, 225, 226, 242–251, 258, 261n
Hart, Joseph C., 20, 121–123, 125, 127, 176,
Harvey, Gabriel (1552–1631), 25n, 41–43, 58, 60, 71, 85, 147, 151n, 170, 228n, 246, 256
Hate-Virtue, 250
Heminge, John, 27–29, 258
Henry IV, Part 1, 47n, 65, 95, 151, 191, 193, 195,
Henry IV, Part 2, 65, 95, 151, 191, 193, 195,
Henry V, 61, 94, 95, 135, 189, 193, 199, 201, 216, 217, 239, 241,
Henry VI, Part 1, 80n, 84, 94, 95, 96, 190, 218, 224, 250n
Henry VI, Part 2, 84, 94, 95, 96, 190, 195, 201, 218, 224, 242
Henry VI, Part 3, 84, 94, 95, 96, 190, 195, 201, 218, 224, 242
Henry VIII, 69, 95, 97, 179, 224, 225
Henslowe, Philip (1555–1616), 20, 109, 113–115, 116, 117, 118, 119, 120, 121, 122, 124, 127, 146, 152, 161, 176, 186, 201, 204, 250, 251n, 253, 260

Herbert, Philip (Earl of Montgomery), 27, 63, 170
Herbert, William (Earl of Pembroke) 27, 63, 67, 147,
hermeneutics, 90–92, 158, 173n, 234, 235, 256
Heywood, Thomas (1570s–1641), 25n, 84, 117–118, 119, 146, 160, 200, 205, 207
Hirsch, E. D., 233n, 235
Hoffman, Calvin, 143–144
Homer, 14, 16, 22, 41, 49, 55–56, 58, 70, 77n, 82, 84, 87–88, 92, 101, 111, 123, 126, 127, 142, 194, 254, 257
Hotson, Leslie, 21, 167, 173–174
Howl 35, 158

Iliad, 14, 16, 55–56, 88, 111, 132, 151n
Ireland, William Henry, 107–109, 256
Is Shakespeare Dead?, 140–141, 184–185
Isle of Dogs, The, 44, 136, 146, 154n, 216, 228, 251n

James, Brenda, 216, 225–226
James, Henry, 20, 141
James, William, 141
Johnson, Samuel, 19, 93–94, 264
Jonson, Ben (1572–1637), 23, 26–27, 29, 31–33, 44, 52, 56, 65, 67, 123, 126, 145–152, 201, 205, 216–218, 228, 258, 260
Julius Caesar, 32, 33, 65, 95, 148n, 183, 198–199, 251n

Keats, John, 15, 56
Kesey, Ken, 36
King John, 95, 97n, 197, 198, 201, 213n, 218
King Lear, 61, 63, 100, 141, 170, 194, 201, 218, 241n, 248
Kuhn, Thomas, 176n, 177n
Kyd, Thomas (1558–1594), 25, 45, 47, 48, 118, 139, 154, 161, 180, 190, 194, 197, 202, 203, 204, 207, 215, 244, 245, 246, 247, 250

Larkin, Philip, 180
Lee, Sidney, 139, 140, 142, 164, 249n
Lincoln, Abraham, 213
Locrine, 31, 109, 204
Lodge, Thomas (1558–1625), 36, 38–40, 48, 60, 63, 65, 80, 84, 100, 105–106, 121, 139, 147, 149, 162, 186n, 190, 194, 198, 199, 202, 204, 209n, 215, 222, 242, 247, 248–250, 251n, 262, 263
London Prodigal, 31, 205
Looney, James, 20, 133n, 167, 168–169, 171, 173, 200
Love, Harold, 87, 103–104, 182–183, 183n, 236, 237, 262
Love's Labour's Lost, 53, 94, 100, 122, 135, 142, 192, 195, 218, 223
Love's Labour's Won, 192
Love's Types of Authorship, 236–238
Lyly, John (1553–1606), 37–38, 41, 42, 44, 48, 80, 115, 154, 163, 170, 171, 185, 186, 191, 192, 193, 197, 202, 209n, 215, 222, 247

Macaulay, Thomas, 33, 102
Macbeth, 49, 56, 97, 100, 109, 118, 135, 154n, 177, 179, 197, 199, 216, 225, 248
Machiavelli, Nicolo, 78, 80, 259
Maguire, Laurie, 159n, 259n
Malone, Edmond, 19, 69, 94–97, 99, 108, 114
Manners, Roger (Earl of Rutland), 20, 142, 208n, 224
Marlowe, Christopher (1564–1593), 13, 20, 21, 22, 25, 30, 36, 44, 45–48, 56, 69, 80, 81, 82, 85, 88, 131, 132, 136, 139, 142–144, 150, 153, 163, 167, 173–174, 185, 190, 192, 197, 198, 202, 204, 207, 211, 215, 222, 223–224
Marston, John (1576–1634), 136, 147–148, 205, 216, 218n, 222, 223, 229
Martin Marprelate, 22, 42, 154, 174
Massinger, Philip (1583–1640), 136, 146–147, 200, 201, 206
Matus, Irvin, 21n, 110n
McCarthy, Dennis, 77n, 101, 225, 226, 259n
McCrae, Scott, 21, 183
Measure for Measure, 93, 118, 179, 199, 216n, 261
Menaphon, 41, 95–96, 244
Mendenhall, Thomas, 143
Merchant of Venice 83–84, 95, 122, 167, 169, 191, 218, 224
Meres, Francis, 73, 76, 82–85, 86, 94, 95, 97, 118, 163, 189, 190–200 passim, 207, 214
Merry Devil of Edmonton, 205
Merry Wives of Windsor, 123, 193, 201
Michell, John, 21n, 48n, 68n, 129n,

173n, 182, 183n, 242n
Middleton, Thomas (1580–1627), 21, 118, 136, 146, 177, 179, 183, 199, 205, 206, 216n, 222, 251n
Midsummer Night's Dream, 49, 83, 95, 100, 193, 218
Milkmaid and Bucket, 102–104, 108, 109, 161, 209, 255
Montaigne, Michel de, 99, 100, 101, 104, 105, 126, 136–137, 200, 251n
Montgomery, Robert, 33
Montserrat, Gilles, 178
Moral Philosophy of Doni, see *Panchantra*
More, Sir Thomas, 153
Mother Goose, 180
Mucedorus, 204, 205, 207
Much Ado About Nothing, 95, 96, 192, 193, 199, 216n
Munday, Anthony (1560?–1633), 80, 115–116, 119, 148, 153n, 154, 160, 170, 185, 186, 192, 198, 204, 222

Naked Lunch, 35, 44n
Nashe, Thomas (1567–1601), 36, 41–44, 48, 56, 57, 63, 66, 70, 74, 77, 80–82, 95, 105, 115, 131n, 146, 147, 151, 154, 170, 180n, 182, 186, 198, 202, 209n, 211, 215, 216, 222, 228, 242, 244–245, 248, 249, 250n, 251n, 256, 263
Nelson, Alan, 70n, 169n, 185–186
Neville, Sir Henry, 21n, 22, 154, 224–225
New Shakespeare Society, 139
Newhart, Bob, 213
Nietzsche, Friedrich, 105, 241n, 259
North, Thomas (1535–1604), 22, 77n, 100, 101, 126, 190, 198–199, 200, 216, 225–226
Northumberland Manuscript, 135, 223, 225

octavo (defined), 26
Odyssey, 77n, 88, 111
Ogburn, Charlton, 21, 169n, 181, 185n, 232
Ogburn, Dorothy and Charlton, Sr., 173
On Poet-Ape, 217–218
Othello, 94, 97, 116, 195, 225, 238, 251n
Oxford, Earl of, see de Vere, Edward
Oxford's Bible, 173, 181–182

Palladis Tamia, see Meres, Frances

Panchatantra, 101, 102, 106, 110, 172, 226
parallelisms, 130, 135, 143, 158, 160, 161–163
pareidolia, 16
Parnassus Plays, 148–151
Parsifal, 157
patternicity, 16
Peele, George (1556–1596), 36, 40n, 44–45, 48, 80, 81, 82, 102, 139, 143, 172, 185, 190, 194, 197, 198, 200, 202, 204, 209n, 215, 222
Pepys, Samuel, 49
Pericles, 31, 179, 190, 194, 200, 203, 214, 216n, 263
Pinner of Wakefield, The 40n, 219–220
Pope, Alexander, 19, 52–53, 55, 84, 93, 111n, 160n, 259
Powell, Enoch, 185n
Price, Diana, 29n, 134, 182
Prior, Roger, 214n
Promus, 135
Puritan, 31, 118, 180, 205
Pyrrho, 104

quarto (defined), 26

Ravenscroft, Edward, 50, 190, 219
Reichenbach, Hans, 175n
Richard II, 53, 66, 67, 94, 95, 101, 136, 154n, 179, 191, 195, 251n
Richard III, 95, 136, 191, 195, 222n, 224
Robertson, J. M., 20, 21, 105n, 139, 140, 162, 163, 175, 209n,
Romeo & Juliet, 49, 84, 95, 96, 147n, 150, 159, 191, 195, 201, 238, 242n, 251n, 261n
Rowe, Nicholas, 19, 50, 52, 93, 144
Rowse, A[lfred] L[eslie], 185n
Rubinstein, William D., 21n, 172n, 216, 225–226

Sackville, Thomas (1st Earl of Dorset) (1536–1608), 22, 61, 226–227
Sams, Eric, 97n, 194, 206, 213n
Satiro-mastix, 116, 148, 151, 152, 201, 215
Schleiermacher, Friedrich, 90, 234n
Schmucker, Samuel Mosheim, 33, 91, 92
Schneider, Ben, R. 105n
Schoenbaum, S[amuel], 21, 149n, 162n, 164, 185n, 186, 257–258

Schopenhauer, Artur, 105, 131, 157
Second Folio, 31
Second Maiden's Tragedy, 118, 180, 206
Seneca [Lucius Annaeus Seneca], 45, 96, 104, 105–106, 194, 199, 243, 244–246, 248, 249, 250
Sextus Empiricus, 105
Shakespeare, William (1564–1616), background 130–132, 211 business dealings 213–215 and see "Clayton Loan" education 131, 211 literary remains 130, 134–135 marriage and children 134, 212 wealth 216–218 Will 74–76, 134
Shall I Die?, 177–178
Shapiro, James, 21n, 69, 81, 87n, 91, 108, 131n, 133n, 134, 173n, 176n, 186–187, 232
Shermer, Michael, 16n, 104, 267
Sidney, Mary (Herbert), 63–64, 65, 66, 67, 170, 171, 200, 225
Sidney, Philip, 43, 58, 60–63, 170–171, 220, 244n, 247, 249n
Sir John Oldcastle, 31, 58, 204–205,
Sir Thomas More, 20, 113, 119–120, 134, 140, 159, 160, 163, 178, 180, 203, 204, 206, 220n, 253
Skepticism, 104, 105
Spenser, Edmund (1552–1599), 29, 41, 58, 60, 68, 68n, 204, 246n
Stanley, William (Earl of Derby), 20, 68n, 141–142, 170, 223
Steely Dan, 44n
Stoicism, 104, 105n
Strittmatter, Roger, 21n, 181, 182n

Tales of Bidpai, see *Panchatantra*
Taming of the Shrew, 95, 97n, 114, 197, 201, 224
Taylor, Gary, 21, 52n, 93n, 95, 118, 177–178, 179, 180, 183, 206, 227
Tempest, The, 49, 64, 96, 99, 135, 200, 223, 249n, 251n
Theobald, Lewis, 19, 53, 92, 93, 94, 101n, 206
Third Folio, 31, 194, 203–205
Thomas Lord Cromwell, 31, 205
Thomas of Woodstock, 206–207
Till Eulenspiegel, 102
Timber, or Discoveries, 32
Timon of Athens, 118, 179, 199
Titus Andronicus, 50, 53, 84, 94, 96, 114, 179, 190, 238
Tolstoy, Leo, 139, 140
Troilus and Cressida, 29, 116, 151, 183n, 194–195, 216n, 251n
Twain, Mark, 20, 139, 140–141, 184–185, 187
Twelfth Night, 49, 135
Two Gentlemen of Verona, 83, 93, 96, 197,
Two Noble Kinsmen, 179, 203, 206, 263

Unitarians, 68n, 88, 92, 94, 125, 127, 129, 142, 172, 179, 181, 183n, 218n, 225, 227, 232, 254, 260, 263
Up From Slavery, 212
Ur-Hamlet, 96, 194, 242, 244, 245, 247
Ur-plays, 96

VALIS, 158
Vedic Expansion, 130, 137, 171, 180, 182, 255, 263
Venetia, 111, 123
Vickers, Brian, 21n, 25n, 101n, 162, 178n, 179, 180, 186, 209, 233, 262

Wagner, Richard, 157, 237
War of the Theaters, 22, 147, 148–149, 152, 218n
Washington, Booker T., 212
Watson, Thomas (1552–1592), 149
Wayte, William, 213, 214n
Webster, John (1580–1634), 113, 119
Welles, Orson, 173
Wells, Stanley, 95, 144n
Whitman, Walt, 20, 141
Wilkins, George (d. 1618), 194, 205, 214, 261n
Will (of Shakespeare), 73–76
Williams Robin P., 63, 225
Winter's Tale, 32, 53, 68, 69, 109, 186n, 197, 200, 262
Wit's Misery, 121, 247, 250

Yorkshire Tragedy, 31, 118, 179, 205

Zeigler, Wilbur Gleason, 143
Zeno, 104

"SAMUEL CROWELL" is the pseudonym of a former college instructor and self-described "loose cannon" who has been fascinated by the Shakespeare authorship problem since he was in grade school. He is a graduate of the University of California (Berkeley), where he studied philosophy, foreign languages, and modern European history before continuing his studies at Columbia University. No stranger to historical controversy, Mr. Crowell is also the author of *The Gas Chamber of Sherlock Holmes and Other Writings on the Holocaust, Revisionism, and Historical Understanding* (Nine-Banded Books, 2011).

NineBandedBooks.com